Accompany Them with Singing—
The Christian Funeral

ALSO BY THOMAS G. LONG
FROM WESTMINSTER JOHN KNOX PRESS

Hebrews
(Interpretation)

Matthew
(Westminster Bible Companion)

Preaching as a Theological Task:
World, Gospel, Scripture
(coeditor)

Preaching from Memory to Hope

Preaching In and Out of Season

The Senses of Preaching

Teaching Preaching as a Christian Practice
(coeditor)

The Witness of Preaching

The Witness of Preaching, 2nd ed.

Accompany Them with Singing— The Christian Funeral

Thomas G. Long

WESTMINSTER
JOHN KNOX PRESS
LOUISVILLE · KENTUCKY

© 2009 Thomas G. Long

First edition
Published by Westminster John Knox Press
Louisville, Kentucky

09 10 11 12 13 14 15 16 17 18—10 9 8 7 6 5 4 3 2

Book design by Drew Stevens
Cover design by designpointinc.com
Cover art by Jonathan Green, The Passing of Eloise

Library of Congress Cataloging-in-Publication Data

Long, Thomas G.
　　Accompany them with singing : the Christian funeral / Thomas G. Long.
　　　p. cm.
　　Includes bibliographical references (p.　　) and index.
　　ISBN 978-0-664-23319-8 (alk. paper)
　　1. Funeral service. I. Title.
　　BV199.F8.L66 2009
　　265'.85—dc22

　　　　　　　　　　　　　　　　　　　　　　　　　　　2009008877

PRINTED IN THE UNITED STATES OF AMERICA

For all the saints who from their labors rest . . . Alleluia!

I will teach you my townspeople
how to perform a funeral . . .
you have the ground sense necessary.
—William Carlos Williams, *"Tract"*

Weep, then, at the death of a dear one as if you were
bidding farewell to one setting out on a journey.

Chrysostom

In the funerals of the departed, accompany them with singing,
if they were faithful in Christ, for precious in the sight of the Lord
is the death of his saints.

—*Apostolic Constitutions, 6.30*

Contents

Acknowledgments

Writing this book has involved a long journey, literally and figuratively. The project began in earnest in 1995, when I was awarded a Henry Luce III Fellowship through the Association of Theological Schools. This generous fellowship allowed me to travel thousands of miles across the United States, from Florida to Alaska, interviewing pastors, funeral directors, hospice workers, cemetery owners, and others, in an attempt to map the ritual life of Americans in regard to death. I am grateful to the Henry Luce III Foundation and to the countless people along the path who shared their insights, experience, and wisdom.

What would we academics do without sabbatical leaves? Much of the actual writing of this book was done during a sabbatical year, in which I was assisted by a grant from the Lilly-funded Louisville Institute of Louisville, Kentucky, for which I am deeply thankful. I want also to express my gratitude to both Princeton Theological Seminary and Candler School of Theology for granting sabbatical leaves for the purpose of pursuing this research.

More than fifty years ago, Professor Paul Irion wrote the pioneering *The Funeral and the Mourners* (Nashville: Abingdon Press, 1954). Not only did this influential book provide much of the original inspiration for my own project; early in my research Paul generously spent a fruitful and delightful day talking things funereal with me and generously shared his vast files on the subject. Of the many funeral directors who have shared their wisdom with me, I want to point out three remarkable and compassionate people who have been particularly helpful: Mark Higgins of Hall-Wynne Funeral Service in Durham, North Carolina; John Horan of Horan and McConaty Funeral Homes in Denver, Colorado; and Thomas Lynch of Lynch and Sons Funeral Directors in Milford, Michigan. Jennifer McBride, director of bereavement support and community education at Horan and McConaty Funeral Homes, provided wise counsel about the ways in which excellent funeral homes provide care for families.

My research assistants, Kristin Saldine, Lance Pape, and Kimberly Wagner, provided excellent support in the research, writing, and editing phases of the project.

I have been trying out many of the ideas found in this volume in various lecture halls and publishing venues. Portions of chapter 2 appeared in *Call to Worship,* volume 38, no. 3 (2004–2005). An earlier version of chapter 4 appeared in *The Cresset,* Lent 2005. Material from chapter 5 appeared in *Theology Today,* January 1999, and portions of chapter 9 appeared in *Journal for Preachers,* Easter 1997 and Easter 2006.

My wonderful editor and friend of many years, Stephanie Egnotovich, died just as this book was moving toward publication. This was one of the last books she edited in her laudatory career in publishing, and, as always, her steady editorial hand brought strength and clarity. I miss her as a colleague and friend, and I am somehow gratified that this project allowed us, in her final months, to converse so deeply about life and death.

Introduction

In June of 1963, a Christian lay dying in Rome. His baptismal name was Angelo Roncalli, but he was then far better known to the world as the beloved Pope John XXIII. The son of an Italian sharecropper, this modest man had earned the affection of the common people and had led the church into a season of dramatic reform. And now "Good Pope John," as he was lovingly called, was facing his final hours on earth. In the days before his death, the pope had received the last communion, and his failing body had been anointed with oil. To those gathered around his bed he spoke warmly, though in a hoarse whisper, of his love for the church, and even as he moved in and out of consciousness, he repeated many times the phrase from the Gospel of John, "*Ut sint unum*" (that they may be one).

When at last it became apparent to all at the bedside that death was at hand, Dr. Piero Mazzoni, the pope's physician, hesitantly spoke to the dying man: "Holy Father," he said softly, "you have asked me many times to tell you when the end was near so you could prepare." The pope's sunken and pale face bore the marks of the cancer that would soon take his life, but he smiled nevertheless.

"Yes. Don't feel badly, Doctor," he replied. "I understand. I am ready."

Loris Capovilla, the pope's secretary, collapsed beside the bed weeping. The pope reached out and touched him tenderly, caressing his head. "Courage, my son. I am a bishop, and I must die as a bishop, with simplicity but with majesty, and you must help me. Go get the people together."

"*Santo Padre*, they are waiting," replied the secretary.[1]

I must die with simplicity but with majesty. You must help me. Go get the people together. These words flowed from a deep faith, and they emerge from a profoundly Christian understanding of dying. But they point not only to a way of dying but also to a way of commemorating death, to the actions and convictions of the church at the time of death, and indeed to some of the key marks of a Christian funeral: simplicity, majesty, and the gathering of the people.

In a Christian funeral, there is simplicity because there is no need for ornament or ostentation among the saints, no need for lavish expense to trumpet importance. Christians are "lambs of God's own flock, sinners of God's own redeeming,"[2] and they move in simple peace and confidence toward their Good Shepherd. This character of simplicity is in tension, of course, with the costly events that many funerals in North America have become.

A generation ago, Catholic liturgical scholar Robert W. Hovda lamented the "incongruity between the Christian way of life as expressed in the church's funeral liturgy and the customs, practices, expectations surrounding the death of an American in our time" and how funerals can become "a witness to materialism rather than to the faith values of prayer, reverence, honesty, simplicity and community."[3] The result, said Hovda, was that the American funeral was in peril of being trivialized, a trivialization not intended, but

> surely evident: in cosmetic disguise, in limousines and other trappings of high society, in funeral homes refurbished to look like luxury hotels, in caskets so self-assertive that they draw attention away from the body rather than to it, in more and more mechanical contraptions which deprive mourners even of the solace of carrying the casket or touching it or covering it with earth.[4]

If the Christian funeral is marked by simplicity, ironically it is also characterized by majesty. Christians believe that Jesus Christ has called them out as a royal priesthood, a chosen people, the very saints of God; and the funeral of a Christian should reflect the sacred value of the one who has died. This is not to make a distinction of status between Christians and others—as if Christians were somehow chosen and royal and others are not—but in fact to emphasize the opposite. Christian faith views all humanity as created in the image of God, and every human being, rightly understood, is royalty, a child of the heavenly sovereign. For Christians, Jesus is not the founder of some new religion or separate sect, but rather a revelation of what it means to live a fully human life, a life that truly embodies the image of God. To follow Jesus, then, is to walk the royal road intended for all humanity, "a way in the wilderness" (Isa. 43:19) toward God marked out for all people.

One of the earliest descriptions of the Christian movement was "people of the Way" (e.g., Acts 9:2). For Christians, baptism is the starting point of this Way, a journey along a road that Jesus himself traveled. Christians travel this road in faith, not knowing fully where it will lead and sometimes seeing only one step ahead. But they keep putting one foot in front of the other, traveling in faith to the end, and "precious in the sight of the LORD is the death of his faithful ones" (Ps. 116:15). Every Christian funeral, in its grand and sweeping representation of the journey of a saint toward God, tells a story of majesty. Every Christian funeral is, in fact, a royal funeral.

And then there is the presence of the faithful community. As Christians, we do not die alone but in the company of others. "Go get the people together," said the dying pope, calling out to the Christian community. Even when dying takes place in the solitude of a nursing home or the isolation of an intensive-care ward in the depths of the night, the dying are nonetheless surrounded by the prayers of the church, and they will be carried to God by the faithful, singing psalms and hymns as they go.

The primary purpose of this book is to provide a reliable guide for pastors and priests who preside at funerals today, in doing so, to describe the Christian funeral, its history, theology, structure, content, and practical features; and to explore the tensions and possibilities of the Christian understanding of funerals in a contemporary culture that often holds radically opposed ideas about the meaning of death. Christian funerals and the other faithful rituals around dying are, when they fulfill their promise, a profound witness of the good news in Christ about life and death. Performing these rituals well is not merely an issue of propriety, sensitive pastoral care, or liturgical taste and tradition, but is rather a matter of telling the gospel truth, of giving testimony to the faith, of acting out in the face of grief and loss our deepest convictions about the promises of God in the risen Christ, and enabling us and our children to discover meaning and hope amid the ravages of death.

While this book will keep its focus on the Christian funeral, it will also recognize that a funeral is conducted not in a sterile liturgical laboratory but out in the swirling currents of contemporary society. Some funerals are not funerals at all, but "memorial services," performed without the body of the deceased and sometimes months after death has occurred. Almost all funerals and memorial services involve participants who do not hold to the Christian faith, or perhaps to any faith. And most pastors are invited on occasion to conduct services for people with no connection to the church, or with a relationship long faded into the past. There are other emerging issues to be addressed:

the growing recognition of the importance of ethnic and cultural traditions, the increase in the number of cremations, the rise of concern for ecologically responsible funerals, organ donation and the dedication of whole bodies for medical science. These and other practical and theological matters are explored in these pages.

Preparing this book on Christian funerals has occupied my thought and energy for more than a dozen years now. The great surprise for me as I look back over this time is to discover how much my mind has changed through the process. I have been converted, so to speak, by my own research, and this book challenges many of the attitudes, assumptions, and pastoral instincts I myself held when I started this project. To put it bluntly, I have written this book in many ways against the book I started out to write. When I began working on this book, I knew that a number of fine works on grief and loss were available but that it had been many years since a comprehensive book on the funeral itself had appeared. My intention, then, was to write a solid, state-of-the-art book on the Christian funeral, one that filled a gap in the literature and addressed all the usual topics: care of the dying, the funeral service, the homily or sermon, the process of grief, and the rest. What I did not anticipate was discovering that the reigning understanding of a "state of the art" funeral, which I shared along with many of my colleagues in ministry, was theologically impoverished and that examining the history, theology, and practice of Christian funerals would dramatically redefine what I consider to be a "good" funeral.

For example, at the beginning of my work on this project, I would easily have agreed with what has become a virtual consensus among those who write about Christian funerals: the essential and overriding purpose of the funeral is to provide comfort for the grief-stricken. As one popular book on Christian life rituals puts it, "Every ritual moment in the funeral process should be evaluated in the light of its effect on the process of grieving."[5] I have gradually come around to the conviction that this consensus view is deeply flawed and has done much to weaken and diminish the Christian funeral today. Yes, funerals provide consolation to those who mourn, but they do so as a part of a much broader work involving the retelling of the gospel story, the restoration of meaning, the reaffirmation of the baptismal identity of the one who has died, and the worship of God.

"Every great culture," notes Daniel Callahan, "has a characteristic view of death, ordinarily accompanied by public rituals, customary practices, and time-honored patterns of communal grief."[6] The Christian faith, for all of its diversity, constitutes just such a "great culture," and over the long centuries it has developed a set of views, rituals, patterns, and practices about death that belong to and express this culture. Over the last two centuries, however, many of those rituals, patterns, and practices have been systematically dismantled. Ironically, it happened mostly in the name of good theological intentions and tender pastoral care. Christian pastors have desired to make funerals more personal, more expressive of the desires and lifestyles of the deceased and mourning families, but have ended up allowing them to become more individualistic and even narcissistic. Pastors have tried to make funerals more pastorally sensitive, more comforting to the grief-stricken, but have allowed them to become controlled by psychological rather than theological categories and, therefore, shallower in meaning. Pastors have wanted to free funerals from the morbidity of funeral home cosmetics, but have allowed them to become spiritualized and disembodied. Pastors have desired to make funerals more faithful expressions of hope in the resurrection, but have allowed that strong hope to be edged out by sentimental views of spirituality and immortality.

Many pastors today are aware, at least intuitively, that funeral practices have drifted off course, but we clergy have not known whom to blame. We have often pointed an accusing finger at funeral professionals and the funeral "industry" for commercializing the funeral and taking it away from the church. There are many issues to be examined, of course, in the relationship between the church and funeral professionals, but the hard truth is that the Christian funeral has been damaged the most, not by its commercial rivals or even by its enemies, but by its theological friends. It is we ourselves, as pastors and practical theologians, who have cooperated with cultural trends around us and done much to weaken the Christian funeral.

A second goal of this book, then, is to call for reform in Christian funeral practices. Underlying all Christian funerals is a very basic action shared by all humanity. Someone has died, and the body must be cared for and carried to the place of burial, the place of farewell. From the beginning, however, the church discerned in this simple act of caring for and carrying the dead a symbol of the baptized Christian life. We are, in so many ways, always caring for each other, bearing one another's burdens, and carrying each other along the baptismal journey toward God. Christians do this at the beginning of life, we do it in the middle of life, and we do it at the end of life too. The purpose of a Christian funeral is to enact the human obligation to care for the dead in such a way that we retell the story of baptism, and if we look hard, we can still see the contours of this understanding of the funeral shining out beneath the confusion of what funerals have become. One aim of this book is to encourage the clearing away of as much of this clutter as possible, so that the narrative power of the Christian funeral can be felt more fully.

So this book is an appeal for reform, but certainly not for repristination. There never was a "golden age" to be nostalgic about, a time when Christians somehow got everything right about funerals. Christian funeral practices have from the beginning been tightly woven into their social contexts, and they necessarily adapt and respond to shifts in the culture. We should learn from our history, but whatever shape Christian funerals will take in the twenty-first century, they must not be attempts to re-create practices of the fifth or sixteenth or nineteenth century. Instead they must be doable, plausible, and meaningful in the urban-influenced, fast-paced, multicultural society in which we live. But even as Christian practices adjust and change to new cultural realities, there remain shapes, themes, and trajectories that mark them off as distinctively Christian. I hope to make the case that when Christian funerals are faithful to those shapes, themes, and trajectories, the human spirit is nourished, the community of Christ is strengthened, the gospel is proclaimed, the dead in Christ are honored and remembered, and the light of resurrection hope shines for all to see.

PART ONE

Background

1

Marking Death: Human Rituals, Christian Practices

In the 1960s, an anthropologist exploring a cave in northern Iraq came across the graves of several Neanderthal men, tombs believed to be nearly 50,000 years old and among the oldest human burial sites ever found. Near the remains were discovered pollen grains from grape hyacinth, hollyhocks, and thistles, silent testimony that flowers had once been placed next to the bodies.[1] Thousands of miles away, at Sungir near Moscow, was found a cluster of Cro-Magnon graves, thirty millennia old, in which lie the remains of what appears to be a family. Draped around the bones of the man are necklaces strung with hundreds of painstakingly crafted ivory beads, and nearby are tools carved from mammoth bones. The woman's skull is placed on top of the man's grave, and next to the man and the woman are the remains of two children. They are buried head to head, and around them are scattered more than ten thousand beads of ivory, several rings and bracelets, a collection of spears and daggers, and the teeth of a fox.[2]

Who knows what happened to cause these deaths so many centuries ago, or what ceremonies accompanied these ancient burials? What we do know is that the flowers, the beads, the rings, and the other artifacts bear witness that from the earliest times human beings have cared tenderly for their dead and approached death with awe. Human death has never been simply a fact; it has always been a mysterious ocean summoning those left standing on the shore to stammer out convictions about life and to wonder what lies over the horizon. From the beginning, humans have adorned burial places and the bodies of the dead with tokens of beauty and love, symbols that push back the brute facts and display the hunger for meaning in the shadow of death.

Some sociologists and anthropologists venture that the origins of religion can be found in these ancient death rituals. The ceremonies our early ancestors enacted reflexively in the face of death, they speculate, were the soil in which a sense of the holy grew. Others suggest that it was actually the other way around. An awareness of transcendence lies, they wager, hardwired in human consciousness, and the sense that there is something beyond the limits of life and the abyss of death compelled these earliest humans to adorn the graves of the dead with flowers and beads. Intimations of an unseen world were enacted in the rituals of burial.

Who can say? Which came first, the ritual rhythms of death or religious awe? Perhaps the knowledge that we cannot finally untangle the knot points to the fact that death and the sacred are inextricably entwined. In both, human beings stand on the edge of mystery and peer into depths beyond our knowing. What we do when the shadow of death falls across our life—the acts we perform and the ritual patterns we follow—etches in the dust of material life a portrait of our sense of the sacred. And, in like manner, what we finally believe and trust about the mystery at the heart of things shapes how our bodies move, what our hands do, where our feet take us, and what our mouths speak in the days of grief and loss. The dance of death moves to the music of the holy.

THE CHANGING LANDSCAPE OF FUNERALS

This book is about how one religious tradition, Christianity, with its own sense of the sacred, expresses itself in seasons of death. I want to explore how Christianity's particular understanding of life's holy mystery takes on shape and movement in the customs, practices, and rituals around death. My main interest here is not anthropological, however, but theological and pastoral. I want to explore Christian funerals— what they do, what they mean, how they work. The overarching goal of this book is quite practical. Specifically, it is to help priests and ministers who guide parishioners and congregations at the time of death to preside over funerals that genuinely embody the hope of the gospel. More broadly, this book is aimed at the larger church with the goal that all Christians will move toward ever more faithful practices in the hour of death.

Doing so, however, will involve some hard work. We will need to be more than liturgical interior decorators, trying to figure out how to create tasteful funerals. We will need to step behind the curtain of our current customs to examine what lies hidden in the shadows and to explore the history of how we came to this place in our funeral practices. We will need to rethink basic assumptions about what makes for a "good funeral."

The moment is ripe to explore the Christian funeral. Over the last half century, a number of exemplary funeral liturgies have been developed by the various Christian communions. Many of these have been stimulated by the breathtaking renewal of worship that has occurred among Roman Catholics as a part of the outpouring of reforms from the Second Vatican Council and, in particular, the appearance in 1969 of a new set of funeral rites for the Catholic world: *Ordo Exsequarium*, the *Rite of Funerals.* These new rites reflected an attempt by the Roman Catholic Church to clear away centuries of clutter that had cropped up around funeral practices and to allow the strong bond between the death of a baptized Christian and the hope given in the resurrection of Jesus Christ to shine through more brightly.

Protestants have been prompted by this to do their own rethinking of the funeral, and in North America alone, revised funeral liturgies have been developed by Presbyterians, United Methodists, the United Church of Canada, the Christian Church (Disciples of Christ), the United Church of Christ, Lutherans (twice), and several other denominations, all seeking to join Catholics in creating what Richard Rutherford has described as "truly a human and Christian symbolic language that allows death and the grief of loss their rightful articulation in a living faith community."[3]

As compelling as these new funeral rites are, what is most impressive is how little impact they have had on actual practice. Ironically, right at the cultural moment that these rich resources for funerals have appeared, American Christians, along with the rest of American culture, have become increasingly confused and conflicted about healthy ways to commemorate death. Funeral practices are in a windstorm of change, and old customs are being abandoned right and left, but the new Christian funeral liturgies don't seem to factor much into the equation. What one scholar said about Catholics a decade after the new rite appeared could well apply to Protestants also:

After ten years of official use of the new Rite of Funerals . . . , American Catholics do not seem to be handling death any better than they did before. In fact, since much of the piety and devotion connected with prayer for the dead has fallen into disuse in that same period, there might be a tendency, at least in some parts of the country, to cope with death more poorly than before the reform.[4]

If we ever needed evidence that writing good liturgy does not automatically generate good worship, the current state of the Christian funeral would be a prime case. While liturgical specialists quietly toiled away, crafting funeral services of great beauty and depth, actual Christian funerals were often migrating toward vague "celebrations of life," sometimes with such features as open-mike speeches by friends and relatives, multimedia presentations of the life of the deceased, NASCAR logos on caskets, the deceased's favorite pop music played from CDs, the release of butterflies, cremated remains swirled into plastic sculpture, and cyber-cemeteries.

Even when the changes are less dramatic, it is still true that a general cultural and generational shift toward experimentation, customization, and personalization has impacted the social network of death customs and the Christian funeral along with it. "Leave it to my generation, the baby boomers, to take control," writes Michelle Cromer. She continues:

> We're not only organizing our parents' funerals, but even planning our own in advance, putting our requests in writing and letting everyone know exactly what we want. We're a demographic so totally accustomed to center stage that we will never give it up without some fanfare. I first noticed this in [the movie] homage to my generation, *The Big Chill.* After the priest announces that a college friend will play one of the deceased's favorite songs, Karen [one of the characters] solemnly sits down at the church organ and hits the classic opening chords of the Rolling Stones' "You Can't Always Get What You Want." As that sixties anthem accompanied the funeral procession, I wasn't the only boomer in the audience who thought, *Now that's the way to go out.*[5]

Responding to the demand for funerals with fanfare, one funeral home in Florida has taken to designing elaborate stage sets for theme-based funerals, and a New Jersey funeral director proclaimed that the old-fashioned funeral business is itself on life support. "We can no longer deliver funerals out of a cookie cutter," he said, speaking of funeral professionals. "We must become event planners."[6]

Funeral changes are not just cultural trends and fashion statements. If our theology shapes our funeral practices, and vice versa, then a change in our practice signals a commensurate shift in our theology. Our funerals are indeed changing, and that means something about how we view death theologically is changing as well. At first glance, though, it is hard to assess what is happening. Are we renewing our faith in a different day, or losing our grip? Many funerals today are more upbeat, more filled with laughter, more festive. Is this good or not? Funerals tend to be less formal, less governed by ritual, more relaxed and personal. A gain or a loss? There seems to be less emphasis on the presence of the dead body in funerals, an increase in "memorial services," a measurable rise in the number of people choosing cremation. Worthy, or a cause for concern?

Time magazine correspondent Lisa Takeuchi Cullen, who spent several years studying changing death rituals in America in order to write a book on the topic, concluded that the "new American way of death is personal, spiritual, and emotional. It is altruistic, futuristic, and individualistic." When she began her exploration, she was, by her own description, "an unabashed advocate of the new American way of death, a way I believed involved celebration in place of mourning."[7] But near the end of her research, two beloved members of her family—her grandfather and a cousin—died, and her mother's cancer, once in remission, returned "with blinding speed and terrible fury." These sudden and sobering encounters with mortality prompted Cullen to question her "blithe convictions" about mourning being displaced by celebration. "If [my mother] died," she wrote, "if I lost this woman who raised me, would I have it in me to throw a party?"[8]

The stakes are high here. I am persuaded that in this, our moment in history, we are going through one of those periodic upheavals in the ways we care (or don't) for the dead that are inevitable signs of an upheaval in the ways we care (or don't) for the living. To put it bluntly, a society that has forgotten how to honor the bodies of those who have departed is more inclined to neglect, even torture, the bodies of those still living. A society that has no firm hope for where the dead are going is also unsure how to take the hands of its children and lead them toward a hopeful future.

I also am convinced that there is a broad but identifiable Christianly way to honor the dead, to walk with them in hope, and to mark well the meaning of death and life. Christianity is not simply a set of ideas and doctrines; it is a way of life, and it finally expresses itself, or denies itself, in the patterns of everyday living, in the ways that Christians do such things as raise children, care for the earth, gather at table, show hospitality to the stranger, manage money, and face death. There are Christianly patterns of living, and there are Christianly patterns of dying and caring for the dead. In sum, I believe, amid the swirling changes and uncertainties of American death patterns, it not only makes sense but is in fact an urgent task to describe, nurture, and practice what can be called "the Christian funeral."

NECESSITY, CUSTOM, AND CONVICTION

The fabric of the Christian funeral is not woven entirely from threads of pure spiritual silk. The finger of God did not inscribe a divinely mandated funeral service on Moses' tablets, Jesus gave no teaching about funerals in the Sermon on the Mount, and Paul did not bother the Corinthians with burial instructions. Throughout their history, Christians have always done what every other social group has done: figure things out for themselves and construct death practices out of rock from nearby quarries. When someone dies, Christians, like all other humans, look around at the immediate environment and ask: What do we have to do? What seems fitting to do? What do we believe we are summoned to do? In other words, Christian funeral practices emerge at the intersection of *necessity*, *custom*, and *conviction*.

Necessity

Necessity refers to the fact that a death creates certain social needs and obligations that cannot be avoided. Scholars argue about the existence of human universals, but the debate mostly grows silent when death knocks at the door. It is a universal truth that every human being eventually dies, and all societies have recognized that the physical fact of death cannot be ignored. When someone who was alive a moment ago stops breathing forever, we don't need a law or a creed to tell us that something must be done. It is coded deep in our DNA that a dead body in the presence of the living both poses some kind of threat—of contamination? of impurity? of the loss of human dignity?—and constitutes a summons to dispose of the body with care and reverence.

In this regard, death is like birth. As funeral director Thomas Lynch has noted, "At one end of life the community declares *It's alive, it stinks, we'd better do something.* At the other end we echo, *It's dead, it stinks, we'd better do something.*"[9] A generation ago, when a group in the Church of England made a list of the key tasks of a Christian funeral, at the top of the list was: "To secure the reverent disposal of the corpse."[10] They threw the word "reverent" in to make it sound like theology, but it was mainly just an acknowledgment of human necessity.

So some of what Christians do at the time of death is dictated not by a creed but by the simple truth that a dead body must be moved fairly quickly from "right here" to somewhere "over there." In this regard, Christians are no different from anyone else. When Christians care for, memorialize, and dispose of our dead, we are not doing something only Christian believers do. We are doing something all human beings do, acting on a very human need, carrying out a basic human responsibility.

And that, interestingly enough, *is* a matter of theology. The necessity of tending to dead bodies belongs, as theologians would remind us, to the order of creation. And that means that whatever rituals Christians develop around death, they are faithful only to the extent that they do not obscure the essential humanity of the experience. A Christian funeral should not be a precious ceremony aimed at covering up the fact that someone is really dead and that the people who are around the dead person have to take care of the body. That is the honest-to-God truth of what is going on. When we care for the bodies of the dead, we are not trying to hide an embarrassment behind a screen of piety; we are trying to do a human thing humanely. Jesus does not reveal what it means to be "fully Christian," but rather what it means to be fully human. Part of being human is confessing that we are *humus*. "I would say," writes Robert Pogue Harrison, "that humans bury not simply to achieve closure and effect a separation from the dead but also and above all to humanize the ground on which they build their worlds and found their histories. . . . To be human means above all to bury."[11]

Custom

If simple necessity demands that something be done with the bodies of the dead, local customs dictate, to some degree, what is imaginable and proper to do. Our place in the world—geographically, historically, culturally—both sets limits and offers possibilities for what actions are expected, for what seems fitting to do and not to do at the time of death. I am thinking here less about broad multicultural themes and general ethnic and class styles of ritual observance (although these are certainly not irrelevant) and more about the set of very particular and concrete actions that are built into the repertoire of a community's response to death.

For example, when someone dies in my own family, we call a funeral home to come for the body. We don't think much about other options; this is just what we do. The body is removed, cared for by the funeral professionals, and we are not likely to encounter the body of our loved one again until the time of the funeral. In other families and social groups, however, such behavior would be astonishing, even offensive, since their impulse is to stay with the dead body at all times and never leave the body alone or in the hands of "strangers." If someone from one of these groups were to challenge my family on our behavior and demand to know how we could possibly allow the body of a loved one out of our sight, I imagine that most of us would end up looking puzzled and stammering, "I don't know. That's just the way it's done."

In some Japanese American Christian funerals, there is a ceremony that hearkens back to customs older than Christianity among the Japanese: a floral tribute. Near the end of a funeral service, the congregation processes forward with flowers, which are placed on or in the coffin.[12] As the people pass by, they show respect for the deceased by bowing toward the body, praying while standing next to the body, or by passing by in silence.[13] Once again, an action that would be puzzling or even suspect to some, bowing toward a dead body, seems to others intuitively the way to show respect. It's just the way it's done.

There are many other examples. In many Alabama farm communities, the burial of the dead in the nearby earth within a matter of days after death seems only natural, perhaps the only proper thing to do. But for people in the far north country, where the ground is frozen hard for several months each year; or in New Orleans, where the water table lies just below the surface; or perhaps in Manhattan, where the space for cemeteries has long been exhausted and earth burial has been prohibited for over a century, very different local customs for the disposition of the body arise. Or again, Puritan settlers in Massachusetts would have found the merest discussion of the life of deceased at burial

to be effusive, excessive, and scandalous, whereas in most settings in
our day, with our very different understanding of self and personhood,
refusal to talk at all about the dead person would seem cold and impersonal indeed. Yet again, in the low country of South Carolina, some
African Americans still follow the old African custom of lifting infants
and young children in the air and passing them over the coffins of their
deceased relatives. It keeps the children from "fretting" they say, and
being afraid of the dead.[14] It's just the way it's done.

David Sudnow studied the unwritten local customs and social protocols prevailing in an urban hospital about how word of a death spreads,
about who may and who may not break the news that someone has
died. Two centuries ago, the news of a death would be announced
to the whole community by the tolling of the church bell, but now
it seems to many in our culture more fitting to spread the news of a
death more quietly and privately. Sudnow found that in the hospital (symbolic of urban society as a whole) it is considered proper that
news about the death of a close loved one should be delivered only by
someone who had a significant relationship to the deceased and who
is of high symbolic standing—for example, a physician, a head nurse,
a priest or minister, a close friend, or another relative. It would be a
serious social infraction if a woman, stepping off a hospital elevator on
the way to visit her husband, unaware that he has just suffered a fatal
cardiac arrest, should be told of his death by the man restocking the
vending machine.

So deeply ingrained is this sense of protocol that some hospitals have
policies stating that only the attending physician can report a death.
Hospital staff are compelled, therefore, to develop elaborate techniques
to avoid breaking the news prematurely while at the same time not
lying to the families by implying that their loved one is still alive.[15]

The welter of local death customs in any given social context often
presents a challenge to Christian pastors. On the one hand, funerals
are not universal templates that somehow elbow all local customs and
protocols out of the way. They are inevitably set down and performed
in particular social contexts and among folk with a ground sense of
what is proper and what is not. If an Episcopal priest opens the *Book of
Common Prayer* and begins to read the funeral service in a community
where restrained emotion is the customary way to show reverence, then
the service will proceed in stillness. If, however, the same priest begins
reading the very same service in a community where loud crying and
visible displays of grief are the locally expected way to show respect to

the deceased, then the priest better be ready to have the service periodically interrupted.

On the other hand, some local death customs seem not compatible with the gospel. For example, the Ma'anyan people of southern Borneo have a custom of holding a death festival every few years at which all of the bodies that have been buried since the last festival are dug up and then cremated. The reason for this is the Ma'anyan belief that the souls of the dead linger for a while in the dead body before they depart.[16] This custom of disinterment rests on a narrative about souls and bodies quite different from the gospel affirmation of embodied human beings. Consequently, it would be difficult to imagine incorporating this practice into a Christian funeral liturgy.

The early Christian movement, almost from the very beginning of its life, had to sift the wheat from the chaff in terms of local custom. In the earliest days, when the decision was made to open Christianity to Gentiles, this was, notes liturgical scholar Anscar J. Chupungco, much more complicated and controversial than merely welcoming some new people into the club. Instead, says Chupungco, "it was a question of investing the Christian rites of worship with elements from the culture and traditions of the gentiles."[17] The church realized that if worship was going to be able to communicate the faith to them, it would need to incorporate symbols, ceremonies, and words that were familiar to Gentiles. Chupungco uses a nice phrase to describe this. Worship, he says, had to become "*recognizably incarnate*, that is, as having taken flesh in the cultural milieu of the worshippers."[18]

This does not mean, Chupungco hastens to say, that the church promiscuously welcomed into Christian worship every local custom and ceremony it encountered. In fact, he says, the early church kept its wits about it and was quite careful to avoid "eclecticism," which Chupungco defines as "a random, indiscriminate, and undigested borrowing of alien doctrines and practices regardless of whether or not they accord with the faith received from the Apostles." The early church, he says, despised eclecticism, and it looked at Gentile culture, that is to say at pagan culture, with an appreciative but ever critical eye.

This allowed the early Christian movement, Chupungco argues, to take three basic postures toward local Gentile rituals and customs: it silently ignored what it found unworthy, it denounced what it found dangerous to the faith, and it welcomed what it could reinterpret in the light of the gospel. Thus the church quietly avoided the "unworthy" practice of animal sacrifice in mystery religions, thundered against the "dangerous" and pompous initiation ceremonies of the Roman elite, and altered its baptismal rite to include a "reinterpreted" Gentile custom of drinking of a cup of milk mixed with honey (the Romans gave milk and honey to newborns to ward off sickness and evil spirits). The reason the church welcomed the milk-and-honey custom into worship was, says Chupungco, because it could and did reimagine it as the "fulfillment of God's promise to our ancestors that he would lead them to a land flowing with milk and honey."[19] That wasn't what milk and honey originally meant to the Romans, but it was what Christian liturgy was able to make of it.

So how does this apply to Christian funerals? The Christian faith is firmly, sometimes maddeningly, both countercultural and proindigenization at the same time. That is to say, the Christian faith transcends every tribe, clan, and local custom, while at the same time it seeks to express itself in every local dialect. Funerals should be "recognizably incarnate" in that the funeral combines that which transcends this place with that which embodies this place.

Here's a test case: In some areas of the United States, it is a custom to drape the coffin of a military veteran with a U.S. flag. People who follow this custom could probably advance many reasons why—it shows "respect," it's a symbol of sacrifice, it's a matter of honor, and so on—but mainly it is one of those local customs that for many folk simply seems fitting. The action is deeper than thought or strategy. This doesn't mean it is right or wrong. "It's just the way things are done around here."

Most composers of sound Christian funeral liturgies, however, from their vantage point necessarily at some remove, are not impressed. They cannot imagine that a coffin bearing a national flag would be a proper symbol in a Christian funeral. It would be like carrying a banner in front of the coffin with a picture of a Republican elephant or a Democratic donkey. A funeral should be an occasion to announce that the deceased is a citizen of heaven, a child of the God of all nations and peoples, not a partisan. So, as the authors of one wise and prominent guide for Christian pastors say: "Regardless of whether a pall is used, other decorations, including floral arrangements, flags, and other insignia that distinguish the deceased and suggest that salvation depends on something other than Christ, are removed from the coffin prior to the service."[20]

But is this good advice? I would say it depends. As H. Richard Niebuhr reminded us, for a Christian the ethical question, What should

I do? is always preceded by another question: What is going on?[21] If what is going on, in fact, is that the American flag is draped over, let us say, Fred's coffin as a sign that "salvation depends on something else than Christ," then stars and bars be gone. Interpreted this way, prominently parading a national symbol down the aisle should in no way be permitted in a Christian funeral. As the early church did when facing such practices, we should either omit the custom (which is what the liturgists suggest) or denounce it (preferably not at the funeral!). Moral philosopher Alasdair MacIntyre would probably urge the latter, since he finds the blending of symbols of the sacred, the nation, and death to be a particularly noxious combination. He writes:

> The modern nation-state, in whatever guise, is a dangerous and unmanageable institution, presenting itself on the one hand as a bureaucratic supplier of goods and services, which is always about to, but never actually does, give its clients value for money, and on the other as a repository of sacred values, which from time to time invites one to lay down one's life on its behalf. As I have remarked elsewhere, it is like being asked to die for the telephone company.[22]

But what if something else is going on here? In most cases, I suspect that the flag on Fred's coffin is not anything close to a rejection of salvation in Christ alone or triumphant nationalism on the part of anyone. In fact, coffins have a hard time, I would think, symbolizing much more than the dead persons inside them. The flag on Fred's coffin likely stands for something about Fred, something fairly difficult to name, something perhaps like Fred was a "good" man, a good citizen, a man who answered without hesitation when duty called, or perhaps even that there was a moment in Fred's life when he gave himself to something outside of his small space in society. What would stripping off the flag at the entrance to the church actually mean then to the people who are present? "*Solus Christus!*" or simply a diminishment of Fred?

So what do we do about the flag on Fred's coffin? Do we remove it at the beginning of the funeral? Do we attempt to reinterpret it by putting a Christian pall over the flag, by placing a cross on the coffin, or by saying somewhere in the service, "Fred was an Army veteran and served bravely in Vietnam, but what is even more important to know about him is that he belongs to Jesus Christ and the great company of the saints"? Or do we just let it go? Deciding wisely will require a pastor's eye and a pastor's good judgment, which has always been the case in Christian worship. The church's first liturgists, observes Chupungco, were pastors and catechists who had a keen perception of how their people lived their lives in the cultural milieu of the time. They were profoundly cognizant of their people's rituals, needs, and aspirations. These they introduced into the liturgy, so that people could worship with their feet on the ground, so that the liturgy would not be divorced from the reality of human life. They were great liturgists because they were pastors.[23]

Conviction

Combing through the pages of church history, we soon become aware that there is not now, and there never has been, any single, ideal pattern for Christian funerals. Christians have developed many ways to baptize, to marry, to pray, and to feast, and the same is true of marking death. Christians have stood beside graves in silent and prayerful reverence, and they have shouted defiantly at death with loud songs of victory. They have marched to the cemetery in solemn cadences, and they have danced to graveyards with the joyful rhythms of jazz bands. Christians have buried their dead, and they have cremated them. They have kept coffins open during the funeral, and they have insisted they be closed. They have wrapped their dead in simple shrouds, and they have adorned them with royal vestments. Christians have prayed lavish funeral liturgies, and they have stood at the grave with only a few words wrought from the heart.

The variety of Christian funeral practices stems partly from historical, ethnic, cultural, and denominational differences, but there is also no one pure form of Christian funeral because there is no one pure form of Christian. Christians do not live or die in the abstract. They are real people who live real lives, and they die real and very different deaths. They die young, and they die old and full of days. They die in the flames of brave martyrdom, and they die cowering in fear. They die as saintly sinners; they die as sinful saints. They die of crib death, of cancer, of old age, and by their own hand. They die full of joy, and they die despairing. They die in Hartford and Buenos Aires, Karachi and Toronto, Nairobi and rural Nebraska—in the places where they have lived and loved and in places where they are strangers and exiles. They die in hospitals and nursing homes, along highways, at sea, and at work. They die surrounded by those who love them, and they die alone.

No ideal, crystalline form of the Christian funeral shimmers above these personalities, places, and circumstances. And yet, amid all of this diversity, there is nevertheless a unifying force in the practice of Christian funerals: the gospel narrative. All Christian funerals—formal or informal, high church or low, small or large, urban or rural—say, in essence, "Look! Can you perceive this? The life and death of this one who has died can be seen, if you know how to look, as shaped after the pattern of the life and death of Jesus." Through the telling of the sacred story, we have seen Jesus be baptized, we have seen him walk his life's pathway in obedience, and we have seen him die and be buried. We have encountered him in the glory of his resurrection, and we have watched with the disciples as he departed from us and ascended into heaven. This is the story the New Testament tells about Jesus, and this is the story the funeral tells about the Christian who has died.

In a Christian funeral, the community of faith is invited once more, and in dramatic fashion, to recognize that the Christian life is shaped in the pattern of Christ's own life and death. We have been, as Paul says in Romans, baptized into Jesus' death and baptized into Jesus' life:

> Do you not know that all of us who have been baptized into Christ Jesus were baptized into his death? Therefore we have been buried with him by baptism into death, so that, just as Christ was raised from the dead by the glory of the Father, so we too might walk in newness of life. For if we have been united with him in a death like his, we will certainly be united with him in a resurrection like his.
>
> (Rom. 6:3–5)

This is what gives unity to the fragments and particularities of a Christian funeral. At death, we are, like all human beings, under the necessity of moving the dead body from "here" to "there," but it is the gospel story that tells us the truth about where "here" and "there" are in the Christian life, that names the "here" as the life we have shared in faith and the "there" as the place in the arms of God toward which our sister or brother is moving. Only because Jesus has traveled this path toward God before us are we able to travel it ourselves, but because "of the new and living way that he opened for us" (Heb. 10:20) we do put one foot in front of the other on this journey. Here, then, is the conviction of faith that draws together all the necessity and custom of death into a funeral that bears witness to the gospel: a baptized saint, a child of God, one who has been traveling the path of faith, is now "traveling on." This brother or sister, precious in the sight of God, is moving along the last mile of the way, and we, his or her companions in Christ, are traveling alongside to the place of farewell. As we travel, we sing and we pray, we tell once again the gospel story, we say farewell, and in faith we return this our friend to God with thanksgiving.

Christian rituals of death have varied from age to age and from culture to culture, but in all times and places they have expressed this conviction that a saint is "traveling on." Some Christians—but not all—dress the deceased in a white baptismal robe for the journey. Some Christians—but not all—stay awake with the body in the hours before the funeral, telling stories and sharing memories, not so much to guard the body or to shoo away the forces of evil, but as fellow pilgrims on the path, as a symbol of the communion of the saints and the unbroken connection with the saint who is "passing on," not just passed away. Some Christians—but not all—open the coffin and look at the face of the deceased, perhaps several times in the course of the funeral and burial, not because they are morbidly curious about death, but because they are saying farewell to a sister or brother. Some Christians—but not all—carry the coffin into the sanctuary, pausing at stations to recount the liturgy of baptism. Some Christians—but not all—walk or march or ride in procession to the place of burial, giving shape to the conviction that the deceased is journeying to the other shore, to the "land that is brighter than day." Some Christians—but not all—sing "From earth's wide bounds, from ocean's farthest coast, through gates of pearl streams in the countless host" and others sing "When we meet on that beautiful shore" and still others sing "O when the saints go marchin' in," but all Christians, in their own ways, mark the milestones of the saintly journey and the progress of a pilgrim toward "a safe lodging, and a holy rest, and peace at the last."

In his memoir *Open Secrets: A Spiritual Journey through a Country Church,* Richard Lischer tells about his early years as a Lutheran pastor in the farm community of Cana, Illinois. "In Cana we baptized our babies, celebrated marriages, wept over the dead, and received Holy Communion, all by the light of our best window."[24] What Lischer calls "our best window" was a stained-glass depiction of no less than the doctrine of the Trinity, set high into the east wall of the sanctuary above the altar. Though it was a piece of "ecclesiastical boilerplate," as Lischer describes it, from a studio in Chicago, it was nonetheless impressive both for its rich colors and its sturdy insistence on classical theology. A large central triangle labeled "DEUS" was surrounded by three smaller triangles, marked respectively "PATER," "FILIUS," and "SPIRITUS SANCTUS." Each smaller triangle was connected to the larger DEUS triangle by a line labeled "EST" (is), and each smaller triangle was connected to the other small triangles by lines marked "NON EST" (is not). In sum, the window announced the very nature of the Trinity: the Father is God, the Son is God, and the Holy Spirit is God, but the Father is not the Son, the Son is not the Spirit, and so on. "Our window's geometric design," observes Lischer, "seemed to say, 'Any questions?'"

Thinking about the relationships between this window, his ministry, and the life of his congregation, Lischer observes,

> We believed that there was a correspondence between the God who was diagramed in that window and our stories of friendship and neighborliness. If we could have fully taken into our community the name Trinity, we would have needed no further revelations and no more religion, for the life of God would have become our life.

The window, in other words, was no mere theological abstraction, but a map of the Christian life. Lischer goes on to say,

> An aerial photographer once remarked that from the air you can see paths, like the canals on Mars, that crisscross pastures and fields among the farms where neighbors have trudged for generations, just to visit or help one another in times of need. These, too, are the highways among *Pater, Filius,* and *Spiritus Sanctus* grooved into human relationships. The word "religion" comes from the same root as "ligaments." These are the ties that bind.[25]

The Christian funeral is, in a way, like that great window in that little church in Illinois. It brings to the chaos and fragmentation of death the light of the one narrative that can hold things together, that can disclose what "is" and "is not" true, even as we face the cold glare of the last enemy, that can reveal amid the severed cords of loss the strong ligaments that bind the story of Jesus to the story of our lives.

Annie Dillard once compared worship to a play we "have been rehearsing since the year one. In two thousand years," she says, "we have not worked out the kinks."[26] True, but we don't rehearse this play hoping to work out the kinks—that will never happen, not in this life anyway. We rehearse this play called Christian worship in order to participate once more in the story and to refresh our memory about our part in it. This is what a Christian funeral is all about. Someone we love has died, and so once again we get out our old scripts, assemble on stage, and act out one more time the great and hopeful drama of how the Christian life moves from death to life. None of us is an expert at this. Some of us limp, all of us have trouble remembering our lines, and many are weeping even as they move across the stage. We are who we are, flawed to a person, and we will never work out the kinks. But that's not the goal; the goal is to know this story in this play so well that we know it by heart.

Nearly every weekday afternoon, I drive myself from my office at the university to my home several miles away. I have done this countless times, and I know the way by heart. Some afternoons my mind is so preoccupied by the events of the day that I find myself almost home, yet I cannot remember having made the trip, not in detail anyway. I think I have been an alert driver, braking and accelerating at all the right times and paying attention to the traffic around me, but I have traveled over several miles of road and made several turns along the way, and I cannot recall any of it. Whatever else this may say about me, it means this: my body knows the way home.

That is what we want in a Christian funeral. We do this again and again, every time someone dies, because it is important for our bodies to know the way home.

2

On Bodies Shunned and Bodies Raised

The wisecracking hosts on the morning drive-time radio show could hardly believe their luck. Hungry for fresh comedy material, they had spotted a delicious piece on the newswire that Costco, the discount retailer, had decided to sell caskets on an experimental basis in a few of their leading stores. Unlike the usual tired material—smirking about the latest celebrity in rehab or sending up the latest loser on some reality show—this discount casket stuff was hot, and the deejays wasted no time mining it for laughs.

"Geez, can you imagine?" said one of them. "You go into Costco and say, 'I think I'll buy forty-eight rolls of toilet paper and, hey, while I'm at it, I'll pick up a casket.'"

"Right!" said the other. "Can't you see yourself wheeling that thing out to the parking lot on the buggy? And how are you supposed to get it home? Call your Uncle Leo and tell him to bring his boat trailer over to Costco?"

This was rich, and the deejays giggled like frat boys, but then one of them sounded a more serious note. "Really, I think this is great," he said, not joking now. "It's American free enterprise, competition in the marketplace, bringing down prices. We spend way too much on funerals, and I've told my family, 'When I'm gone, if you need to cut a corner, cut it on the casket. I don't need it. This body is just a shell. The real me will be gone somewhere else. So don't be wasting money on a casket. Get me a pine box. Get me something at Costco!'"

In most respects, this was just a silly exchange tucked between the traffic report, the weather, and the sports, but in some ways it was a snapshot of contemporary cultural attitudes about death. It was all there: the reflexive connection between death and money (Jessica Mitford's scathing attack on the funeral industry, *The American Way of Death*, taught us that); the tittering over the notion of caskets at Costco, which was really nervous laughter about the very idea of death come close enough to touch, death's ashen face peeking out among the refrigerators, lawn furniture, and DVD players of the sub-urban good life. Death in our culture is a mixture of taboo and terror, always fertile ground for whistling-in-the-dark humor, and while some have claimed that North America is a death-denying culture, this is not exactly on target. For Americans, death is more like pornography,[1] endlessly fascinating while at the same time forbidden. No wonder there are nervous giggles over caskets in the housewares department; finding a casket at Costco was like discovering an issue of *Hustler* in the choir loft.

But perhaps the most revealing comment by the radio jock came not in the juvenile jokes but in his more serious reflection, in his observation that his body is "just a shell" and that the "real me" has nothing to do with the dead body, that the "real me" is elsewhere after death. This was said as a matter of fact. Of course the body is just a shell. Of course "the real me" goes elsewhere after death. Of course it would be foolish to waste time, attention, and money on a casket for a discarded and useless body that will only decay. He wasn't arguing the case. He didn't need to. He was assuming it, merely stating the obvious, like gravity and the rotation of the earth.

If his only point was that human bodies eventually turn to dust after death and that lavish expenditures for coffins are unnecessary and maybe foolish, then it would be a point well taken. But this was not his point, not really. What he said, I believe, betrayed the deeper world-view out of which he spoke, a very old and widely shared religious per-spective in its own way, that the "real me" is an immortal soul and that souls and bodies are two separate things—that is to say, "the real me" and the body that hauls the "real me" around have only a temporary and stormy relationship. When death occurs, the pure soul is released at last from the always limited, occasionally troublesome, and decay-prone body, leaving behind . . . well, "just a shell." The fact that he could assume that all of his listeners shared this dualistic view of souls and bodies is a sign of just how deeply a pop form of Platonism has embedded itself in the contemporary worldview. In fact, except for the jokes and the giggles, Plato himself sounds a lot like the deejay.

> In this present life, I reckon that we make the nearest approach to knowledge when we have the least possible intercourse or communion with the body, and are not surfeited with the bodily nature, but keep ourselves pure until the hour when God himself is pleased to release us. And thus having got rid of the foolishness of the body we shall be pure and hold converse with the pure, and know of ourselves the clear light everywhere, which is no other than the light of truth.[2]

BODIES AND SOULS?

This sharp separation of spirit and body, and the devaluing of the body that inevitably accompanies it, runs like a ribbon through Western thought. Descartes's mountaintop moment of revelation, so influential to shaping the contemporary epistemological landscape, was announced as *"Cogito, ergo sum."* I *think*, therefore I am. Not "I enter into relationships, therefore I am," or "I eat or walk or work or make love or bear children, therefore I am," but I *think*. In short, the fact that I am, the essence of "me-ness," is understood to be a disembodied mental or even spiritual process. Sociologist Emile Durkheim kept the beat going when he said, "[T]he soul is invested with a dignity that has always been denied the body, which is considered essentially profane, and [the soul] inspires those feelings that are everywhere reserved for that which is divine. It is made up of the same substance as are the sacred beings: it differs from them only in degree. A belief that is as universal and permanent as this cannot be purely illusory."[3]

There you have it, a belief so universal and permanent it *must* be true: the soul is divine, the body profane, an idea with a long and deep pedigree in philosophical and popular thought. Small wonder, then, that many people in our culture, having drunk deeply from this flask of old wine, view dead bodies as "just shells" left behind after the soul has flown away. The logic of this unfolds inexorably for the funeral. If the "real me" is a soul and not the body, then the presence of my body at a funeral is unnecessary, indeed a costly distraction, an inconvenience, or—let us press the case to its conclusion—even a morbid and vulgar embarrassment to the more rarefied spirituality of the moment.

Not only do bodies get in the way of freedom-seeking souls; their sheer fleshiness makes things awkward for freedom-seeking moderns too. "The body's a downer, especially for boomers," said Mark Duffey, a former funeral-home owner who started, of all things, a funeral concierge service, which helps families plan new-age memorial services. "If the body doesn't have to be there [at a memorial service]," Duffey goes on to say, "it frees us up to do what we want. They may want to have it in a country club or a bar or their favorite restaurant. That's where consumers want to go."[4]

The Christian view of human beings and human bodies, which in large measure was inherited from Judaism, forms a sharp contrast to this prevailing view and is, in fact, countercultural in two directions at once. On one front, Christians reject as reductionist the view that human beings are *only* bodies. Some philosophers and neurophysicists believe that Western philosophy's whole flirtation with the idea of "souls" has been a misadventure in speculative metaphysical hooey and that what we call a human being is simply a set of biochemical and electrical processes. That is all there is; there is no "ghost in the machine." On the other front, though, Christians with equal force reject the Platonic view that human beings are essentially nonmaterial and immortal souls, temporarily housed in disposable and somewhat loathsome bodies.

Christians believe instead that the best way to understand what makes for a human being is disclosed in that wonderful image in the Genesis account of creation where God creates the first human being, not by snatching some immortal soul out of the air, sticking it into a body and forcing it to work the garden. The picture is far more tender. God takes dust, ordinary dust from the ground, and breathes into the dust "the breath of life." Dust into which God has breathed life: that is what living human beings are in biblical understanding. Christians, to sum up, do not believe that human beings are *only* bodies, nor do they believe that they are souls who, for the time being, *have* bodies; Christians affirm, rather, that human beings are *embodied*. What others call "the soul" and "the body," Christians call the "breath of God" and dust; and when it comes to living human beings, they form an inseparable unity. There is no such reality in the Christian lexicon as "the real me" apart from "the embodied me." Moreover, the "embodied me" is a creature, created by God. Human life flows entirely from God as a gift. Take away the breath of God, and there is no immortal soul left over to make a break for it to freedom; there is just dust.

Christians do, from time to time, use the language of "soul," as in, "When the ship went down, many souls were lost at sea," or "Bless your soul!" or the famous statement of Sister Pollard from the Montgomery, Alabama, bus boycott, "My feets are tired, but my soul is rested." "Soul" in these cases does not mean some immortal spark within, but refers to those times when we become especially aware that we are standing in the presence of God. On those rare occasions when the New Testament uses the Greek word for "soul," it refers, N. T. Wright has said, "not to a disembodied entity hidden within the outer shell of the disposable body but rather to what we would call the whole person or personality, as being confronted by God."[5] Or as Barth said of human beings, "[T]hey themselves are their souls, for their souls are the souls of their bodies."[6]

The biblical view of embodiment connects firmly to the ways that we experience ourselves and other people in everyday life. Take, for example, a good friend. We have come to know this friend over time in the thousands of things this friend has said and done in our presence. We have seen our friend laugh at these kinds of things and cry in those experiences. Our friend has shown up at our side in times of need, his need and ours. We have watched our friend take care of his children, stand up for his convictions, show stress under pressure, and express delight in a day at the beach or over a plate of enchiladas. In other words, the way we get to know a person is through a lifetime of small embodiments. We are, in essence, what we choose to do with our bodies. When we say we know our friend's "soul," we do not mean something apart from his body; we are describing the character and personality we have seen through his cumulative embodied actions. If our friend should suddenly and uncharacteristically lash out at us in rage, we say to ourselves, "That's not like him." What we mean is that this moment of embodiment is unlike the many other embodiments of him we have experienced before.

Since we are not immortal, when the body dies, the whole person dies, period. We don't have deathless souls, spirits, or anything else. Only God is immortal (1 Tim. 6:16), and Christians speak of anything human as "immortal" only in a derivative way. Paul tells the Corinthians that "this mortal body must put on immortality" (1 Cor. 15:53), but he is not spouting Platonism; he is preaching resurrection. He is saying that God's love for human creatures is so powerful and steadfast that God will not allow anything—not even death—to drive a wedge between us. "The trumpet will sound, and the dead will be raised imperishable" (1 Cor. 15:52). This is not about deathless souls shedding bodies; this is about embodied mortals being given new and glorified *bodies* by the grace and power of God.

THE SACREDNESS OF HUMAN LIFE

While Christians do not believe human beings are immortal, they do believe that human beings—these creatures of dust into which God has breathed life—are sacred, and that includes the sanctity of the body. In the secular world, the affirmation of the sacredness of human life has been translated into talk of "human dignity," and the medical, legal, and ethical literature is filled with debates about "dying with dignity" and even the human right to a "dignified death." The quest for death with dignity is laudable, but we should be careful about swapping terms. Seeing human beings as sacred is not exactly the same as saying that human life has dignity, and dying with dignity is not equivalent to dying as a saint. "Dignity" is rooted, etymologically and philosophically, in the concept of merit.[7] Dignity is an achievement, a rank, and therefore it can be lost. Sacredness is a divine gift, and it can never be taken away, even when the old thieves, disease and death, pillage us of our dignity.[8]

Early in his book *How We Die*, physician Sherwin B. Nuland tells the story of a woman in her forties who had been left emotionally distraught by the experience of watching her mother die in agony of breast cancer. "It was nothing like the peaceful end I expected," she told Nuland. "I thought it would be spiritual . . . [but] there was too much pain, too much Demerol." And then she added angrily, "Dr. Nuland, there was no dignity in my mother's death!" Reflecting on this exchange, Nuland says,

> All of her efforts and expectations had been in vain, and now this very intelligent woman was in despair. I tried to make clear to her that the belief in the probability of death with dignity is our, and society's, attempt to deal with the reality of what is all too frequently a series of destructive events. . . . I have not often seen much dignity in the process by which we die.[9]

Christians do not romanticize death, and while they join with others in working for human dignity in death and hope for their own deaths to be marked by dignity, they are not banking on it. Death often steals dignity, and Christians don't stop loving and caring for people when there is little dignity left. Death is a liar, trying to conceal the sanctity of humanity under the disguise of devastation. While death may approach us holding out as a lure the crown of dignity, it always pulls it back in favor of the sword of destruction. Any idea that death—cold and unmitigated death—can be "spiritual" is Platonic wishful thinking. Yes, some deaths are more peaceful than others, some are less painful than others, some can even be taken to be blessings; but death itself is not holy. God is holy, and human holiness comes because God's breath formed us in the very image and likeness of God. Christians understand, then, that human beings are like icons of God, sacred even when the disfigurements of sin, the ravages of disease, and the final despoilments of death have stripped away the last shred of dignity like the robes of deposed emperors.

So what I am claiming here is that, when it comes to death and Christian funerals, it is important to keep our sources straight. As for the nature of human bodies, Christians draw not on Platonism, not even on ethically derived notions of "dignity," but on a theology of creation. Even when illness and aging have turned once-supple bodies into sagging flesh and inflicted upon them the indignities of impaired mobility and the loss of memory and rationality, we nonetheless are called to see holiness shining through the decay and to honor fathers and mothers "that your days may be long in the land that the LORD your God is giving you" (Exod. 20:12). And when death invites us to gaze upon the lifeless clay and despair, we are called instead to remember that this very body was formed by God in beauty and holiness from the dust of the earth.

HONORING THE BODY

In her essay "Love Songs to the Dead," Catherine Madsen of the National Yiddish Book Center describes the Jewish ritual of *Tahara*, the preparation of the dead for burial. It is, she says, "work that is close enough for indignity." The ritual is performed by the *Chevra Kadisha*, the "holy society" of those who have volunteered to take on this emotionally demanding task. The members of the society come into the presence of the dead body—men to prepare a man, women to prepare a woman—and address the body by its Hebrew name, asking forgiveness "for any indignity they may visit on it as they work." Madsen continues:

There are smells, there is sometimes blood, the body is heavy and cold, the work reminds nearly everyone of handling a huge chicken. The body is washed twice. First the practical washing, in warm water: the fragile skin cleansed with washcloths, the ears swabbed with Q-tips, the hair combed, the toenails and fingernails cleaned. At this point the body is treated almost as if it were still alive, as if it could feel warm water, as if it could feel shame; only the part being washed is uncovered to view. Then the sheet is removed for the ritual washing. Naked, the body is sluiced with floods of cold water. It is not embalmed. It is dried and clothed in the garments of a priest of the Temple, and the hood is pulled over the face. It is put in a pegged wooden coffin; no nails are used, so that body and box may return entirely to earth.[10]

But what Madsen calls "the most disorienting feature of this pro-foundly disorienting ritual" happens while the body is being washed with warm water. Those who are doing the washing begin to sing, and the words they sing from the Song of Songs are a sacred love song, which the indignity of death cannot silence:

His head is the finest gold; his locks are wavy, black as a raven. His eyes are like doves beside springs of water, bathed in milk, fitly set. His cheeks are like beds of spices, yielding fragrance. His lips are lilies, distilling liquid myrrh. His arms are rounded gold, set with jewels. His body is ivory work, encrusted with sapphires. His legs are alabaster columns, set upon bases of gold. His appearance is like Lebanon, choice as the cedars. His speech is most sweet, and he is altogether desirable. This is my beloved and this is my friend, O daughters of Jerusalem.

(Song of Songs 5:11–16)

"When a man is dying," Sherwin Nuland wrote, "the walls of his room enclose a chapel, and it is right to enter it with hushed rever-ence."[11] Those who perform the *Taraha* recognize that the sacredness does not end at death and that reverence can be shown with a love song as well as with silence. Madsen observes that if anyone today tried to invent this ritual and then persuade a synagogue or church to perform it, it would almost certainly be voted down. "There would be nervous giggles about homoeroticism and necrophilia; the plan would be hotly discussed at one or two committee meetings, roundly declared inappro-priate, and quietly dropped." In the meantime, the volunteers in the *Chevra Kadisha* are learning that "one cannot handle the dead kindly without feeling tenderness," and are grateful for the old tradition that frees them "to be fully alive on behalf of the dead."[12]

Early Christianity inherited the treasure of this Jewish understanding of the body and intensified it with strong convictions about the incarnation and the bodily resurrection of Jesus. Doing so stirred Christians not to idealize bodies (as the Greeks did in their perfect sculptures) or to romanticize them (as *Sports Illustrated* does in its swimsuit issue), but to care for bodies, real bodies, both living and dead, in ways that perplexed and confused their pagan neighbors. The Greco-Roman world was thoroughly Neoplatonic, maintaining a fire wall between pure souls and corrupt bodies, but "[t]he historical fact that Christ as God entered the world of nature, bodies, and objects," writes Margaret Miles, "meant to the Christians of the first three centuries that a cosmic seismic shift had occurred in the condition of being human."[13]

The world mattered, bodies mattered. The world and bodies mattered to the Christian community because they clearly mattered to God, who loved the world so much that the divine became flesh and dwelled among us. This led the early Christians "to have some strange preoccupations and activities," says Miles. They gathered before dawn as a body for worship, they sang hymns together as a body, and they shared a common meal, which they described in such bold and graphic bodily terms ("this is my body. . . take, eat") that some shocked Romans accused them of cannibalism. What was even odder to Roman eyes was that the Christians "volunteered to take care of bodies, both living and dead bodies," writes Miles, "not just of their own families but also of the poor surrounding them. . . . This immediate, almost instinctive urge of Christians to care for the sick, the hungry, the old, and the poor aroused comment from their neighbors."[14]

But the most bizarre activity of all these bodily activities, as far as Roman citizens were concerned, was the Christian practice of burying the dead—not just their own dead, but the poor as well. In Roman society, the bodies of poor people, if left unattended, were dumped in a common pit, a paupers' grave. Respectable Romans were horrified by the inhumanity of this, and some of them even formed burial societies to ensure that no person would go without a proper burial. However, despite the lofty rhetoric of these charitable organizations, nobody actually wanted to do the dirty work of burial, of handling a dead body—except the Christians. Not only did they volunteer to bury the dead, Miles says, they "insisted on gathering the bones of those who had been executed for refusal to renounce the Christian sect.

They put these bones in a place of honor and described them as capable of possessing the sanctity of the living holy person."[15] Educated secular Romans were convinced that all of this concern among Christians for bodies could only be the product of ignorance. One well-placed Roman, Miles reports, speculated that the Christians who were willing to bury the dead as an act of service were surely "fleeing from the light," in short, ignoring the enlightened wisdom that only minds and souls were spiritual, while bodies were corrupt "bags of dung" and worth nothing except to be despised.

In other words, Christian attitudes toward the body were as countercultural in antiquity as they are today, if not more so. They did not derive their attitude toward the human body from their Roman neighbors, from the great philosophers, or even from their own inner goodness, but from their theology of creation and their experience of Jesus Christ. "I emphasize the oddness of Christians' behavior in the context of Roman culture," writes Miles,

> in order to indicate that behavior we may be tempted to characterize under "general goodness," was in fact not something they could have learned from secular life. Rather, they cared for living bodies and dead bodies because they understood that the Incarnation of Christ had once and for all settled the issue of the value of human bodies.[16]

THE UNBEARABLE LIGHTNESS OF DISEMBODIED FUNERALS

Would that it were true that the value of human bodies had been settled once and for all. Unfortunately, Platonic dualism is a powerful ideology, and within a few centuries of the beginnings of the Christian movement, Neoplatonic attitudes began to seep into Christian thought, enduring to this day. The earliest Christians could never have anticipated how thoroughly we contemporary Christians would be willing to trade our incarnational birthright for a bowl of warmed-over Neoplatonic porridge. Antipathy to the body now carries the day in many a Christian funeral, particularly among suburban, educated, white Protestants, where the frank acknowledgment of the pain of death and the firm hope in the resurrection of the body get nosed out by the sort of vague, body-denying, death-defying blather expressed in this popular anonymous funeral poem.

Do not stand at my grave and weep;
I am not there, I do not sleep.
I am a thousand winds that blow.
I am the diamond glints on snow.
I am the sunlight on ripened grain.
I am the gentle autumn rain.
When you awaken in the morning's hush
I am the swift uplifting rush of quiet birds in circled flight.
I am the soft stars that shine at night.
Do not stand at my grave and cry;
I am not there,
I did not die.

"I am a thousand winds that blow. . . . I did not die" is certainly a far cry from "Death has been swallowed up in victory. . . . Thanks be to God who gives us the victory through our Lord Jesus Christ" (1 Cor. 15:54, 57). Somehow we have been lured into "I am not there" sentimentality. Dead bodies, however, are definitely there, and they have become unfortunately an embarrassment to us, a vulgarity, so much so that we have arrived at a place unprecedented in history: conducting Christian funerals without the presence of the dead.

The retreat from embodiment cuts against the grain of Christian community. The brother or sister in Christ who has died has been known to us in embodied ways—in fact, only in embodied ways—and it has been a sacramental knowing. The body is the way we have received God's gift of life in this person. We have washed the body of this one in baptism, fed this body at the Lord's Table, prayed together with the words of our mouths, joined hands with this one in service to the world in the name of Christ, and touched this person's body in holy blessing and peace. And now bearing the dead body of this saint is the way we will experience and bear witness to the transition from this life to the next. So we need to wash this body once more and to anoint it, to treat it with reverence, to carry it to the place of farewell. To do so is more than a duty; to do so is a holy privilege and a joy.

We may say, though, "We don't want to focus on the dead body; we want to keep our eyes on God and provide a hopeful witness to the resurrection." But what can this shielding of our eyes from the body of our friend in Christ mean, except that we have begun to prefer the god of Plato and the purity of the immortal soul to the messiness of declaring, in the teeth of death's apparent victory, the good news of the resurrection of the body and the life everlasting? Pastors who would never imagine that a celebration of Holy Communion would somehow be "more spiritual" without the signs of the body, the bread and the wine, seem often ready to banish the dead from their own funerals. A pastor once told me that she preferred to do a private graveside service, followed by a memorial service without the deceased, because "the burial was like Good Friday, and then the memorial service was like the joy of Easter." But do we really want to leave the dead behind at Golgotha and not welcome them to Easter? Is Easter about only a resurrection of our memory, or is it about the resurrection of the body?

Theologian Paul Hoon called this retreat from the sheer facts of death and bodies a kind of "psychological regression." He wrote:

> One symptom of this may be the glibness with which we conceptualize the nature of the funeral in theological cliches: "to communicate the Christian hope," "to celebrate life," "to proclaim Christ's victory," "to comfort those who mourn," and so on. Certainly these are not untrue but often they strike me as convenient fall-backs, "rhetorical theology" I call them, that does not penetratingly grasp the real situation.[17]

Perhaps psychological regression or revived Platonism aren't the problems. Perhaps we have a perfectly good theology of the incarnation and the resurrection, but we just are not convinced by this that a good funeral demands a body. After all, we say, the person is there "in spirit," and the presence of a casket can be more of a clumsy distraction to worship than an asset. We are not amused, though, when a church member heads off to the golf course on Sunday morning, reassuring us that they will be present at worship "in spirit." The body does not lie. Ethically and theologically, we are not where we put our good intentions; we are where we put our bodies. Where your treasure is, where your stuff is, where your body is, there will your heart be also. We would not perform a wedding without the bride, a baptism without the baptismal candidate; so why a funeral without the deceased?

Or perhaps we are simply convinced that the migration of the funeral, away from a worshipful procession to the place of farewell and toward a moment focused on grief work, is a good thing. Here is the way one pastoral care–oriented book on liturgy expresses it:

> We need to rethink the funeral ritual process in response to the radical changes in patterns of living that affect and sometimes hinder the possibilities of grieving. . . . [I]t may be beneficial to suggest an

alternative order in which the vigil and committal occur before the memorial liturgy. The pastoral advantage of this sequence is that the ritual of closing the story at the committal, usually limited to close family and friends, could occur relatively quickly, before the celebration within the faith community. The approach presumes that a body not be present as a sign of closure for a memorial to be an effective ritual moment that enhances grieving.[18]

There are many things to object to in the previous paragraph. The assumptions here are that the funeral is not about theology but psychology, not primarily about the grand drama of the gospel but about the smaller landscape of grief, not about the story of the resurrection but the story of us. The goal of the committal is "closure," and that is best done as a more private matter with close family and friends, freeing up the public memorial service to be about the business of enhancing grieving without the clutter of the body being present.

Why would we contemplate such a truncated and diminished ritual? The real reason why we would do such a thing—and here's the rub—is that we are no longer persuaded that funerals are about the embodied person who has died. If we are walking the last mile of the way with a saint, then the saint needs to be there for the journey. But if the dead are just plain dead, or if they are disembodied souls floating in the gnostic ether, then the story line of the funeral has changed. The revised funeral story is that we are simply summoning memories, comforting each other, invoking some inspiring thoughts, doing effective "closure," and managing our grief; so it is better not to have an embarrassingly dead body cluttering up our meditation.

Of course, as a practical matter, Christians can raise the resurrection song when there is no coffin, no ashes, no body. Sometimes there is no way a body can be present, because bodies are lost, destroyed, or donated to science. And, of course, there are also ways, even if the body is absent, to honor the body in our words and prayers and holy imaginations (and we will discuss some of these in chapter 7). But as a cultural and ecclesial trend, a funeral minus the presence of the one who has died is a curious development. Why would we encourage it? If it is because we think that the body is a lesser thing, an unworthy presence in Christian worship, or if it is because we esteem the spirituality of the mind over the materialism of the body, then we are not paying full attention to biblical anthropology. We are not even paying attention to our deepest human impulses. People may say that the body is "only a shell," but let someone be lost at sea or crushed in the World Trade Center collapse, and society sacrifices time, money, and energy trying in every way imaginable to reclaim the body, even a small portion of the remains. Let the manager of the Tri-State Crematorium in Georgia actually treat bodies as refuse, stacking them like cordwood in a shed instead of cremating them as promised, and society cries out with a deep wound. We may say in moments of bravado, "A dead body is just a lump of clay, a mound of flesh bound for decay," but when the manager at the crematorium actually tosses bodies cavalierly into the back lot, our sensibilities are alerted that some sacred boundary has been crossed, some holy thing blasphemed.

Jessica Mitford touched a cultural nerve, though, when she wrinkled her nose at the idea of a body being present at a funeral, and especially at a ritual that at any point involves the viewing of a body, a practice Mitford found to be altogether barbaric and unseemly. She cites with approval a London undertaker's remark that viewing a dead body is "contrary to good taste and proper behavior."[19] At the time Mitford's book was published, funeral professionals had played right into her hands by trying to persuade an increasingly wary public that viewing an embalmed corpse smeared with a heavy layer of face powder was somehow both therapeutically necessary, because it allowed for "closure," and aesthetically desirable, because it transformed the last sighting into a "beautiful memory picture."

Christians, however, are not the least interested in "closure." Yes, death marks a dramatic transition, and it is important to recognize the change that has taken place in our relation to the dead. But in Christ the dead have an open future, and in the communion of the saints there is no "closure," but unending praise and participation in the ceaseless creativity of God. When the early Christians buried the abandoned corpses of the poor, there were no "beautiful memory pictures" to be seen. Christians are not afraid to look at the hard truth of death. As Oscar Cullmann has said, "Death in itself is not beautiful, not even the death of Jesus. . . . Whoever paints a pretty death can paint no resurrection. Whoever has not grasped the horror of death cannot join Paul in the hymn of victory: Death is swallowed up—in victory!"[20]

The point, then, is not about futile efforts to preserve the "beautiful" body with embalming fluid and waterproof burial vaults or to reinforce false distinctions of social class with expensive caskets and "floral tributes." The point is about giving thanks to God for a life we have known only in embodied ways, in what the dead did and said, in what they crafted with their hands, in where their feet took them, in the intimacy they experienced by giving themselves bodily to others, in the commitments they signified by their choosing to place their bodies here rather than there. The point is not to spread enough pancake makeup on the deceased to make them appear not to be dead. The point is to look into their faces and to see saints.

But even though Jessica Mitford had her fun with the silliness of "beautiful memory pictures," the fact is that her attitude toward dead bodies was reheated Neoplatonism, with a dash of Edwardian snobbery thrown in for good measure. When it comes to the Christian understanding of the sanctity of the body, though, Mitford was way out of her depth. In his book *The Undertaking*, funeral director Thomas Lynch comments on the "just a shell" theory of dead bodies. "You hear a lot of it," he observes, "from young clergy, old family friends, well intentioned in-laws—folks who are unsettled by the fresh grief of others." He remembers a time when an Episcopal deacon said something of this sort to the mother of a teenager, dead of leukemia, and promptly received a swift slap. "I'll tell you when it's 'just a shell,'" she retorted. "For now and until I tell you otherwise, she's my daughter."[21] Lynch goes on to say,

> So to suggest in the early going of grief that the dead body is "just" anything rings as tinny in its attempt to minimalize as if we were to say that it was "just" a bad hair day when the girl went bald from chemotherapy. Or that our hope for heaven on her behalf was based on the belief that Christ raised "just" a body from dead. What if, rather than crucifixion, he'd opted for suffering low self-esteem for the remission of sins? What if, rather than "just a shell," he'd raised his personality, say, or The Idea of Himself? Do you think they'd have changed the calendar for that? . . . Easter was a body and blood thing, no symbols, no euphemisms, no half measures.[22]

One of the clearest and most needed reforms in the funeral practices of many Christian communities is the honoring of the bodies of the deceased. The Christian dead should be welcomed once again to their own funerals. If they cannot literally be there in bodily presence, then we must summon every gift of language we have to establish their embodied presence in our memories and imaginations. How else are we going to experience the blessed burden of carrying them to the waiting arms of God, singing as we go?

3

The Future of the Dead in Christ

Everything we have said so far about the sanctity of human life and the honoring of bodies rests, of course, on a Christian theology of death. Actually in the face of a mystery so profound as death and a tradition so diverse as Christianity, it is more accurate to speak in the plural, of Christian theologies of death. When Christian faith reflects on any of life's great issues, it is not possible to catch it all up in a single stitch. Multiple vantage points are both inevitable and needed. As New Testament scholar Norman Perrin is reported to have said one day to theologian Langdon Gilkey, "Well, Langdon, which of my fifty-seven New Testament christologies do you want to use today?"[1]

This is not the place to rehearse the full chorus of Christian voices about the meaning of death, but in order to understand how a funeral is a ritual enactment of the promise of the gospel in the presence of death, we need at least to sketch a broad theological picture of the sort of Christian thinking about death that undergirds funerals. Funerals are capable, of course, of expressing the wide range of inflections in Christian theology, from liberal to evangelical to feminist to liberationist and so on, but amid those many perspectives, funerals have, as does worship in general, a conserving function. The funeral liturgy remembers the gospel in its most basic form and holds it in trust for us, knowing that we will urgently need it when death throws us into confusion and tries to make a mockery of faith.

CAPITAL-*D* DEATH, SMALL-*d* DEATH,
AND DEATH IN CHRIST

The funeral process begins, of course, with a person's death, so we begin this theological exploration by noting that, when it comes to human death, the Christian faith identifies two essential forms of death, or two ways of construing death, to which it then adds a third. The two essential forms of death are natural death (which we might call "small-*d* death") and Death as mythic force, as the enemy of all that God wills for life (which we might call capital-*D* Death). The third form of death, added by the gospel, is death in Christ.

Small-*d* death is simply the recognition that human beings are mortal. We have a life span, short or long; we are born, we live, we die. This form of death marks us off as human and not divine, and it is a mixed blessing. On the positive side, our mortality teaches us "to count our days that we may gain a wise heart" (Ps. 90:12). The fact that we do not have infinite time, infinite options, and infinite opportunities to loop back around and do things over makes our decisions count and makes our choices significant. It generates human creativity and faith. It relieves us of the burden and terror of living forever as frail and failing bodies. As God says in Genesis, "My spirit shall not abide in mortals forever, for they are flesh" (Gen. 6:3).[2] This form of death can come with peace and kindness, and it is what allows a deeply grieving spouse to say when death has ended agony and suffering, "My heart is broken, but in some ways this comes as a blessing."

On the negative side, this death holds a threat above our heads everyday that tomorrow we will be gone, forgotten, nothing. "As for mortals, their days are like grass; they flourish like a flower of the field; for the wind passes over it and it is gone, and its place knows it no more" (Ps. 103:15–16). This causes the anxiety of impermanence, which in turn stimulates us to rebel against our mortality, either by fabricating the illusion that we are immortal gods or, conversely, by turning against ourselves in despair and wasting our selves, our gifts, and our time, stamping out the very life we have been given. In short, awareness of our mortality both prompts us to wisdom and prompts us to sin.

Capital-*D* Death is a different reality from small-*d* death. It comes toward us never as a friend but as an alien and destructive force. There is nothing natural about it. It is our enemy, and it is God's enemy; indeed, Paul calls it "the last enemy" (1 Cor. 15:26). Death in this form is out to steal life from human beings, but it does not stop with individuals. Death wants to capture territory, to possess principalities. It desires to dehumanize all institutions, poison all relationships, set people against people in warfare, replace all love with hate, transform all words of hope into blasphemy, to fuel the fires of distrust, to lead people to the depths of despair, to shatter all attempts to build community, and to make a mockery of God, faith, and the gift of life. It is "the pestilence that stalks in darkness" and "the destruction that wastes at noonday" (Ps. 91:6).

It is important to maintain, at funerals and otherwise, the distinction between these two categories: death and Death. If we thunder out only denunciations of Death, the final enemy, we may obscure the fact that death, biological death, can sometimes come as a friend, ending pain and halting the merciless fall of sufferers into despair. On the other hand, if we forget about Death's bloody saber and focus only on death as a part of the natural flow of life, we can be seduced into bland and finally unchristian bromides about death. We can overlook the poisonous fangs of the old serpent and blather about the naturalness of death, of death as "the final stage of growth" or an experience to greet with open arms and "acceptance,"[3] as in the sentiment of the Nancy Byrd Turner poem that makes an appearance in many funeral sermons: "Death is only an old door set in a garden wall. On quiet hinges it gives at dusk, when the thrushes call. . . . There is nothing to trouble any heart, nothing to hurt at all. Death is only a quiet door in a garden wall."[4] Jesus, however, did not complacently face the prospect of his own death as "a quiet door," but instead was "deeply grieved, even to death" (Matt. 26:38) and died "with loud cries and tears" (Heb. 5:7).

Consider, as yet another example of well-meaning Christians overoptimistically sanding off all of death's rough edges, the following naive, death-embracing language taken from a denominational study document on euthanasia:

> Death for an older person should be a beautiful event. There is beauty in birth, growth, fullness of life and then, equally so, in the tapering off and final end. There are analogies all about us. What is more beautiful than the spring budding of small leaves; than the fully-leaved tree in summer; and then in the beautiful brightly colored autumn leaves gliding gracefully to the ground? So it is with humans.[5]

Perhaps we should not be surprised by this sweetly fond embrace of natural death and near total disregard for the destructive character of Death, since the church is sometimes the first to lose its grip on its own bold and clear-eyed theology. When lay theologian William Stringfellow visited Harvard University in the early 1960s, he was to speak on the theological theme of the powers and principalities of death loose in the world. In fact, he was scheduled to speak twice on the same day, once at the business school and then at the divinity school. Stringfellow thought about modifying his talk for the business school by eliminating any explicit biblical references or apocalyptic language, but he finally decided to go with the same speech for both audiences. Ironically, the students in the business school turned out to be far more responsive and alert to what he was talking about than were the divinity students. The business students kept Stringfellow long past the scheduled hour, offering numerous examples of the death-dealing powers at work in corporations and the business world. The seminarians, however, mostly yawned, saying that talk of "powers and principalities" was "archaic imagery having no reference to contemporary reality."[6] Evidently there is nothing like a little experience on Wall Street to reinvigorate awareness of the powers of Death.

Human life is bounded by mortality, by small-*d* death, and savaged by the voracious appetite of our old enemy, capital-*D* Death. Reinhold Niebuhr pictured well the human condition. Human beings are set down in the midst of history, and we give our energies to making the best life we know how to make for ourselves, forming relationships, daring to bring children into the world, working at our trade, building up and nourishing communities. And yet we have a sense that life, while not other than this, is somehow more than this, that we are more than this. Life is more than the sum of its parts, and we cannot be fully summed up by the mere biographical details—that we were born in Seattle, went to Central High, worked in a hardware store, joined the Rotary, married our high-school sweetheart, and had three children. This is our life, yes, but not all of it. We are more than our little lot in life; we are creatures of freedom who live with our eyes fixed on a distant horizon. Human beings yearn for our labors to count where we are but also to count beyond this one little place where we stand on the earth and to endure beyond this one tiny moment in time. Thus every person, said Niebuhr, "has a direct relation to eternity, for he seeks for the completion of the meaning of his life beyond the fragmentary realizations of meaning which can be discerned at any point in the process where an individual may live or die."[7]

But death has no patience for this; death scorns human beings who are set down in the middle of history with aspirations for eternal worth.

As for history, along comes small-*d* death to kill us and to end our life in time and place. "The wind passes over it and it is gone." As for eternity, along comes capital-*D* Death to sneer at our hopes, to take away our freedom, and to turn us into slaves paid only the wages of sin, which severs our relationship to the eternal God. If we seek evidence for this, we can go to the shopping mall, and there we will see us, fevered consumers ready to throw off all hints of the eternal for the ceaseless consumption of bread that does not nourish, while Death stands in the shadows and laughs. It is not as though we have a choice. As theologian Arthur McGill has said,

> [T]here is no point in leveling an attack against selfishness, or in exhorting people to get busy and help others . . . [for] whether people serve themselves or serve others is not in their power to choose. This is decided wholly in terms of the kind of world in which they think they live, in terms of the kind of power they see ruling the roost. The issue lies at the level of the god they worship and not in the kind of person that they may want to be. In New Testament terms, they live or die according to the king that holds them and the kingdom to which they belong.[8]

If, as McGill says, we live or die according to the king that holds us and the kingdom to which we belong, then we are held by King Death and we die. We are trapped; we cannot escape the clutches of death, and, as Niebuhr knew, "Only God can solve this problem."[9] Paul too knew: "Wretched man that I am!" he cried. "Who will rescue me from this body of death?" (Rom. 7:24).

CROSS AND RESURRECTION: CHRIST'S VICTORY OVER DEATH

Paul, of course, knew the answer to his own anguished cry. What he knew is the truth that forms the gospel proclamation about our liberation from both death and Death that Christians echo at funerals: "Thanks be to God through Jesus Christ our Lord! . . . For the law of the Spirit of life in Christ Jesus has set you free from the law of sin and death" (Rom. 7:25; 8:2).

Now how did this act of liberation take place? How have we been set free from sin and death? It was not done by a command from afar, by an edict from a distant throne. According to the gospel, it was done in the middle of history, the same history in which we find ourselves, through the death of a man on a Roman cross. The death of Jesus is an event so near to us, so close to our own experience, that we can reach out and touch it. Jesus, a human being like us, with a life arced toward the eternal, just like us, got killed and died, just as we will die. Even for Jesus, Death and death apparently won, as they always do. Despite its cruelty, despite the fact that Jesus was God's own Son, Jesus' death was an event of history so ordinary that we can even mark in the obituary the day on which it happened; it was a Friday.

And yet, according to the witnesses, on Sunday morning this ordinary end of a mortal man was transformed into the truly extraordinary. God raised Jesus from the dead. The death and resurrection of Jesus is an event so full of meaning and mystery that, as Eberhard Jüngel has observed, even "the New Testament offers us no single, uniform doctrine" to account for it.[10]

This much we are told: Jesus was raised bodily. The Gospel writers are keen to make that point. Jesus, who was physically present to his followers before his death, was an embodied presence to them afterward, and the resurrection was no mere mental state or inner illumination or spiritualized vision. "The relation of Jesus to his disciples . . . is not suddenly privatized," writes Rowan Williams. "In his ministry, Jesus created and sustained the community of his friends by speech and touch and the sharing of food; and so, after his resurrection, that community is sustained in the same way. It is not taken away from history, from matter, from bodies and words."[11]

But the resurrection was not a supernatural magic trick in which Jesus, who was a dead body, is now—presto!—a live body, back just as he was. The Gospel writers are keen about this too. The risen Jesus was embodied, but it was not precisely the same body he had once had. There were continuities; the body of the risen Jesus was in some ways like his former body, like our bodies. His followers looked at his face and recognized him, he ate food with them just as before, and he invited them to touch his flesh so they would know he was not a ghost or a dream. But there were also discontinuities; his risen body was not like his former body and not like our bodies. He could stand beside someone in a garden or walk along a road with followers, people who had known and loved him, and yet his identity somehow remained hidden from their eyes. He walked through doors and could vanish in an instant. This was not just the old Jesus given a shot of new life. These New Testament stories of the strangeness of Jesus' risen body are saying that this was a transformed Jesus, and a glorified body. This was not a resuscitation; it was a resurrection.

The bodily resurrection of Jesus—so troubling to philosophers, so perplexing to scientists, so repulsive to gnostics—is a crucial claim, but not a crudely literalistic one. It is not as if God gathered together all of the cells and molecules of Jesus' body, including the DNA he left on the chalice at the Last Supper and on the cross beam, reassembled them, and set Jesus back walking the streets of Jerusalem. The claim is that God raised the fullness of Jesus, the person of Jesus, from the dead. God raised *Jesus*, the Jesus who was known and experienced in the things he said and did with his body—not the idea of Jesus, not the spirit of Jesus, but *Jesus*; and that is an embodied reality.

Reinhold Niebuhr, while rejecting a literalistic interpretation of the bodily resurrection, reported in the middle of his theological career that what he had once doubted—the bodily resurrection of Jesus—had become central to his theology. In his own theological development he had gradually come to understand that the words of the ancient creed, "I believe in the resurrection of the body," name an indispensable aspect of the Christian faith:

> These closing words of the Apostolic Creed in which the Christian hope of the fulfillment of life is expressed, were, as I remember it, an offense and a stumbling block to young theologians at the time my generation graduated from theological seminaries. . . . We were not certain we could honestly express our faith in such a formula. . . .
>
> The twenty years that divide that time from this have brought great changes in theological thought. . . . Yet some of us have been persuaded to take the stone which was then rejected and make it the head of the corner. In other words, there is no part of the Apostles' Creed which, in our present opinion, expresses the whole genius of the Christian faith more nearly than just the despised phrase: "I believe in the resurrection of the body."[12]

When the early Christians began to reflect on the meaning of this startling Easter encounter with the risen and embodied Jesus, they came to the realization that, of the many things Easter meant for them, one of the most astonishing was that, in the death and resurrection of Jesus, Death itself had been defeated. When the man Jesus was hanging on the cross, dying the kind of death that all humans must die one way or another, God had fully identified with Jesus. The God they had always known before was immortal, untouched by death, always at infinite distance from human mortality. But in Jesus, God had done the unimaginable, had become one with humanity even in death. As Jüngel states, "in the death of Jesus [God] endures contact with death. By identifying himself with the dead Jesus, God exposed himself to the alienating power of death. God exposed his own divinity to the power of negation. And God did this precisely in order to be God for all [people]."[13]

The motivation for this action on the part of God was love, pure and simple—or love, pure and not so simple. "God, through love, shares the pain of death,"[14] and in the resurrection, God gives humanity victory over Death. Humanity, as Niebuhr said, has always yearned to gather the bits and fragments of its historically bounded life together and make of it something eternal, but the gate was always blocked by the poisonous scorpion of Death. But in the cross and resurrection of Jesus, God has opened the gate by taking into the very life of God the scorpion's sting and exhausting it. "Where, O death, is your sting?" (1 Cor. 15:55). Death's sting is in the very life of God, overcome in the cross and resurrection of Jesus. God swallowed up death in victory. In the words of Jürgen Moltmann, "Death will die, not-being will be no longer, hell will go to hell."[15]

In the resurrection of Jesus, the death sentence pronounced upon all humanity has been reversed in the highest court, the court of heaven, and as a consequence all hell has broken loose in hell. The closing words of the stirring ancient Easter sermon, often attributed to John Chrysostom, picture Death and hell thrown into a frenzied uproar because of Easter:

> Let no one fear death, for the Death of our Savior has set us free.
> He has destroyed it by enduring it.
> He destroyed Hades when He descended into it.
> He put it into an uproar even as it tasted of His flesh.
> Isaiah foretold this when he said,
> "You, O Hell, have been troubled by encountering Him below."
> Hell was in an uproar because it was done away with.
> It was in an uproar because it is mocked.
> It was in an uproar, for it is destroyed.
> It is in an uproar, for it is annihilated.
> It is in an uproar, for it is now made captive.
> Hell took a body, and discovered God.
> It took earth, and encountered heaven.
> It took what it saw, and was overcome by what it did not see.

O death, where is thy sting?
O Hades, where is thy victory?
Christ is risen, and you, O death, are annihilated!
Christ is risen, and the evil ones are cast down!
Christ is risen, and the angels rejoice!
Christ is risen, and life is liberated!
Christ is risen, and the tomb is emptied of its dead;
for Christ having risen from the dead,
is become the first-fruits of those who have fallen asleep.
To him be glory and power forever and ever. Amen![16]

The risen Jesus stands in that doorway between ordinary time and eternity, the threshold between historical reality and the reign of God. That is why his risen body is ambiguous, both continuous and discontinuous with his body before. He is in history and time, and his body is familiar and recognizable, bearing yet the wounds of his cruel death. But he is also transfigured in glory, a part of the eternal, no longer mortal, and we are not fully able to see and comprehend what he has become.

Jesus did not die as a hero to be admired or a role model to be emulated. He died as an obedient Son of God, and he rose as a savior. Without him, we still must face the lonely and mortal combat with death, and the outcome is inevitable. There is no destiny for us but the grave. With him and because of him, there is a way forward, a truth to trust, and a life to be preserved. This, then, is the third form of death, added by the gospel: death in Christ, death defeated, death as experienced in and through Christ. When God joined God's very self to Jesus on the cross, God opened the divine life to the reality of death, and then defeated it. When we join ourselves to Jesus in baptism, our death becomes gathered up into Jesus' death and, therefore, into God's victory over death. "If we have been united with him in a death like his, we will certainly be united with him in a resurrection like his" (Rom. 6:5). In the death and resurrection of Jesus, God defeated our ancient nemesis Death, and the path to life has been opened to us. Because God did not raise only the idea of Jesus or the spirit of Jesus but the body of Jesus, what makes up the embodied stuff of our lives—our relationships, the words we have spoken, the acts of love we have done—counts, counts eternally. The commitments of our lives and the places we have placed our bodies are gathered up by the power of God and transformed in the resurrection into the very life of God: As Niebuhr said,

The hope of the resurrection reaffirms that ultimately finiteness will be emancipated from anxiety and the self will know itself as it is known. . . . The idea of the resurrection implies that the historical elaborations of the richness of creation, in all their variety, will participate in the consummation of history. It gives the struggles in which [people] are engaged to preserve civilizations, and to fulfill goodness in history, abiding significance and does not relegate them to a meaningless flux, of which there will be no echo in eternity.[17]

A FUNERAL THEOLOGY

We can now bring this Christian theology of death home to the funeral itself. In a Christian funeral, we are telling two stories at one and the same time. The first story is that a sister or brother in Christ has died, and we are reverently carrying the body to the place of disposition. We cannot hide the sheer facts of this story, and we should not try. Someone is dead, and the old enemy death has apparently claimed yet another trophy. Even if the deceased is a ninety-five-year-old Sunday school teacher who died peacefully in her sleep, this death is not altogether sweet and beautiful. Death has once again severed the cords of love, shattered community, and destroyed a life. Someone is dead. Something must be done with the dead body, and we do it with care and love.

But we are also telling another story, a story made possible by Easter, a story that unmasks death's lies. This story is that a saint of God, precious in the sight of God, is being carried by the faithful, not to the abode of the dead, but into the arms of God. We tenderly carry the body of the one we have loved to the place of farewell, weeping perhaps, but also singing psalms and Easter songs as we travel. This body of the saint is a sign of remembrance and thanksgiving for all that we have received in and through this person's life and also a sign of hope that death has done its worst and lost, because the God who defeated death in the raising of Jesus Christ has also raised this child of God in an imperishable and glorified body.

The intermingling of these two stories at a funeral makes room for grief as well as joy. It also raises questions: When is this dead person raised in Christ? In what form? And is this true only for those who have faith in Christ, or others too? These are challenging questions, and the church has always had difficulty providing clear answers. But they are important and pressing questions, so we must try to say what we can.

As for the question of when a person is raised to new life, the New Testament provides evidence for two quite different answers. On the one hand, Paul told the Thessalonians that the dead would lie in state, as it were, until the last day, when all of the dead in Christ will be raised together to the sound of a trumpet: "For the Lord himself, with a cry of command, with the archangel's call and with the sound of God's trumpet, will descend from heaven, and the dead in Christ will rise first. Then we who are alive . . . will be caught up in the clouds" (1 Thess. 4:16–17). On the other hand, Paul told the Philippians that he could not make up his mind which was better, to "depart and be with Christ," which Paul preferred, or to stick around and do more ministry with them (Phil. 1:23), which sounds as if he thinks that death means going right away to be with Christ. Jesus told a story about a poor man named Lazarus who died and was immediately "carried away by the angels to be with Abraham" (Luke 16:22), and he said to the thief on the cross, "Truly I tell you, today you will be with me in Paradise" (Luke 23:43).

So, which is it? Do the saints go immediately to God at death, or do they go into some kind of holding pattern, waiting for the general resurrection of the dead? There is trouble, it seems, whichever way we answer that. If we say, as most funeral liturgies seem to imply, that the person is raised immediately to be with God, then we have the problem of facing up to our experience and common sense that remind us that there is a body or a box of ashes somewhere out there slowly turning into very earthly dust. And we also have by implication a quite individualistic picture of the eternal life being populated one saint at a time.

The answer that the dead wait for a general resurrection seems, at first glance, to solve the problem of individualism, since the dead are raised en masse, and it has the added virtue of making it clear that the ultimate victory of God over death is not just about human life but about the whole of creation. Ultimately God is going to make "a new heaven and a new earth," to use the traditional language, and the human dead are but a part of this vast act of new creation.

But soon problems about this answer stir our minds; particularly, if the dead are raised together at the end of time, we have the dilemma of *where* to park the dead in our theological imaginations in the meantime. The church has managed to come up with three broad answers to the question of the when of the resurrection and the whereabouts of the dead, none of them very satisfactory.

The first answer is that when someone dies, the soul and body immediately separate. The soul flies away to God, and the body goes into the ground. Here, for example, is a description of the state of the dead found in a classic seventeenth-century creed of the Reformed theological tradition, the Westminster Confession of Faith:

> The bodies of men, after death, return to dust, and see corruption; but their souls (which neither die nor sleep), having an immortal subsistence, immediately return to God who gave them. The souls of the righteous, being then made perfect in holiness, are received into the highest heavens, where they behold the face of God in light and glory, waiting for the full redemption of their bodies; and the souls of the wicked are cast into hell, where they remain in torments and utter darkness, reserved to the judgment of the great day. Besides these two places for souls separated from their bodies, the Scripture acknowledgeth none.[18]

The virtue of this statement is that it at least recognizes that neither being "asleep in Jesus" (that is, being somehow in Jesus' presence but unconscious of that fact) nor being temporarily dead (that is, completely dead but "in storage" until the last day) is a theological live option for the fate of the Christian saints. Beyond that, though, this notion of souls and bodies being apart from each other until judgment day does not have much to commend it. To begin with, it is fully Platonic in origin and carries with it the unbiblical idea that it somehow makes sense to speak of human beings as "souls" apart from bodies. Even the normally reliable Scottish theologian John Baillie gets in the act:

> The orthodox teaching, both Roman and Protestant, is that until the last day the souls of both the blessed and of the damned remain *disembodied*, though already dwelling in what is to be their final place of abode; but on that Last Day there will be a General Resurrection whereby the souls of both are reunited to their old bodies.[19]

Not only is this view infected with dualism; it also carries with it some strange twists of logic. It implies, as James Barr has pointed out, that, when people die, their immortal souls go wafting off to final destinations, presumably either heaven or hell, until judgment day, when they swoop back down to earth and pick up their new bodies, only to return again to where they had been all along since death, which would be pretty funny if it were not serious theology. "There is no indication," says Barr wryly, "of what difference this may make."[20]

A second view of just where the dead may be and when they are to rise is one that has recently gained an advocate in the fine New

Testament scholar N. T. Wright. In two books, *For All the Saints?*[21] and *Surprised by Hope*,[22] Wright is eager to squash the notion, so dear to romantic piety, that Christianity is all about individuals "going to heaven." The idea that individuals, one by one, make their personal pilgrimages to an ethereal oasis in the afterlife is not, Wright argues, what the New Testament has in mind. He makes a vigorous case instead that the Scripture describes one and only one resurrection of human beings, namely, the general resurrection of the dead as a part of God's new creation of the earth at some specific time in the future. Salvation is not about individuals escaping earth and going to heaven, Wright insists; it is about God's intention to renew the earth and to involve us in this act of re-creation.

According to Wright, then, there is one general resurrection, and that happens in the future when God in Christ re-creates all things. But in the meantime, where are the dead until that day when God renovates the earth? "I arrive at this view," says Wright, "that all the Christian departed are in substantially the same state, that of restful happiness."[23] When Jesus said to the thief, "Today you will be with me in Paradise," Wright argues, "paradise" did not mean "heaven," but what paradise means in some other Jewish contexts, namely, "the blissful garden, the parkland of rest and tranquility, where the dead are refreshed as they await the dawn of the new day."[24]

So the dead are in a blissful garden of rest and tranquility awaiting the day of resurrection. This sounds nice, at least until one again raises the questions of bodies, at which point things get a bit dicey. Are these dead, who are residing temporarily in "restful happiness," embodied? Wright is not clear on this point. On the one hand, he is a fierce critic of Platonic dualism and its doctrine of the disembodied immortal soul. So if he says, no, the blissful dead do not have bodies but are temporarily disembodied "persons," waiting until the new creation for their resurrected bodies, then the Platonism he slew at the front door has slipped in, dagger in hand, through the back way. If, on the other hand, he would say, yes, the blissful dead are indeed embodied in their state of "restful happiness," then where are they, and what sort of bodies do they have? Either they are out there in the cemeteries in their old bodies, which are crumbling rapidly away, a strange thought, or they already have their glorified bodies, in which case, what's the point of lying around in paradise park? Wright claims support for this "two-stage post-mortem future" in patristic and medieval theologians,[25] but regardless of where this view originates, it results in a kind of Protestant purgatory, an intermediate state for the Christian dead, only this time without the purgation.

The third possibility for where the dead may be at the moment, a modified version of the first view, is indeed the classical doctrine of purgatory. As it was in the first view, dead bodies go to the earth until the general resurrection. Souls fly away, but not to God—not yet anyway. They are not ready yet to be fully in the presence of God, but must be cleansed of the sin that still clings to them. They go then to purgatory to have their souls rid of impurity.

By the eve of the Reformation, the idea of purgatory had become fixed in Western church doctrine. For the most part, even very faithful Christians were thought to have died with enough corruption in their souls to render them not yet fit to join the communion of the saints. These not-quite-saints were no longer on earth, but they weren't in paradise or heaven either. They were instead in a middle place or a state of in-betweenness (purgatory was described both ways), and they would remain there until they had been, as the name purgatory implies, purged of their sins.

Purgatory involved suffering and punishment, and therefore it was not a place where one wanted to spend much time or wished for a loved one to be, either. Fortunately, there was a way to hasten the purification process. The living could help souls in purgatory by arranging to have Masses said on their behalf, giving alms in their name, fasting in their memory, doing good deeds in their honor, and, most important, praying for them. All such acts of devotion were thought to be beneficial to the dead, making their time in purgatory shorter and less severe. Eventually, as is well known, the system led to greed and corruption, as various church authorities collected vast sums of money from the faithful in exchange for "indulgences," which were in essence promises that the sentence of time in purgatory would be shortened or commuted.

Even without the corruption, though, the whole system of purgatory was a vexatious social burden. In some ways purgatory was like today's nursing homes: it was filled with multitudes of not-quite-departed people who needed the assistance of the living and who were, therefore, the moral and financial responsibility of the younger generation.[26] Eventually the burden became too heavy to bear, and the time grew ripe for a revolt. It came most powerfully with the Reformation and its claim that people were saved not by works but by faith alone. The idea that one could do some meritorious act of devotion, lubricated by a little cash, that would somehow nudge the dead out of purgatory and closer to heaven was one of the major grievances against Rome that provoked the Reformation. For the Reformers, the whole idea of purgatory was not only a church scandal; it was also thoroughly unbiblical and unjustified theologically. The Reformation may have given theological voice to the protest, but purgatory, as a tax on the living, was already doomed. Even without Luther's revolt, the living were already quite weary of carrying the dead on their backs.

Today, the medieval doctrine of purgatory, with its full array of gears and pulleys, has few friends, and good riddance. Many contemporary Catholic theologians, while in some ways obligated to keep the idea of purgatory going, are nevertheless drastically redefining purgatory along more biblical and christological lines. For example, in his book *Eschatology*, Joseph Ratzinger (now Pope Benedict XVI), reframes purgatory not as some "supra-worldly concentration camp" but as a description of a process of transformation, namely, the one that happens in the twinkling of an eye to the dead who ultimately encounter the refining fire of Christ's mercy. Purgatory becomes that flashing instant between who we are at death and who we will be in the full presence of God, an instant in which all that is stubble and straw is burned away by grace.[27] This turns purgatory from a place to a moment, from a region to an experience of transforming mercy, and makes purgatory close, if not identical, to Paul's statement that "this perishable body must put on imperishability" (1 Cor. 15:53).

Most of this mischief and confusion about the place of the dead was stirred up not only by Platonic dualism but by biblical literalism and, perhaps most of all, by the perfectly understandable attempt to work all of this out using only the metrics of linear, historical clock time, with its fixed notions of before and after, now and then. But when we speak in a Christian sense about death and resurrection, we are working not in clock time alone, but in at least two time frames: ordinary historical time and eschatological time (or perhaps more accurately, the eternal that transcends time). Moltmann points in a better direction when he argues that the raising of individuals at the hour of their deaths, which we in our world of clocks and calendars experience one by one in linear chronological fashion, and the general raising of all the dead in Christ on the Day of the Lord should be thought of not as events that happen one before the other in temporal sequence but as simultaneous events:

> But how ought we to imagine a "resurrection at death"? The starting point must again be eschatology: the "Last Day" is not just the

chronologically final day in the calendar. It is eschatologically the
Day of the Lord, and therefore the Day of Days. If this is the day
when the dead are raised, then it appears to all the dead simultaneously, "in a moment"—that is diachronically—irrespective of when
in time they died. If this is correct, then we must be able to say the
converse, too: that the hour of every individual death in this present
time leads directly into that eternal "Day of the Lord."[28]

The theological possibility that Moltmann sketches here certainly
addresses, even if it does not completely solve, the problems in the
other views. Scripture gives us the image of the great Shalom of God,
the vision of God reconciled to and at peace with all (Col. 1:20), of a
new heaven and a new earth and God in union with all humanity (Rev.
21:3), of a reality devoid of suffering and death (Rev. 21:4), of God
being "all in all" (1 Cor. 15:28). How shall we picture this reality, this
reign of God, in relationship to ourselves? Is this great Shalom a reality
that stands in our future, in the sense that as we turn the pages of the
calendar we are getting closer and closer to this day, like the arrival of
Christmas? Or does God's Shalom transcend all historical time?

Imagine one of those line drawings used to show something about
how perception works. If one looks at the line drawing *this* way, it is
clearly a picture of a candlestick, but if one adjusts one's perception and
looks at the drawing *that* way, it suddenly appears to be the profile of
two faces looking toward each other. Same drawing, two perceptions.
So look at the reign of God from two perspectives. First, from our
vantage point in the middle of history, defined as we are by the march
of time, the reign of God lies in the future. It presses in on the present,
even spills over into the present in signs and wonders, but the Parousia,
that "Great Gettin' Up Morning," as the old spiritual called it, is yet
to come. From our place in the flow of time and history, here is the
truth about the dead expressed in the best way it can be said, with all
the verbs in the future tense: There is coming a day when "the trumpet
will sound, and the dead will be raised imperishable, and we will be
changed" (1 Cor. 15:52).

But if we adjust our perception and look at the same image another
way, if we look at the reign of God framed differently, the candlestick
becomes the two faces. We see something that, as history-bound creatures, we can hardly imagine: the reign of God without time, the eternal God as all in all. Time seems to us to be a given, a quality that could
not possibly *not* be. But this is not true. Time is not God; God created
time. There was no time until God made it—"there was evening and

there was morning, the first day" (Gen. 1:5). Time is one of God's many good gifts to us. God makes time for us; God has time for us.[29] But time is a feature of the creation, and it will pass away. For historically bound creatures, if time stops for us personally, we have run out of time and we are dead. If time stops for the whole earth, the world has run out of time and come to an end. But God is not a creature; God is the creator. In the life of God, there is no time as we know it, and there is no running out of time, no death, and no end.

How do we speak of this timeless reality? What language shall we borrow to describe eternal life and our relationship to it? We have no language really. We cannot pick ourselves up out of time to speak of that which has no time, so we pick the best word we can: "Today." "Today" sounds, of course, like a time-bound word, but we do not mean "today," like Monday or Saturday or tomorrow afternoon, but "Today," as in the Day of Days, the Day when there is no night, the Day when there is no "when," the Today of God, the great Sabbath Day of rest, the Today spoken of in Hebrews: "[God] sets a certain day—'today'" (Heb. 4:7), the Today as in "Today you will be with me in Paradise."

These two perspectives come together in John 11 in the conversation between Jesus and Martha, the sister of Jesus' friend Lazarus. In that way of the author of John—superimposing two kinds of time, ordinary and eternal, layering the candlestick and the faces in the same text—we are shown Martha, who is in clock time, historical time, and we are shown Jesus, who is eternal, not constrained by time. Martha is distraught because her brother Lazarus has died and Jesus was not there to help. From Martha's perspective, they have run out of time.

"Lord, if you had been here, my brother would not have died." Measured by the turning of the clock and the march of days, Jesus was, frankly, late . . . too late.

But then eternity speaks into temporality: "Your brother will rise again."

Martha hears and responds as one whose perception is constrained by time and history. "I know that he will rise again in the resurrection on the last day."

But eternity speaks not of "the last day" but of Today.

"I *am* the resurrection and the life," Jesus tells her.

Returning to our question of the where and when of the dead, we experience human deaths one after the other in time. Augustine dies, then Catherine of Siena, then Luther, then Wesley, then Mother

Teresa, and on goes the line. When does God raise them from the dead and give to them glorified bodies? Immediately. Death does not have one second's worth of victory over them. But it is also true that they rise, along with all the other saints, together at the same time.

If this seems like theological sleight of hand, having our cake and eating it too, I would simply point out that, since Einstein, even in the natural and physical world we have been able to grasp the fluid character of time. In an Einsteinian universe, time can move forward and time can reverse; events in time can happen both in sequence and simultaneously. I am not suggesting that contemporary physics's view of time and a theological understanding of time are to be equated. I am simply saying that one helps us imagine the plausibility of the other.

One last question remains: Who are the dead who are raised imperishable? Who participates in Christ's victory over death? Christians only? All of "the righteous," whoever that might be? Every human being, good or bad? How broad is the way of Christ, how expansive the sheep who belong to Jesus but who are "not of this fold" (John 10:26), how wide the mercy of God? The question is an important and vexing one, and it tends to divide the house.

While the biblical evidence is mixed, the overall thrust of the biblical witness seems to encourage a hope for the redemption of all humanity. We are promised that God will be all in all, and we are told of a God who takes "no pleasure in the death of anyone" (Ezek. 18:32), a God who is patient, "not wanting any to perish" (2 Pet. 3:9) and who "was pleased to reconcile to himself all things" (Col. 1:20). The notion that the eternal fate of people swings on whether they decide to allow Jesus Christ into their hearts is ruthlessly individualistic and runs counter to the biblical hope of a new creation. Putting the weight of God's intent to redeem creation on a series of personal choices is something like a man in a cottage on the coast of Normandy in June of 1944, as the Allied forces swept across the beaches, thinking that he had to choose whether to be liberated or not. Moreover, such a view of salvation puts God's will at the mercy of human decision making. As Moltmann observes:

> Can some people *damn themselves,* and others redeem themselves by accepting Christ? If this were so, God's decisions would be dependent upon the will of human beings. God would become the auxiliary who executes the wishes of people who decide their fate for themselves. If I can damn myself, I am my own God and judge. Taken to a logical conclusion, this is atheistic.[30]

On the other hand, a sweet and easy universalism itself infringes on the freedom of God (God *must* redeem every human being, because, after all, that's what *I* would do) and runs into problems with ethics. Theologian Miroslav Volf makes the case that when Christians call people in the midst of a bloody and unjust world to turn the other cheek and to respond to violence with nonviolence, this ethical call rests logically on the promise that God will judge the wicked and violent. "[I]f God were not angry at injustice and deception," writes Volf, "and *did not* make the final end to violence God would not be worthy of our worship."[31] Volf recognizes that the notion of God as judge of the wicked "will be unpopular with many Christians, especially theologians in the West," but he invites his skeptical readers to engage in a thought experiment where ideas about the nonjudging God are tried out in the middle of a bloody war zone:

> To the person who is inclined to dismiss [the idea that God will judge the violent], I suggest imagining that you are delivering a lecture in a war zone. . . . Among your listeners are people whose villages have been first plundered, then burned and leveled to the ground, whose daughters and sisters have been raped, whose fathers and brothers have had their throats slit. The topic of the lecture: a Christian attitude toward violence. The thesis: we should not retaliate since God is perfect, noncoercive love. Soon you would discover that it takes the quiet of a suburban home for the birth of the thesis that nonviolence corresponds to God's refusal to judge. In a scorched land, soaked in the blood of the innocent, it will invariably die. As one watches it die, one will do well to reflect about many other pleasant captivities of the liberal mind.[32]

Volf is correct to warn us away from a warm and fuzzy, justice-free picture of God, of a God whose love lacks any wrath against those who commit violence against the innocent. I do not believe that this prevents us from leaning our hope in the direction of redemption for the whole of creation, including all human beings, but that we should be modest in our claims, willing to entrust this finally to the God whom we know in Jesus Christ. Many years ago, as an assignment in a seminary course, I spent several weeks as an observer in a municipal court. Day after day, I watched as defendants charged with everything from assault to robbery to public intoxication were brought to trial. Going in, I had assumed that these trials would be like the courtroom dramas I had seen on television, with prosecutors and defense attorneys battling it out over the question of guilt or innocence. I soon found this expectation was naive. In fact, almost 100 percent of the defendants were guilty. These were repeat offenders, petty criminals, caught for the most part red-handed once again committing petty crimes. The real question in the trials was not guilt or innocence—*everybody* was guilty. The real question was, Who is the judge today? The municipal court had a staff of judges, some hard and tough and some more lenient, and for most defendants their hopes rested not on being declared innocent but in drawing a merciful judge.

The bad news is that everybody in this court is guilty; the good news is that the judge of the "quick and the dead" is Jesus Christ. "Who is to condemn?" asked Paul. "It is Christ Jesus, who died, yes, who was raised, who is at the right hand of God, who indeed intercedes for us" (Rom. 8:34).

As Niebuhr put it:

> It is therefore important to maintain a decent measure of restraint in expressing the Christian hope. Faith must admit "that it doth not yet appear what we shall be." But it is equally important not to confuse such restraint with uncertainty about the validity of the hope that "when he shall appear, we shall be like him, for we shall see him as he is."[33]

4

Whatever Happened to the Christian Funeral?

When Elizabeth Janzen died in a Minneapolis nursing home in October, the staff immediately notified the closest relative, her daughter Sarah in St. Louis. Sarah, who had faithfully visited her mother once a month, arranged for Elizabeth to be cremated, for the ashes to be sent to St. Louis, and for an obituary to be placed in the Minneapolis newspaper. In early November, Sarah took the ashes to a lake in rural Minnesota, where Elizabeth and her family had often vacationed, and scattered them on the water.

A week later, a memorial service was held in the chapel of the Minneapolis church where Elizabeth had kept her membership, though her health had prevented her from attending for a number of years. On a table at the entrance to the chapel were placed several photographs of Elizabeth at various stages in her life, her Bible, a ceramic vase she had made, and a few other personal mementos. At the service, Sarah read one of her mother's favorite poems, Elizabeth's younger sister told an amusing story about their childhood, the chaplain from the nursing home read Psalm 23 and prayed a brief prayer giving thanks for Elizabeth's life, and two of Elizabeth's former students (she had taught high school for more than thirty years) read fond reminiscences of her as a teacher. After a time of quiet reflection, during which was played a recording of Judy Collins's rendition of "Amazing Grace" (one of Elizabeth's favorite hymns), the small group in the chapel silently dispersed.

Elizabeth Janzen is fictitious, but the rituals marking her death represent the truth about a rapidly emerging trend in Christian funeral practices. With surprising swiftness and dramatic results, a significant segment of American Christians has over the last fifty years abandoned previously established funeral customs in favor of an entirely new pattern of memorializing the dead. This new pattern is not firmly fixed (indeed, variations, improvisations, and personal customizations are marks of the new rituals), but it generally includes the following characteristics:

—a memorial service instead of a funeral (i.e., a service focused on remembering the deceased, often held many days after the death, with the body or the cremated remains of the deceased not present)
—a brief, simple, highly personalized and customized service, often involving several speakers (as opposed to the standard church funeral liturgies presided over primarily by clergy)
—a focus upon the life of the deceased (often aided by a physical display of photos and other mementos)
—an emphasis on joy rather than sadness, a celebration of life rather than an observance of the somber reality of death
—a private disposition of the body, often done before the memorial service, with an increasing preference for cremation

The shift toward this new pattern has not happened everywhere, of course. Currently it is most pronounced among white, suburban Protestants, and the older customs often still prevail in rural areas, among nonwhites, and in many Catholic parishes. But these differences seem more a matter of lag time than anything else. The trend lines are clear, and it is apparent that funeral practices for all Christians, as a part of the larger culture, are moving at various rates of speed toward this new pattern.

A significant number of Christian clergy, especially those who are more progressive and better educated, applaud many of these changes. While they may be troubled somewhat by the open-mike atmosphere of these new services or by the inevitable banalities of some of the poems, songs, readings, and other elements imported into them, they nevertheless find them preferable to the older, often depersonalized, and more somber rituals of the past, primarily for two reasons. First, the preference for memorial services, the emphasis on joy or even on laughter, the deemphasis on the body of the deceased, and the celebration of the personal aspects of the life of the one who has died all seem more commensurate with the Christian witness to the resurrection. Second, the valuing of simpler, less formal services provides leverage for people to break loose from the stranglehold of showy, expensive, and burdensome funeral practices so prized by the funeral industry.

These clergy are unquestionably well-intentioned and they are right to find some encouraging signs here, but I want to raise some basic theological questions about this emerging pattern of death practices. I would like to suggest that these newer rituals, for all of their virtues of freedom, simplicity, and seeming festivity, are finally expressions of a corrupted understanding of the Christian view of death. These newer practices are attractive mainly because they seem to offer relief from the cosmeticized, sentimental, impersonal, and often costly funerals that developed in the 1950s, which were themselves parodies of authentic Christian rituals. Contemporary Christian funeral practices certainly need to be changed, but refreshing our memory about what is at stake in funerals makes it clear that this change should be more a matter of recovery and reformation than innovation and improvisation.

In order to make this case, we need to look at the essential and definitive pattern of Christian death practices, which developed gradually over the first five centuries of the church's life.

THE ORIGINS OF THE CHRISTIAN FUNERAL

The Christian church began in Roman-occupied Palestine as a group within Judaism. As such, early Christian funeral practices were woven from threads borrowed first from Jewish and then from Roman death customs. Significantly, both Jewish and Roman funeral practices were themselves in a period of flux and reformation in the first century. In Judaism, reform efforts that were aimed at simplifying funerals and reducing their cost and extravagance were beginning to take hold. Lavish feasts, ornamental funeral biers, and costly funeral garments—all of which flattered the wealthy, shamed the poor, and exhausted the resources of many in the middle—were coming under critical fire from the rabbis.

In Roman society, a remarkable and somewhat puzzling shift away from the practice of cremation was occurring. Cremation had been the prevalent custom in Roman society for several centuries (writing near the turn of the first century, Tacitus could describe cremation as the "*Romanus mos*," the Roman custom[1])but concurrent with the appearance of Christianity, Romans began slowly to return to the more ancient practice of earth burial. By mid-third century, burial had replaced cremation as the usual custom throughout the whole Roman world.[2]

Why did this happen? The reasons are disputed. Some scholars interpret the Roman shift to earth burial as essentially an economic and fashion trend. Earth burial was attractive to the poor, since a cremation pyre and the necessary fuel were quite costly. Also, carved sarcophagi and other forms of showy cemetery architecture were becoming status symbols among the rich, making burial a more popular option. Earth burial thus provided a savings for the poor and a public stage for the ambitions of the rich.

Other scholars, however, suggest that the change occurred because Roman religious sensibilities were shifting away from Greek skepticism toward a deeper and more positive interest in the afterlife and the fate of the dead. A typical early first-century inscription on Roman graves, inspired by Epicurean and Stoic skepticism, read, "*Non fui, fui, non sum, non curo*" (I was not, I was, I am not, I don't care), an epitaph so common that it was often simply abbreviated as "*nf f ns nc.*"[3] But the growing popularity of mystery religions, neo-Pythagorean ideas, and, perhaps later, Christianity itself were eroding the older images of death as a shadowy world and replacing them with pictures of the dead living a blessed new existence in the heavens.[4] As this argument goes, the Romans saw burial as "a gentler and more respectful way of laying to rest the mortal frame which has been the temple and mirror of the immortal soul and enduring personality."[5]

Jewish Funerals

Most of the earliest Christians were, like Jesus, Palestinian Jews and were, also like Jesus, buried according to Jewish custom. The practice was simple and driven by necessity. Dead bodies decomposed rapidly in the hot climate of Palestine; so when a first-century Jew died, burial took place as soon as possible, usually by sunset of the day of the death.[6] Failure to bury a body promptly was considered a sin and a social shame. Family members, usually led by the eldest son if there was one, would close the eyes of the deceased, place cloth in the bodily orifices, close the mouth of the corpse and tie it shut with a cinch, wash the body,[7] and anoint it with aromatic spices.[8] The body would then be wrapped in linen cloths and placed on a bier or in a coffin. When all of the mourners had gathered, the body was carried by pallbearers to the place of burial, accompanied by mourners, family, and sometimes paid flute players (see Matt. 9:23).

The procession traveled to the place of burial, the mourners crying laments and chanting psalms. The place of burial was usually a small family tomb with room for a few graves, located outside the town or village. Along the way, if the funeral entourage encountered a wedding procession, the funeral yielded the right of way to the bridal party, not only to honor the bride, but also as a sign that death must give way to life.[9] When the burial party arrived at the tomb, a brief eulogy and prayers were spoken. The body would be placed in the tomb, ordinarily in a niche carved into rock, a grave dug in the earth, or, in the case of the very rich, a freestanding sarcophagus. The funeral procession then returned to the home of the deceased for a time of condolences and the serving of a meal, which was evidently prepared only for the male mourners.[10]

We can hear echoes of this Jewish funeral pattern in the New Testament description of Jesus' burial, the only deviation being that the anointing with spices was delayed, probably owing to the abnormal manner of Jesus' death and the fact that, as Jesus was buried, the Sabbath was fast approaching:

> [Joseph] went to Pilate and asked for the body of Jesus. Then he took it down, wrapped it in a linen cloth, and laid it in a rock-hewn tomb where no one had ever been laid. It was the day of Preparation, and the sabbath was beginning. The women who had come with him from Galilee followed, and they saw the tomb and how his body was laid. Then they returned, and prepared spices and ointments. On the sabbath they rested according to the commandment. But on the first day of the week, at early dawn, they came to the tomb, taking the spices that they had prepared.
>
> (Luke 23:52–24:1)

The Jewish burial ritual, from death to entombment, occupied only a few hours, but the mourning rituals took many months to complete and, according to Byron McCane,[11] were divided into three periods. The first period, known as *shivàh*, was a period of intense mourning on the part of the family, lasting seven days. During this period, family members covered their heads, engaged in ceremonies of lamenting, received the comforts of relatives and friends, and refrained from work. Couches in the family home were turned over as a reminder that sexual intercourse was forbidden, and mourners were forbidden to travel, except to the grave.[12]

During the first three days of *shivàh* (known as "the three days of weeping"), the tomb of the deceased, still unsealed, would be visited by family members both to mourn and to ensure that the deceased was actually dead (premature burial not being an entirely unknown phenomenon). Palestinian Jews shared a common Middle Eastern view that the soul of the deceased lingered near the body for three days, but when three days had passed and the inevitable change in facial appearance made it clear that death had indeed occurred, the resigned spirit departed.[13]

The narrator of the Gospel of John notes that when Jesus arrived in Bethany, his friend Lazarus "had already been in the tomb four days" (John 11:17), a clear signal to the reader that Lazarus was irretrievably and permanently dead. The point is made again when Jesus calls for the stone covering the tomb to be removed and Lazarus's sister Martha protests, "Lord, already there is a stench because he has been dead four days" (John 11:39). Both of these references to four days presuppose the "three days of weeping" and underscore the fact that Lazarus's subsequent raising by Jesus was a true miracle.

The second period of mourning, known as *shloshim,* lasted up to thirty days and consisted of less severe forms of grief. Family members continued to stay at home to mourn, and they could not cut their hair or participate in normal social events After *shloshim*, mourners reentered the world of normal social relations, but for a period of one year they were commanded as an act of devotion and mourning to recite the Kaddish, the ancient prayer that ended every synagogue service and has as its theme not psychological grief but external praise. This recital forms the third period of mourning, and in its earliest retrievable form the Kaddish reads as follows:

> Exalted and hallowed be his great name
>   in the world which he created according to his will.
> May he let his kingdom rule
>   in your lifetime and in your days and in the lifetime
>   of the whole house of Israel, speedily and soon.
> Praised be his great name from eternity to eternity.
> And to this say: Amen.[14]

After a year of mourning, Palestinian Jews engaged in a rather unusual ritual known as *ossilegium*, or secondary burial. Someone from the family of the deceased, customarily the eldest son, would reenter the tomb, gather the bones of the deceased, and then rebury them, either in a an ossuary (a stone container), a niche hewn in rock, or an earth grave.[15] The *Semahot*, a part of the Babylonian Talmud, gives quite explicit, even clinical, instructions for the practice:

> The bones of the corpse should not be taken apart, nor the tendons severed, unless the bones have fallen apart of themselves and the tendons of themselves have been severed. Rabbi Akiba says, "The bones may not be gathered until the flesh has wasted away. Once it has the features are no longer recognizable in the skeleton."[16]

Secondary burial occurs in a number of cultures, many of them quite removed and disconnected from ancient Palestine, but among the Jews of the first century, *ossilegium* had specific theological import. The Jews of that period believed that the wasting away of the flesh represented the person's gradual purification from sin and corruption. People atoned for their sins partly through the decay of their flesh. When the body consisted only of bones, the person was cleansed from impurity and ready for the afterlife and even, among some Jews, the resurrection from the dead.[17] If the deceased was a condemned criminal, it was required that he or she be buried away from the family, but once the process of decomposition—and, thus, purification—had taken place, the bones could be placed in the family tomb.

To return to the tomb a year after a death and to see that the bones of an ancestor were reburied in an ossuary was an act of great respect and a testimony to the conviction that the ancestor, now cleansed from sin and corruption, was now among the righteous. Archaeological evidence from Palestine during the Roman period shows that 92 percent of all excavated tombs contained some sort of *ossilegium*.[18] Thus we can be certain that the first Christians, who in this early period followed local Jewish burial customs in all other respects, also practiced secondary burial.

The very earliest Christian funerals, then, were Jewish funerals in all respects. However, Christians gradually, on the basis of their own theology, began to challenge and change some aspects of Jewish funeral customs. The most striking example of a shift away from traditional Jewish practice concerns the notion of the ritual impurity of a dead body. In traditional Jewish thought, touching a dead body rendered one unclean, as the Torah specified:

> Those who touch the dead body of any human being shall be unclean seven days. They shall purify themselves with the water on the third day and on the seventh day, and so be clean; but if they do not purify themselves on the third day and on the seventh day, they will not become clean. All who touch a corpse, the body of a human being who has died, and do not purify themselves, defile the tabernacle of the LORD; such persons shall be cut off from Israel. Since the water for cleansing was not dashed on them, they remain unclean; their uncleanness is still on them.
>
> (Num. 19:11–13)

Obviously, those who washed and carried the deceased came into contact with the body, so ritual washings and periods of separation lasting up to seven days were required to restore them to a state of purity. The Babylonian Talmud tells the story of a dying father who from his deathbed urged his son to bury him according to the traditional customs but without touching even his father's bones, so as to avoid contamination:

> Rabbi Eleazar bar Zadok said, "Thus spoke father at the time of his death, 'My son, bury me at first in a fosse [temporary grave?]. In the course of time, collect my bones and put them in an ossuary, but do not gather them with your own hands.'"[19]

This notion of death and contamination stands in the background of Jesus' statement, "Woe to you, scribes and Pharisees, hypocrites! For you are like whitewashed tombs, which on the outside look beautiful, but inside they are full of the bones of the dead and of all kinds of filth" (Matt. 23:27). A Jewish tomb in Palestine would be whitewashed, not as a decoration but as a warning. Graves were often painted white, especially prior to the Passover festival, to enable pilgrims to avoid becoming unclean through inadvertent contact with the place of the dead. The Lukan version of the same statement of Jesus makes this clear: "Woe to you! For you are like unmarked graves, and people walk over them without realizing it" (Luke 11:44).

Many Christians were persuaded that Jesus had replaced external purity rules with the idea of inward purity: "Listen to me, all of you, and understand: there is nothing outside a person that by going in can defile, but the things that come out are what defile" (Mark 7:14–15). Thus, they gradually began to alter their funeral ritual significantly. Instead of avoiding contact with the deceased as sources of contamination, they began to view the dead as holy saints worthy of being touched and caressed. In a pastoral letter from the middle of the third century, cited by Eusebius, Dionysius of Alexandria described how the Christian community handled the bodies of fellow Christians who had died in a plague:

> With willing hands they raised the bodies of the saints to their bosoms; they closed their eyes and mouths, carried them on their shoulders, and laid them out; they clung to them, embraced them, and wrapped them in grave clothes.[20]

As is almost always the case with ritual change, the shift from an older pattern to a newer one did not occur smoothly or with equal speed in all places. The author of the fourth-century *Apostolic Constitutions* urges Christians not to avoid contact with the dead, couching the counsel in the typical polemic of the time. This sharp language used to reject the Jewish purity laws, including funeral practices, betrays, of course, the fact that such practices were still being observed by some Christians:

> For He is thy Lord, and the Lord of the universe; and meditate in His laws without observing any such things, such as the natural purgation, lawful mixture, child-birth, a miscarriage, or a blemish of the body; since such observations are the vain inventions of foolish men, and such inventions as have no sense in them. Neither the burial of a man, nor a dead man's bone, nor a sepulcher, nor any particular sort of food, nor the nocturnal pollution, can defile the soul of man; but only impiety towards God, and transgression, and injustice towards one's neighbor. . . . Wherefore, beloved, avoid and eschew such observations, for they are heathenish. For we do not abominate a dead man, as do they, seeing we hope that he will live again.[21]

And again:

> Do not therefore keep any such observances about legal and natural purgations, as thinking you are defiled by them. Neither do you seek after Jewish separations, or perpetual washings, or purifications upon the touch of a dead body.[22]

Another area in which Christians began to depart from traditional Jewish practice had to do with the importance of the place of burial. One of the reasons often given for the widespread Jewish adoption of secondary burial was that it allowed for Jews throughout the Diaspora the possibility of being buried in Israel.[23] This connected to a larger goal of being buried in the same land and in the same place as one's ancestors. Over time, however, Christians increasingly began to visualize the company of the faithful in eschatological terms rather than geographical ones. Christian dead were understood to be journeying to the place of heavenly banquet and not simply to the resting place of the ancestors.

When Augustine's mother entered her final illness, she told Augustine and his brother that she did not wish to be buried in her homeland but, rather, in the land where she died. Augustine kept quiet, but his brother protested, responding to their mother that she should instead be buried not in a foreign land, but beside her husband in her own land. Augustine describes what happened next:

> She, with an anxious look, stopped her son with her eyes, for that he still savored such things, and then looking upon me, said, "Behold, what he said. Instead, lay this body anywhere and let not the care for that any way disquiet you. This only I request, that you would remember me at the Lord's altar, wherever you be." And having delivered this sentiment in what words she could, she held her peace, being exercised by her growing sickness.[24]

Roman Funerals

As Christianity spread throughout the ancient world and began to incorporate more and more Gentile adherents, many Christian funerals moved away from Jewish patterns and increasingly became modifications of Roman funerals. A death that took place in a Roman home would typically happen this way.[25] When death was near, family members and close friends would gather at the deathbed, providing comfort and expressing grief. As the death throes began, those at bedside would begin to stretch out the hands and the feet of the dying person, and the nearest relative would hover close by, ready to give the last kiss, which was an attempt to catch the soul as it departed from the body. When the kiss had been given and it was clear that death had occurred, this same relative would close the eyes of the deceased, while all others present began loudly calling the departed's name (partly in grief and partly to be sure that the person was actually dead) and ritually crying out laments.

The deceased was then lifted from the death bed and placed on the floor, where the body was washed, anointed with scented oil, and dressed in a cloth wrapping, a tunic, or a toga. Sometimes, if the decedent was a male of prominence, a crownlike wreath was placed on his head. A coin, to pay the fare of Charon, the ferryman of the dead, for passage to the next world, was placed under the tongue of the deceased, and the body was lifted again onto a bed, feet toward the door of the house, to lie in state for a period up to seven days, during which a mournful wake was held. From time to time during the wake period, the name of the deceased would again be shouted aloud.

In the case of the wealthy, the funeral ceremonies that followed were often quite elaborate and were turned over to professional undertakers, but families of ordinary means would make the arrangements themselves. When the time came for the funeral proper, which was almost always held at night, the body would be carried on a bier by male bearers (as few as four or, in the case of the rich, as many as eight) to the place of burial, followed by a torch-bearing procession of family and friends, all wearing black or red garments, the colors of death. Sometimes a member of the funeral procession would wear a clay death mask bearing the visage of the deceased and, as the group moved toward the grave, would perform an imitation of the deceased.

In rural locales, graves were in separate family plots, but every city had at least one "city of the dead" (necropolis) located, by Roman law, outside of the city, usually alongside a major road. When the procession arrived at the place of burial or cremation, some dirt would be thrown on the corpse and, if the body was to be burned, a finger or other small portion of the body (known as the *os resectum*) was cut off for burial. Cremations were done on a rectangular pyre. The eyes of the corpse would be reopened and, as the body was burned, sometimes pets were killed around the pyre so that these animals could accompany the deceased into the afterlife. The burned bones and ashes were collected by relatives and, after being drenched in wine, were placed in a basket, box, or urn, which was buried, along with the *os resectum*. Most Romans, however, were not cremated but were buried, being placed either directly in the ground (in the case of the poor) or in a wood or lead sarcophagus, which was then placed in a chamber tomb or into the ground, often with items the dead might need in the afterlife—jewelry, dishes, lamps, dice and other games, toilet articles, and, in the case of children, toys.

When the burial of the body or the ashes was complete, a pig was sacrificed at the site to make the place of burial a legal tomb, and a funeral feast was eaten at the grave. When the family returned from the grave, they went through a ritual of purification involving fire and water and entered into a nine-day mourning period. On the ninth day, the family returned to the grave for another meal, which involved pouring wine on the grave and leaving food for the deceased. This concluded the official season of mourning, but during the year—on the birthday of the deceased and during the annual festival of the dead—the family would return to the grave for meals, always providing a serving for the deceased. These graveside feasts were sometimes raucous occasions, heavy with wine, and some Roman graves were constructed with pipes leading from the surface to the corpse so that wine and food could be deposited directly on the remains. Some mausoleums were built with kitchens to facilitate these ceremonies.

Early Christians, especially Gentiles, were influenced by these Roman practices and followed them in general, but altered them according to Christian beliefs and understandings, adopting some customs outright, rejecting others, and amending still others.[26] Christians, too, gathered at the bedside of a dying loved one, offering support and grief. However, since Christians did not believe that the spirit of the dying could be "caught" and preserved by the living, there was generally no attempt to give a last kiss to the decedent. On other occasions, Christians did carry out the gesture of the last kiss, but reinterpreted it, not as a capture of the spirit, but as a simple act of tenderness (an interpretation that was gradually taking hold in Roman society more generally). This is the way that Bishop Ambrose of Milan explained his actions at the death of his own brother in 375 CE:

> It profited me nothing to have received your last breath, nor to have breathed on you in your dying moments. And yet, I thought that either I myself should receive your death, or that I should pour out my life into you. O that sad, yet very sweet pledge of the last kiss.[27]

Christians believed that their dead were traveling to God, not to the land of the dead of Roman mythology, so they did not place coins in the mouths of their dead. However, they did add a corresponding custom to the process of caring for the dying: the administration of the Eucharist. The idea was that the food of the Lord's Supper would provide nourishment for the dead as they traveled to God, and the goal was for Christians to die with the Eucharist in their mouths. If death was delayed, the Eucharist was administered frequently, as often as several times a day. This final eucharistic meal came to be called the viaticum, the same Latin term used to describe the coin to pay the ferryman of the dead. So important was this meal for the journey to God that an abuse of the practice, namely, the giving of the Eucharist to those who were already dead, developed. As early as the Council of Hippo in the late fourth century, the practice was condemned, but it evidently continued to spread widely until at least the seventh century.

When death occurred, Christians generally followed local practice regarding the closing of the eyes, and the washing, anointing, dressing, and laying out of the dead, but they did not loudly cry out to the body. Christians clothed their dead in linen cloth or the best of the clothes possessed by the deceased, but they did not use wreaths or crowns, insisting instead that God was the Christian's crown. "Athletes exercise self-control in all things," wrote the apostle Paul; "they do it to receive a perishable wreath, but we an imperishable one." The poet of *The Odes and Psalms of Solomon* states, "I was crowned by my God, and my crown is living."[28] Gradually Christians began to clothe the dead in more and more lavish and expensive clothes, a practice that was roundly criticized in several of the patristic writings.

Christians followed local custom regarding the timing of the burial. In Jewish areas, the deceased was buried the same day, but in Gentile areas the burial could be delayed as long as a week. Christians would hold periods of mourning and attending to the body, or wakes for the dead, either in the home (the Roman custom) or at the grave (the Jewish custom). After Constantine, Christians often held the "waking of the dead," the vigil service held in the presence of the body, in church buildings.

The most significant change instituted by Christians regarding the wake has to do with the character of mourning. Christians experienced sorrow in death, of course, but they sought to subdue the loud and excessive Roman displays of grief with reverent quietness, the chanting of the psalms, the singing of hymns, and confident expressions of resurrection hope. "We do not want you to be uninformed . . . about those who have died," wrote Paul, "so that you may not grieve as others do who have no hope" (1 Thess. 4:13). Chrysostom, noting that Jesus cast out the mournful wailers around the deathbed of Jairus's daughter, rebuked those of his congregation who engaged paid mourners to increase the level of grief. "Weep, then, at the death of a dear one as if you were bidding farewell to one setting out on a journey," he urged.[29] "We grieve Christ," said Tertullian, "when we do not accept with equanimity the death of those who have been summoned by God, acting as if they were to be pitied."[30] Augustine's description of his own impulse to grief at the death of his mother, Monica, is fairly representative of early Christian views:

> On the ninth day then of her sickness, and the fifty-sixth year of her age, and the thirty-third of mine, that religious and holy soul was freed from the body. I closed her eyes, and there flowed a mighty sorrow into my heart, which was overflowing into tears. My eyes at the same time, by the violent command of my mind, drank up their fountain wholly dry; and woe was me in such a strife!
>
> When she breathed her last, the boy Adeodatus burst out into a loud lament, but then, stopped by us all, he held his peace. In like manner also a childish feeling in me, which was, through my heart's youthful voice, finding its vent in weeping, was checked and silenced. For we thought it not fitting to solemnize that funeral with tearful lament, and groanings; for thereby do they for the most part express grief for the departed, as though unhappy, or altogether dead; whereas she was neither unhappy in her death, nor altogether dead. Of this we were assured on good grounds, the testimony of her good conversation and her faith unfeigned.[31]

When the time came for burial, the body of a Christian would be carried by other Christians in the community in a simple procession to the grave. Early Christians uniformly practiced earth burial, rejecting altogether the practice of cremation as a blasphemy against the body as a temple of the Spirit and a rejection of the bodily resurrection. Christians believed that they were taking their dead, not to the final resting place, but to the place of departure, the point of embarkation as the deceased traveled to God. "In the funerals of the departed, accompany them with singing," urged the *Apostolic Constitutions*, and instead of dirges and sad songs of flute players, Christians walked to the grave with only the music of human voices singing psalms and hymns. "What is the reason for the hymns?" asked Chrysostom in a sermon:

> Is it not that we praise God and thank him that he has crowned the departed and freed him from suffering and that God now has the deceased, freed from fear, with him? Is this not the reason for the singing of hymns and psalms? All this is a sign of joy, for it is said, "Is anyone cheerful, let him sing."[32]

Gradually Christian leaders encouraged the faithful to replace the black and red mourning garments typical of the Romans with white funeral clothing, the garments of baptism and eternal life. Unlike those of the Romans, Christian funeral processions were usually held during broad daylight, and the use of candles and torches was avoided, because of the connection of fire with both cremation and pagan cults of the dead. The fourth-century apologist Lactantius argued, "No one in a right mind would offer candles and tapers to God who is the author and giver of light. . . . Their gods, however, because they are of the earth, need light lest they be in darkness."[33]

When the procession arrived at the gravesite, prayers would be said for the deceased, and sometimes a funeral sermon or oration would be given. Then, in a remarkable and unique gesture, the faithful would, as an act of farewell, kiss the forehead or cheek of the deceased. This was the "kiss of peace," the same sign of forgiveness and reconciliation that took place in Christian worship at the table before the Lord's Supper.[34] Then, with a final word of farewell—often "May you live in God! Rejoice forever!"—the body would be placed in the ground, and a eucharistic meal would be observed either at the grave or in the home.

The Essential Christian Funeral

Christians, therefore, gradually formed over the earliest centuries of the movement a set of distinct funeral practices that, while woven from local customs, still reflected Christian theology. At the beginning of the third century, Tertullian could already speak of an "appointed office" for Christian burial in North Africa, and certainly by the late fourth century, we can begin to see the contours of a basic and distinct Christian funeral rite. Simply put, this rite was composed of three movements: preparation, processional, and burial. In the preparation movement, the body was washed, anointed, and clothed in garments representing baptism. In the processional phase, the body was carried to the grave, and sometimes the procession entered the church on the way for prayer and the reading of Scripture. The burial phase took place at graveside and included the commendation of the deceased to God and the actual burial of the body. During each movement, the church prayed, chanted psalms, and sang hymns of joy. Often a Eucharist was held, either in the church or at the grave. The theme of the service was the completion of baptism, and the church accompanied a brother or sister to the place of union with God through the resurrection of Christ. Taken as a whole, the early Christian funeral was based on the conviction that the deceased was a saint, a child of God and a sister or brother of Christ, worthy to be honored and embraced with tender affection. The funeral itself was deemed to be the last phase of a lifelong journey toward God, and the faithful carried the deceased along the way to the place of final departure with singing and a mixture of grief and joyful hope.

In subsequent centuries, this basic funeral pattern sometimes struggled for visibility against cultural and theological changes. For example, the joyful Easter motif of the early Christian funeral was nearly submerged by a gloomy "Day of Wrath" theology of the late Middle Ages, and the Puritans in England and later in America, offended by what they saw as excesses in Anglican funerals, tried, unsuccessfully as it turns out, to get rid of funeral ceremony altogether. Nevertheless the basic pattern and practices of Christian burial managed to weather the storms and continued to exert a strong force on Christian funerals until the late nineteenth century, when their influence began to erode.

WHAT HAPPENED?

This review of the development of classic Christian funeral practices should make it evident that the new pattern for funerals now appearing is not simply a modernization and adaptation of traditional customs but a radical, and finally diminished, replacement of Christian ritual. For example, the current shift to a memorial service with the body absent means that Christian death practices are no longer metaphorical expressions of the journey of a saint to be with God. The saint is not even present, except as a spiritualized memory, a backdrop for the real action, which happens in the psyches of the mourners. The mourners are the only actors left, and the ritual now is really about them. Funerals are "for the living," as we are prone to say. Instead of the grand cosmic drama of the church marching to the edge of eternity with a fellow saint, singing songs of resurrection victory and sneering in the face of the final enemy, we now have a much smaller, more privatized psychodrama, albeit often couched in Christian language. Taking the plot of the typical memorial service at face value, the dead are not migrating to God; the living are moving from sorrow to stability.

How did the church shift from the understanding of a funeral as the joyful accompanying of a saint on "the last mile of the way" to a reflective, disembodied, quasi-gnostic cluster of customs and ceremonies? Although the dramatic changes in practice begin to be widespread in the middle of the twentieth century, we can trace the roots of many of them to the latter part of the nineteenth century. Because this is precisely the time that embalming became widespread and the modern funeral parlor developed, it is almost irresistible to blame the newly minted funeral professionals for all the mischief. As the argument goes, undertakers reinvented themselves as "funeral directors" and rode the technological advances in embalming all the way to the bank. They first took the dead away from us in order to embalm them, and then they took the funeral itself away and turned it from a worship service into a vulgar display of conspicuous consumption.

The truth, however, is that a guild of embalming technicians could never have become "directors" of any sacred Christian ritual, could never have taken the funeral away, had not church and culture been more than ready to hand it over. Almost every developed society, even ancient Rome, has had "undertakers" who assist with the preparation of the dead, but even if nineteenth-century undertakers had hatched a plot to hijack the Christian funeral, it would have failed if our death rituals had been healthy and full of meaning.

If Christian funerals today are impoverished, we must look primarily to the church's own history and not look with scorn at the funeral director. The fact is that many educated Christians in the late nineteenth century, the forebears of today's white suburban Protestants, lost their eschatological nerve and their vibrant faith in the afterlife, and we are their theological and liturgical heirs. It was not, of course, as if the whole of nineteenth-century Christian society woke up one morning and suddenly found that they no longer believed in eternal life. The loss of conviction about the otherworld came slowly and gradually.

In the decades after the Civil War, the quite literal views of many American Christians regarding heaven, hell, the end of the world, the resurrection of the body, and the second coming of Jesus began to ebb away. A recent study by Drew Gilpin Faust points out that the sheer devastation of the Civil War itself, the staggering number of dead, the violence and loss of life out of all proportion to the ability of most people to make meaning from it, accelerated the nineteenth century's already growing crisis of faith. She writes:

> Civil War carnage transformed the mid-nineteenth century's growing sense of religious doubt into a crisis of belief that propelled many Americans to redefine or even reject their faith in a benevolent and responsive deity. But Civil War death and devastation also planted seeds of a more profound doubt about human ability to know and understand. . . . The Civil War compelled Americans to ask with

intensified urgency, "What is Death?" and in answering to find themselves wondering why is death, what is life, and can we ever hope to know? We have continued to wonder ever since.[35]

Part of the crisis of faith was about eschatology. In the 1840s, some Christians confidently calculated the exact date of Jesus' return, only to have their hopes, and for many of them their naive faith, crushed when Jesus did not come, a time that came to be called the Great Disappointment. Even less-advent-minded Christians of the time had to reckon with the impact of the rising sciences, of Darwinism, and of the new skeptical philosophies imported from Europe. Consequently, the literalisms of the past came under severe stress. Pictures of Jesus coming in the clouds, of the dead rising bodily from the graves, of the saints arrayed in glory, became less and less imaginable, less and less plausible. The notion of heaven was not altogether abandoned. Instead, it was revised and domesticated. Heaven was reimagined as a place very much like the best of earth, sometimes not a "place" at all but simply an intensification of earthly delights, and the idea of the resurrection of the body yielded to the more gentle and continuous notion of the immortality of the soul. One late nineteenth-century clergyman characteristically said, "To me, heaven means only myself with larger opportunity. It means this earth-life grown into perfection."[36] Lucy Larcom, in a devotional essay characteristic of the period, wrote:

Surprises doubtless await us all, across the boundaries of this earthly existence. But none, perhaps, will be more surprised than those humble, faithful, self-sacrificing souls who have often almost dreaded the strange splendors that might open upon them beyond the gates of pearl, when they find that it is the same familiar sunshine in which they have been walking all their days, only clearer and serener. They will wonder that they have no new language to learn, no new habits to form, almost no new acquaintances to make. They will at last discover what their humility hid from them here, that while on earth, without knowing it, they had already been living in heaven.[37]

No wonder the metaphor of journeying to be with God began to break apart at the seams. If people had "already been living in heaven," then there was, after all, nowhere for the dead to travel, and without letting go of the vocabulary of the otherworld, mainline Protestants in the late nineteenth century, long before the Beatles, could well "imagine there's no heaven."

A second significant nineteenth-century development was the creation of rural cemeteries, located some distance away from towns and villages. At first, cemeteries were separated from the living because of the notion that putrefying bodies produced miasmas, noxious gases that caused disease, but by the end of the nineteenth century, rural cemeteries were less about avoiding pollution and more about aesthetics. They were landscaped, gardenlike environments designed to encourage quiet and restful contemplation of nature, immortality, and the meaning of life.

The more practical effect of these remote cemeteries, as Susan J. White has pointed out, was the division of the previously unified funeral ritual into two discrete parts: the funeral in the church and the burial in the distant cemetery.[38] It was not long before this separation in distance became a separation in liturgical fact and in theological symbolism. The funeral was no longer a journey to the place of burial; it became a stationary event completely contained within the church building. The graveside ritual became a mere optional afterword. As White observes, "[T]he removal of the gravesite to a location far away from the precincts of the church depletes a fund of theological and communal images and severely reduces the sense . . . that the living and the dead are part of one 'holy communion.'"[39] So, with heaven gone and with the cemetery miles away, neither the dead nor the living had anywhere to go, and the metaphor of the journey to God collapsed.

Surely the task before the church now is to retrace our steps and to recover the grand liturgical theater in which Christians embrace their dead with tender affection, lift up their voices in hymns of resurrection, and accompany the saints to the edge of mystery. This will not involve a mere repristinating of funeral practices or a rejection of cremation, but a recovery in our time and in contemporary forms of the governing symbols of the communion of the saints, the resurrection of the body, and the journey of Christian dead toward the life everlasting.

In the meantime, though, the seeds planted in the nineteenth century continue to bear weeds. Since literalistic views of heaven and the saintly journey are no longer plausible to us, and we lack the theological imagination to grasp the poetic truth and power of these metaphors, dead Christians have nowhere to go but to evaporate into the spiritual ether and into our frail memory banks. With heaven domesticated, the soul morphed into an immortal gas, the corpse become a shell, and the cemetery moved out of sight, it was almost inevitable that the dead with their embarrassing bodies would be banned from their own funerals and the living would be condemned to sit motionless, contemplating the meaning of it all and pretending to celebrate life as the nephew of the deceased sings "When Irish Eyes Are Smiling."

Surely our culture will eventually weary of such liturgical and spiritual thinness and be ready for more depth, for more truth—for our sake and for the sake of those we love. When we are, the great drama of the journey to God will be there, beckoning us to join the procession of the saints. We will travel toward eternity with those we have loved, singing as we go and calling out to the distant shore in words of confident hope, like these from an ancient Coptic funeral prayer:

> Let the shadows of darkness be full of light.
> Let the angels of light walk before him.
> Let the gate of righteousness be opened to him.
> Let him join the heavenly choir.
> Bring him into the paradise of delight.
> Feed him from the tree of life.
> Let him rest in the bosom of our ancestors, Abraham,
>   Isaac, and Jacob, in your kingdom.

5

The Funeral as Worshipful Drama

A central idea to keep in view in understanding a Christian funeral is this: a funeral is essentially a piece of religious drama. It has a script, a plot, actors, and a stage on which it is performed. When we remember this, much else about the funeral falls into place. Planning for and presiding at a funeral becomes more than simply choosing the right Scripture readings, selecting suitable music, and composing a fitting homily. It is akin to directing a play, making sure that the actors know their parts and that the words and actions of the funeral enact the story that needs to be told.

There is nothing particularly remarkable about claiming this. Funerals are, after all, acts of worship, and Christian worship is intrinsically a form of drama, liturgical theater in which the people of God re-present the gospel story. Indeed, all Christian ritual, spanning across the whole of the Christian life, is the way that the church both acts out its faith and absorbs what the faith is all about. As theologian Shannon Craigo-Snell has said, the church performs the gospel, not because it already has the gospel mastered, but instead as a means to figure out what the gospel means:

> In church, as in theatre, interpretation is neither an individual, nor an exclusively mental, matter. Indeed, it involves the entire person— mind and body, voice and spirit— and the entire community. Acting out of their relationship with Scripture, Christian communities

shout and dance, they get happy and they mourn together, they bake casseroles and sing hymns and comfort one another and open soup kitchens and raise money for the homeless. If Christian interpretation is really like theatrical performance interpretation, then these events and activities are not merely the results of an understanding that comes from interpretation: they are part of the interpretive process. We do not interpret, understand and then act on our understanding, but rather our actions are part of our interpreting, constitutive of our understanding.

The emphasis on ritual and community found in the church underlines the fact that the connection between comprehension and behavior runs both ways. We teach our children to sing "Jesus Loves Me" not as an affirmation of something they know, but as a way for them to know it. We bow our heads, bend our knees, lift our arms and raise our voices, not merely to express an understanding previously gained, but in order to comprehend more fully the reality and meaning of the Word of God.[1]

In a funeral, what is true about all worship, namely, that the gospel story is reenacted in dramatic form, comes to particular focus around the occasion of a death. The major theme of a funeral is the gospel story, and the life story of the person who has died is a motif running through this larger theme; perhaps more precisely, a funeral is about the intertwining of these two narratives. At a funeral, the faithful community gathers to enact the promises of the gospel and the convictions of the Christian faith about life and death, as they are refracted through the prism of the life of the one who has died.

To say that a funeral is a gospel liturgical drama seems simple and true, but this is precisely one of the aspects of the Christian funeral most obscured and crusted over by so many contemporary funeral customs. When it is clear that the funeral is a dramatic reenactment of the gospel, this shines a bright light on what a funeral is *not*. Despite popular misconceptions, a funeral is not primarily a quiet time when people gather to reflect on the legacy of the deceased, a devotional service dealing with grief, a show of community support for the mourning family, or even a "celebration of life." Good funerals, in fact, do all of these things—console the grief-stricken, remember and honor the deceased, display community care, and give thanks for all the joys and graces experienced in the life of the one who has died. But these are some of the consequences of a good funeral, not its central meaning or purpose.

THE FUNERAL AS DRAMA: THREE KEY INSIGHTS

If we keep our sights firmly set on the idea of a funeral as a piece of religious drama, three key insights for understanding and planning funerals emerge.

1. While it is true that the gospel is proclaimed in the words of the funeral, it is also true that the gospel is proclaimed in the actions of the funeral. The whole funeral, as an act of drama growing out of baptism, proclaims the gospel.

When a Christian dies, the church gathers to act out the story of what this death means in the light of the gospel, but it is a story that began long before the person died. It is a story that began at baptism. Since a funeral is built on the foundation of baptism, we cannot fully grasp the dramatic aspects of a funeral without seeing them in baptism as well, and it is there that we must begin.

On the banks of Louisiana's Ouachita River, the congregation of St. Paul's Baptist Church, an African American congregation, gathers every year, after several days of fervent prayer meetings and vigorous revival preaching, to baptize new converts to the Christian faith. The older members of the church call this spot on the river "the old burying ground," because of what Paul said about baptism: "Therefore we have been buried with him by baptism into death, so that, just as Christ was raised from the dead by the glory of the Father, so we too might walk in newness of life" (Rom. 6:4). Here, in the flowing currents of the Ouachita, sinners are plunged beneath the waters symbolically to die with Christ, to be washed clean, and to be raised up to a new way of life.

On those days when the congregation of St. Paul's gathers for baptism, the Ouachita River is, of course just the Ouachita, but in the drama of baptism it becomes much more. It is the Red Sea, the waters through which the children Israel passed on their way to freedom and to the promised land. On baptism day, the Ouachita is also the Jordan River, the place of Jesus' baptism, and it is the "river of the water of life, bright as crystal, flowing from the throne of God and of the Lamb" (Rev. 22:1) through the heavenly city. "We gather here on this old river that drifts into the sea," said the pastor of St. Paul's, standing hip-deep in the water one baptismal day, "because we have come back here. Things may have changed uptown; banks may have gone out; shopping centers may have closed, but this old river just keeps on. So we thought the church would come back here and tell the Lord, we thank him for this old river."

The candidates for baptism, wearing cotton robes sewn especially for them by the older women in the congregation, "the mothers of the church," stand on the riverbank waiting. At the beckoning of the pastor, the deacons take each of them by the hand, one by one, and lead them down into the river, as the congregation sings old hymns and spirituals like "Take me to the water; take me to the water; take me to the water to be baptized."

When those baptized come out of the river, they are taken to an improvised dressing room, from which they emerge dressed in dazzling white "Sunday clothes," and they go back to the river to sing and pray while others are baptized. Then the whole congregation goes back to the church building for a festive ceremony in which these new Christians are "fellowshipped into the church."[2]

Notice that the Baptists of St. Paul's Church don't just talk about their convictions concerning baptism; they act them out in a dramatic piece of what could be called Christian community theater there on the river. Baptism is about dying and rising with Christ. Baptism is about being washed clean from sin. Baptism is about being welcomed into a community of the faithful as a brother or sister in Christ. Baptism is about responding to a holy call and setting out on an adventure of faith. Every one of these claims about baptism, and more, is acted out in the drama of the baptismal service.

The same is true whenever and wherever baptism is performed. Whether it is the Baptists assembled on the banks of the muddy Ouachita or a Lutheran congregation around the font in a candle-lit church in Wisconsin or an assembly of Catholics observing the sacrament of baptism in a Texas cathedral, though the details may differ, the essential baptismal drama is the same. In the waters of baptism—river, lake, pool, or font—Christians "die" to the old self, and emerge from the waters to set out on a journey of new life. One of the earliest names for the Christian movement was "the Way" (Acts 9:2), because the faith was not understood as a set of ideas or intellectual beliefs, but as a journey down a road, a way of life. Just as Jesus came up out of the baptismal waters of the Jordan River and set out on the road to the cross, just so, Christians pass through the waters of baptism and begin to travel, following in the path of Jesus. Christians do not take this road alone, but, as the baptismal drama makes plain, they travel in the company of the saints. Those being baptized are visibly and audibly surrounded by the faithful, who pray and sing these new Christians along their baptismal way. The prayer for the baptismal journey in the Episcopal *Book of Common Prayer* points toward the road: "Send them into the world in witness to your love," and then names the destination, "Bring them to the fullness of your peace and glory."[3] The church promises in the words of the Presbyterian *Book of Common Worship*, "to guide and nurture [them] by word and deed, with love and prayer, encouraging them to know and follow Christ."[4]

A Christian funeral is a continuation and elaboration of the baptismal service. If baptism is a form of worshipful drama performed at the beginning of the Christian life, a funeral is—or should be—an equally dramatic, and symmetrical, performance of worship performed at the end of life. When Christians traveling along the baptismal path die, the company of the faithful who were there to guide them at the beginning are also there to carry them at the end. In baptism, new Christians are "buried with Christ by baptism into death," and they come up from the waters raised to "walk in newness of life." In funerals, these same Christians, having traveled the pilgrim way, are once again buried with Christ in death in the sure confidence that they will be raised to new life. In baptism, the faithful sang them into this new way of life; now they gather around to sing them to God in death. Just as they washed the new Christian in the waters of baptism, they now lovingly wash the body of the deceased. Just as they adorned the newly baptized Christian with the garments of Christ, they now adorn the deceased in clothes fitting to meet God and perhaps place a pall, a symbol of the garments of baptism, over the coffin. As the church has been traveling with the baptized saint along the road of faith, the church now walks with the deceased on "the last mile of the way" to the place of farewell.

The funeral, then, is not just a collection of inspiring words said on the occasion of someone's death. It is, rather, a dramatic event in which the church acts out what it believes to be happening from the perspective of faith. In this sense, a Christian funeral is a piece of theater, but it has more in common with ancient forms of religious drama than with popular theater. The philosopher Martha Nussbaum once contrasted ancient Greek drama with more contemporary Broadway-style theater. Today, observed Nussbaum, a playgoing audience sits quietly in a darkened theater, "in the illusion of splendid isolation," and watches the actors perform on a stage "bathed in artificial light, as if it were a separate world of fantasy and mystery." Not so in ancient

Greece. Greek plays "took place during a solemn civic/religious festival, whose trappings made spectators conscious that the values of the community were being examined and communicated." Also, the plays were performed in broad daylight and "in the round," that is, in the midst of the community. People could look across the stage and see the faces of their neighbors and fellow citizens on the other side. "To respond to these events," says Nussbaum, "was to acknowledge and participate in a way of life." Greek drama, like other forms of art, "was thought to be practical, aesthetic interest a practical interest—an interest in the good life and in communal self-understanding. To respond in a certain way was to move already toward this greater understanding."[5]

Just so, at a funeral the congregation does not gather as an audience to hear and see a production performed "on stage" at the front of the church or funeral home chapel. In fact, the congregation at a funeral is not an "audience" at all; they are the actors, and they are themselves on stage, moving and gesturing at the right times; singing, speaking, and praying their lines in the great drama of death and life. "[A]ll Christians are performers," claims Craigo-Snell, "and the entire Christian life is a performance in which we attempt to enact and create the events called for by the script/Scripture. Those who sit in the rear pew on Sunday mornings are no less actors than the clergy up front."[6] Even those neighbors, friends, and family members who are not a part of the church but who have come for this funeral are welcomed with the hospitality of God and invited to take up powerful roles in this drama.

2. Because the funeral is a piece of drama, it is crucial to enact the gospel script, that is, to be sure that it is the Christian narrative being performed at a funeral, not some other story.

We have been making the case that a Christian funeral—its words, gestures, and movements—ought to be understood as a dramatic event. We have done this mainly to counter the widespread assumption (held with particular tenacity by many white, educated, suburban folk, but by others as well) that a funeral is merely a quiet, even passive, gathering of people who have come together to hear soothing and inspiring words of comfort.

Looked at another way, though, the dramatic quality of funerals is inescapable. A funeral is a drama, whether we like it or not, and even an attempt to be "nondramatic" is its own dramatic form. Consider, for example, the somewhat sad and extremely spare memorial service that Jessica Mitford thought worthy of approval in *The American Way of Death*, her diatribe against funerals and funeral professionals. The service, for a local judge who had died, was held in a Unitarian church in a symbol-free environment where there were "no decorations" save a bowl of flowers and a "single, store-bought wreath." After an organ prelude, four men—a state supreme court judge (wearing his robe), a rabbi, a Congregational minister, and a Unitarian minister— walked up to the platform and gave "warm and vivid" addresses on the deceased judge's life and character. That was it. "When the last speaker had concluded, all four rose and descended from the platform, indicating that the service was over. There being no casket 'to view,' we in attendance filed directly out into the lobby."[7]

Although this memorial service seems nondramatic, perhaps even intentionally antidramatic, it cannot escape being a form of theater. Those in attendance probably thought of themselves simply as "paying their due respects" to the deceased and engaging in a proper and dignified ceremony of remembrance. Viewed as drama, however, this service reveals much more, and it is not difficult to read it. For example, the choice of an "organ prelude" was not a neutral element, but was borrowed from the usual Sunday liturgy and served as a signal that a quasi-worshipful time was beginning. Even though this memorial service was quite secular (no Scripture read, apparently no divine praise or prayer), the organ music, along with the flowers and the wreath, evoked a vague impression of the sacred. This was "church light," a secular ceremony held in a house of worship and emitting the faint fragrance of a religious ritual left far behind. Where was the deceased? His casketed body was banished from sight, and he became a purely mental event, a "warm and vivid" memory to be evoked with words. The peak moment in the drama was the giving of tribute speeches by the four men, who served in priestly roles (even the judge wore a robe), and the sacred text for the hour was the biography of the deceased. Through evocative words summoning memories of this "humane and dedicated, almost saintly" man (again quoting Mitford), these priestly figures invoked a spiritualized presence of the one who had died.

What we have here is a performance of minimalist theater. Someone had died, and those who loved and respected the deceased gathered so that priests could utter powerful words of evocation. Though probably no one present would have thought of it this way, this little bit of drama was actually something of a secularized séance. The actual dead man was nowhere around; in fact, *not* having his body around was part of the theatrical point. What was desired was his *spirit,* and the four "priests" were there to invoke it in the form of positive memory.

But where did this drama go? Where did the plot of this play lead? If the traditional Christian funeral reenacts the baptismal journey, this service enacted a pilgrimage to nowhere. The only signal that the drama had ended was that the speakers abruptly left the stage. Instead of ending up at the graveside, giving the deceased into the hands of the God who can be trusted, this service merely petered out "into the lobby."

Years ago, in the middle of the major-league baseball season, a popular player was killed in an accident at the height of his career and promise. A vigorous young sports hero who had been full of life on one day was unexpectedly dead on the next, and it was a tragic loss for his family, his team, and his city. The next night after the death, his team was scheduled to play a home game, and everyone knew that something must be done, some ceremony should be observed, but what? On that night, after the playing of the national anthem, the stadium announcer asked everyone in the stands to rise in silence, and as the crowd stood up, the dead player's teammates, wearing black armbands on their uniforms, ran out to the pitcher's mound and embraced each other in grief. It seemed a fitting thing to do, and for a brief time those on the field and in the stands were caught up in the power of the moment. But then the occasion turned to awkward. After the players embraced, what were they to do next? It seemed graceless for them simply to trot out to their positions, slapping their gloves, but they couldn't embrace each other forever. Finally, one by one, they broke their huddle and slowly and uncomfortably walked away. Like the memorial service described by Mitford, this ritual had no place to go, not because the participants lacked conviction or cleverness, but because the underlying narratives on which these rituals were based were stories of the dead with no destination.

In the Christian faith, the dead are going somewhere. That is the gospel truth. When we recognize that all funerals are, in one way or another, a form of ritual drama, the significant question becomes, is it good theater or bad theater? Or to put it more theologically, does the drama narrate the truth about life and death, or not? For a Christian funeral, the question is even sharper: does the drama tell the gospel truth, or does it convey some other version of reality?

Here, once again, is the basic plot of the worshipful drama we call the Christian funeral: A child of God, a baptized Christian, a follower

of Jesus Christ, a saint has died. The Christian community lovingly prepares the body for burial (or cremation, bodily donation, etc.). When
the time has come, the community that has been walking with this
saint along the way of faith now carries the body to the place of departure, worshiping as they travel, a journey both necessary because of the
fact of death and symbolic of the baptismal journey now coming to
completion. At the place of farewell, with tears and thanksgiving, they
give their loved one into the hand of God. What are the truths being
told in this drama? The deceased is a saint; the body is to be honored;
God is worthy of trust even in the face of death; the baptismal journey
leads to the arms of God and the communion of the saints; and death
changes but does not destroy the relationship with the deceased.

There are many different ways to perform this basic dramatic plot.
Some Christians prepare the bodies of their dead themselves, while
others entrust this sacred task to a funeral home. Some lift and carry
the coffin from the church to the graveyard, some load the coffin onto
a hearse to travel to a cemetery miles away. Some pause at the church
for a formal funeral service, others go directly to the graveside. But the
basic shape of the drama remains the same.

Unless we hold firmly to the value of this gospel drama performed at
death, the Christian funeral becomes fragile, and there is constant cultural pressure to distort the script, to play out in a funeral some other
story than the gospel story. Here, for example, is my description of a
rather typical funeral, some version of which serves as the customary
pattern for many Christian funerals today, and a funeral that, in terms
of drama, has gone awry:

> The funeral is held at 2:00 p.m. on a Tuesday in the chapel of a
> local funeral home. Architecturally the chapel both gives and takes
> away. On the giving side, it is designed to evoke the impression of
> a church (or synagogue), with pews and pulpit, flowers and stained
> glass set in gothic-shaped windows. On the taking side, it must serve
> the needs of the funeral home's many clients; so it is bereft of any
> symbol that would anchor it to a specific faith tradition or, to put it
> another way, that would begin to tell any particular sacred narrative.
> It is generically "religious." There are candles but no cross, no font
> or baptismal pool, no Bible, no altar or communion table. There are
> attractive images in the window art, but nothing identifiable; just
> pretty designs.
>
> The people attending the funeral, a few dozen neighbors, fellow
> church members, and friends of the deceased, gradually gather as the

hour approaches, while an organist, hidden from view by a louvered wooden screen, softly plays a medley of hymns. Those attending are met by representatives of the funeral home, who hand them a printed program and point the way into the chapel. At 2:00 p.m. sharp, a small cluster of people, the close members of the family of the deceased, are ushered by a funeral home employee down the center aisle of the chapel, and they are seated in a special, set-apart section of pews.

When the family is in place, a door on the left-front of the chapel is opened, and two funeral home attendants wheel the closed coffin of the deceased, on a casket cart, across the front of the chapel and into position at the center, beneath the raised pulpit. The attendants then reverently move to the side of the chapel, one at the left and one at the right, and stand at attention.

At this point, the minister moves to the podium, reads several passages of Scripture and offers a brief prayer. A soloist sings "Peace Like a River." This is followed by three short speeches recounting touching and humorous memories of the deceased, given by two family members and one close friend. The minister follows these speeches with a brief homily on Psalm 23 and John 10:11–18, in which he assures the hearers that God shepherds us through the "valley of the shadow of death," that Christ is our "good shepherd," and that the deceased is surely among God's flock. The minister also includes in the homily a couple of stories about the deceased that show personal characteristics and traits, and ends by saying, "God is with us in our sorrow, and Sam (the deceased) is with us, too. We will always cherish the memories we have of Sam, and he will never be forgotten by us."

The minister then prays again, this time a longer prayer naming and giving thanks for some of the personal characteristics of the deceased, after which the congregation sings the hymn "In the Garden." The minister pronounces a blessing, and, as the organist plays "Sweet Hour of Prayer," the funeral home attendants who have been standing at the front of the chapel position themselves by the coffin, one at each end, and glide the coffin and cart out of a side door on the left to a waiting hearse. Another funeral home representative guides the family from their seats to the side door. They get into waiting cars, and the hearse and cars leave in procession for the cemetery and a brief graveside committal service. The rest of those in attendance make their way out the main door of the chapel and to the parking lot. Most leave at this point, but a few people drive to the end of the procession of cars headed to the cemetery.

It would be quite ungenerous and finally untrue to say that this was not a Christian funeral—it was. But in this ceremony much of the essential drama of the Christian funeral was cluttered, obscured, and to some extent undermined. As a result, the story being told was rendered ambiguous, and some of the power of the gospel available in and through the funeral was siphoned away. I want to engage in a critical analysis of this funeral, but I hasten to add that my intent is not to declare any funeral, past or future, to be illegitimate. People in my own family, cherished loved ones, have had funerals much like the one in our example. No liturgy, no matter how excellent, can force people with stony hearts to worship, and no liturgy, no matter how inept, can keep grateful hearts from praising God and bowing before the gracious mystery of God's presence. I want, therefore, to put this example funeral under a microscope, not to invalidate it, but to sharpen discernment and to move toward greater faithfulness in the performance of funerals. I want to examine four aspects of this funeral: the place where it was held, the participants, the words and actions employed, and its theology:

A. Place. This funeral was held in the funeral home chapel, which, by virtue of its generic architecture and decoration, is inherently a place of ambiguity. Christians are able to worship, of course, in stadiums, cinemas, and pastures as well as cathedrals, and the church can, if need be, faithfully commemorate its dead in the rented room of a funeral home.

Where should the funeral be held? Ought it be in the church, in a funeral home, in a cemetery chapel, institutional chapel, or auditorium, or at graveside? Good arguments can be made for each of these locations, but the issue of place gets reframed when we remember that a Christian funeral is essentially not a sit-down affair but a processional. Although our current funeral customs have often made this hard to see, the main venue for a Christian funeral is not in a room but on a road, the pilgrim way. A funeral does not occur in only one place but moves from location to location.

When a Christian dies, the community goes into action. The body is recovered, cared for, washed, dressed, and prepared for burial. When the time has come, friends and fellow Christians carry the deceased to the place of burial, worshiping as they go. This seamless movement from the place of death to the place of departure is the final sector in the great arc of a Christian's life from baptism to the grave. What the church has been doing all along, walking and worshiping along the way with a brother or sister, it continues to do in the time of death. As we have noted, all of these actions taken together—the care of the body, the worship along the way, the farewell at the grave—all of them constitute the Christian funeral.

Of course, what most people call a "funeral" happens inside a building. People go to a church or chapel, sit down, and participate in a service of worship. But it is best to understand this as only one portion of the whole funeral drama, as a moment when the funeral procession pauses along the way to engage in those acts of worship that can best be done inside a room. In the 1662 Anglican *Book of Common Prayer*, this rubric, or instruction, is provided for the clergy: "*The Priest and Clerks meeting the Corpse at the entrance of the Church-yard, and going before it, either into the Church, or towards the Grave, shall say, or sing,* 'I am the resurrection and the life.'" Can we picture this? Here comes a group of people down the road—family, friends, neighbors, parishioners—carrying in a coffin the body of one who has died. Back at the home of the deceased, the body was laid out on a bed, or perhaps on the family dining table, and was washed and dressed by loving hands. Now the deceased is being brought from the home to the church. The procession makes its way toward the gate of the churchyard, where the clergy stand vested and waiting, and when the pilgrim band arrives, the clergy join the ranks of the procession and begin to sing the promises of the gospel as they make their way either into the church building or toward the grave. If they go into the church, it is only to pause for a few moments of Scripture reading before continuing on to the grave. Of key importance here is the movement; this is an event that goes somewhere. It goes somewhere not only because a dead body must be buried, but also as a sign that a saint of God is "traveling on" in faith. A baptized Christian who has been on a pilgrimage of faith and has now come to the end of the earthly road is going on toward God.

Today the contours of this processional movement have unfortunately been obscured for several reasons. First, much about death has been taken out of the home and out of the hands of loved ones and given over to professionals. People now die mostly in institutions—hospitals, nursing homes, hospice facilities—and bodies are whisked out of sight from bed to morgue to funeral home, where morticians, not family members, prepare them for burial. Thus the continuous trajectory of bearing the dead from home to church to graveyard has been interrupted.

Second, burial grounds were once located more or less in "walking distance," placed either on the family homestead, in the churchyard, or in the center of the village. Gradually, however, cemeteries were moved away from churches and outside of towns. This trend began in Europe during the late fifteenth century, when church burial grounds became seriously overcrowded and were viewed as public-health hazards,[8] and in the New World the development of parklike cemeteries out in the countryside became a trend in the romantic "rural cemetery" move-ment of the nineteenth century.[9]

One result of putting cemeteries at a distance, as we noted in the previous chapter, was the gradual breaking apart of the funeral ritual into two separate services: one done in the church and the second one performed at the grave. As an example of this fragmentation, White traces the evolution from one unified service to two services in the various editions of the *Book of Common Prayer*, pointing out that what happens to the funeral in the *BCP* also occurs in the prayer books of Methodists, Catholics, and most other communions and denominations. As we saw in the rubric from the 1662 edition of *The Book of Common Prayer*, the worship started on the road and con-tinued in an unbroken sequence all the way to the grave. By the 1928 edition, however, we find not a single unified funeral service, but a ser-vice divided into two sections, "The Service in the Church" and "The Burial"; the latest version of the *Book of Common Prayer* now makes the division even more distinct, using names that imply that there are two discrete services, "The Burial of the Dead" and "The Committal."[10]

Thus divided, these two parts of the ritual—the service of prayers and lessons, often conducted in the church building, and the words of committal, spoken at the grave—lost their character as sequential acts in the overall drama of the funeral and became, instead, chess pieces that could be moved around on the board at will. A funeral could include the service in the church but not the burial service, or vice versa. Or both services could be done but, strangely, in reverse order. Indeed, there is an increasing trend today to gather first with the immediate family at the grave for a private burial service, followed by a more pub-lic "memorial service" in the church and without the body present. The argument for doing so is often pastoral and psychological—"let's get the sad part out of the way and then celebrate the resurrection without the dead body present"—but logically the practice is, in some ways, as out of order as a wedding would be if the wedding party were to gather in a private place to pronounce the couple married, and then would go to the church for the recitation of the vows.

Of course, we are not going back to a bygone era. There are exceptions, but most funerals today are not going to be like the village funerals of previous centuries or like jazz funerals in New Orleans. The community is not going to walk from home to church to grave, and most of what happens in the funeral service is going to happen inside a building and not in a procession on the road to the cemetery. If, however, we recognize the value of holding on to the symbol of the processional, we can find good ways to incorporate its power even into a building-centered service (more on this in later chapters).

Returning to the original question, if funerals are going to occur mostly in buildings, which building is best? Theologically, the balance tips decidedly toward the church building. The same building where the community gathers to perform its weekly act of worship is where the community should come for its occasional worship at the time of death. It is in the church that the community welcomed the new Christian in baptism, and it is in the church where the community can best bid farewell.

Sometimes those closest to the deceased object to a church funeral, saying something like, "We don't want Elizabeth's funeral to be in the church; we could never worship there again without being upset. All we would think about in church from now on would be the funeral, her death, our sadness." This reluctance is understandable reluctance, but it should be gently challenged and resisted for at least two reasons.

First, the objection that the mourners would never again be able to come to church without reliving the trauma of death and the sadness of the funeral is, except in rare cases of pathology, simply not true. The intense experience of grief does not persist in the ways they fear.

Second, and more important, making connections between funerals and everything else that happens in the place of worship is a benefit, not a problem to be overcome. The place where the promises of God are proclaimed week after week is the very place to hear them again at the time of death. Most church buildings, through architecture and memory, begin one of the essential tasks of a funeral, namely, telling the gospel. By its design and its association with regular worship, a church building announces the gospel, or at least an angular version of it, in wood and stone. Whether it is a dimly lit Gothic building with candles flickering on the altar, a whitewashed, clear-glassed puritan meetinghouse, or a contemporary sanctuary with projection screens and seating in the semiround, the building speaks to the community of faith that worships in that place, saying, "This is a station of the cross, a shelter for prayer, a feasting place on the Christian Way. This place of worship is a testimony to how we approach God."

All time—festival time and ordinary time, time marked by our births, our marriages, our growing old, and our dying—is offered to God in prayer in the place of worship. There is a deep connection between the regular preaching of the gospel and the declaration "Death is swallowed up in victory!" at a funeral. There is a profound link between the Lord's Supper and the communion of the saints around the heavenly banquet table. At a funeral, in the midst of grief and loss, it is important to remember that this is the very place where the joyous news of Easter has been celebrated, and on Easter morning, amid the trumpets and the lilies, it is good to hear Easter's "Do not be afraid" in the place where we have faced death.

As funeral director Thomas Lynch observes in his book *The Undertaking,*

> [T]he funerals held in my funeral parlor lack an essential manifest—the connection of the baby born to the marriage made to the deaths we grieve in the life of a family. I have no weddings or baptisms in the funeral home and the folks that pay me have maybe lost sight of the obvious connections between the life and the death of us. And the rituals by which we mark the things that happen to us once, birth and death, or maybe twice in the case of marriage, carry the same emotional mail—a message of loss and gain, love and grief, things changed utterly.[11]

As desirable as it is to have a Christian funeral in the church, sometimes practicalities get in the way. Perhaps the church is too small or too large for the expected attendance, maybe there is inadequate access for people with disabilities, or maybe it is necessary for the funeral to take place in a distant city. If the funeral is held in a building other than the church, say in a funeral home or a public auditorium, every effort should be made to mark the space as a place of Christian worship. A cross, crucifix, Bible, banners, or other artwork with Christian symbols can be placed in view.

Another option, of course, is not to pass through the church building at all, but to do as the old prayer books suggested: for the worshipers to process directly to graveside. In this case, the cemetery is itself a sanctuary, often full of Christian symbolism, and the procession of the worshipers to the grave is its own witness of the journey of the Christian life.

B. Participants. This example funeral was sparsely attended, which is not unusual. While there are notable exceptions, the general trend in North America is toward lower attendance at funerals and memorial services, even as, ironically, attendance remains high at wakes, viewings of the body, and other occasions when the family receives friends and well-wishers.[12]

A number of explanations have been offered for this, but many observers place the blame primarily on the changing work patterns of contemporary society. Funerals, such as our example service, are often held during the workday, and the era has mostly passed when the bell tolled in the village church to announce a death, and everyone ceased labor in farm and home to care for the bereaved family and to prepare for the funeral. Now many employers frown on workers taking time off for a funeral (except perhaps for the funeral of a very close family member), and given patterns of commuting and other life obligations, attending a funeral during a weekday can be a hardship.

In an effort to address this problem, some churches encourage families to hold funerals in the evenings or on weekends. One pattern proving to be effective at boosting funeral attendance in some communities is a late-afternoon or early-evening visitation or viewing time at the church, when the family receives friends, followed immediately by the funeral. One problem with this pattern, however, is that it tends to delay burial until at least the next day, since nighttime burials are usually not desirable and many cemeteries have policies prohibiting them. The time gap between the funeral service and the burial, combined with the fact that those who attend the funeral in the evening often don't return for the burial, breaks the ritual flow of the funeral service.

But the problem of low attendance is not entirely a matter of schedule. It is also a sign that the idea of a funeral itself has declined in social and religious importance. Many people today avoid funerals, not mainly because they find it hard to free up the time to go, but frankly because they cannot figure out what good it would be if they did go. Given the current cultural climate, we can hardly blame them. Society has shifted, as we have seen, toward understanding the funeral as primarily an occasion focused on grief management and the comfort of the bereaved. That leaves only two clear reasons why someone would want to attend a funeral: to receive comfort or to give it.

As for the first reason, the local merchant may have served the deceased as a customer, the dentist may have treated the deceased as a patient, the fellow church member may even have worshiped every Sunday only a few pews away from the deceased, but, given the fragmentation of contemporary urban life, chances are good that none of these people feels the bereaved family's wrenching sense of grief, or even the keen sense of loss that people in small communities two centuries ago experienced over the death of a fellow villager. Whatever sadness is felt when the news of death arrives will be mediated by the passing of time. There is no need for a funeral to address what is, after all, only a mild case of sorrow.

But even if the merchant, the dentist, and the fellow church member do not need the comfort of a funeral themselves, they perhaps still want to help and support the grieving family. But once again, it is not evident how this can be done sitting in a pew at the funeral, out of reach of the grieving family, singing hymns, praying, and listening to memories of the deceased. It is clear, though, that showing up for the wake or the visitation can be of practical help, where they can make personal contact with the family and speak directly words of compassion and encouragement.

When the funeral is defined essentially as religious grief therapy, it is no wonder people stay away, preferring more intimate settings where compassion can be more easily expressed to the family. To the extent that we buy into the therapeutic understanding of funerals, we could even welcome and encourage this change in attendance patterns. What would be lost if funerals were to become even smaller events, private ceremonies essentially for family, close friends, and others who are grief-stricken? We could give greater attention to wakes and visitations, where community support could more readily be given. Even in the 1950s, one critic agreed that public funerals had lost their social usefulness:

> The American funeral appears to be an anachronism, an elaboration of early customs rather than the adaptation to modern needs that it should be. . . . Although anthropologists assign a positive function to the rite in primitive societies, no serious scientific effort has been made to ascertain whether a like function is served by the funeral in modern industrialized society.[13]

But as I have been arguing, comfort at the time of grief, as important as it may be, is one of the *outcomes* of a Christian funeral, not its main purpose. The Christian funeral is about meaning, not just therapy. It is a dramatic performance of the gospel, enacting the meaning of life and death for the person who has died, for the Christian community and the communion of the saints and, indeed, for the whole of humanity. Left to its own devices, death always seems to have the last word, even the last laugh. The mourners need to be assured, the church needs to remember, the world needs to be told, that death does not in truth speak the final word. A Christian funeral is the enactment of an alternative narrative, one in which the living God, the God we know in Jesus Christ, speaks the last word. The merchant, the dentist, and the fellow parishioner are needed at the funeral not primarily to give or receive comfort (though that happens), but because they have important roles to play in the drama. They are needed "on stage" to act out the gospel story on the occasion of a death. To perform this drama is urgently to reclaim the gospel promises in the teeth of that reality that seems to deny them, namely, the final enemy of death. To rehearse this drama again and again becomes an essential resource for all Christians, including the merchant and the dentist, in living their own Christian lives and in preparing to face their own deaths as Christians.

C. Words and Actions. As a drama, a funeral is not just a random series of elements—prelude, solo, Scripture lessons, prayers, and so forth—but is rather an ensemble of interrelated actions and speeches. Because of the interaction among the elements of worshipful drama, each action or piece of dialogue has two main levels of meaning. First, an element means something in and of itself. Second, and even more important, an element means something in relation to the totality of the liturgy. Suppose, for example, that at the raw and emotional funeral of a teenager who committed suicide after weeks of anguished depression, the minister chose to read Psalm 22:1–2 ("My God, my God, why have you forsaken me? Why are you so far from helping me, from the words of my groaning? O my God, I cry by day, but you do not answer; and by night, but find no rest"). It would make a significant difference where it was placed. This powerful lament would mean one thing as the opening words of the funeral and quite another if it were to be read as the final word at the graveside. To speak the language of forsakenness at the beginning of the funeral would be an acknowledgment of the pain felt by the deceased and the pain that the mourners perhaps bring to the funeral. To end the funeral with these words of despair, however, could undermine the hope promised by the gospel.

Or to give a nonliturgical example, imagine watching a theatrical version of the fairy tale "Cinderella." We learn at the outset of the play that Cinderella is a young girl whose father, a widower, has married a second wife, who is jealous of Cinderella because she is a finer and more beautiful person than either of the stepmother's two vain daughters. We observe a scene near the beginning where the heartless stepmother forces Cinderella to wash dishes, scrub floors, and behave like a servant toward her own daughters. At the first level of meaning, this early scene is what it is; standing on its own, this moment in the play conveys Cinderella as an innocent victim, and it rouses the empathy of the audience on her behalf. At the second level, though, this early scene is but a gear driving the overall machinery of the plot forward, and it works to set up the play's main tension: the contrast between the Cinderella we see, the ragged and lowly servant girl, and the Cinderella we know is really there "inside," the good and beautiful woman. This tension is, of course, ultimately resolved when Cinderella, helped by a magical fairy godmother, trades her rags for a fancy gown, attends a royal ball, and is discovered by the handsome prince, who marries her, makes her his princess, and lives with her "happily ever after."

Funerals are also composed of several discrete elements or scenes that work together to create a whole. In the case of our example funeral, these elements included the gathering of the community, the positioning of the coffin, music by a soloist, Scripture readings, tribute speeches, homily, prayers, and so on. Each one of these elements has intrinsic meaning and value, but we need to press farther and ask about the larger plot structure they form. In other words, when we put all the pieces of this funeral together, what larger story did it tell?

Honestly, when we step back and take a critical look at the overall dramatic structure of this funeral, the story line becomes muddy. Note, for example, that the major movements of this funeral were led largely by the representatives of the funeral home. They were prominently visible throughout and orchestrated the choreography of the service. At one level, this is innocent, understandable, and helpful. After all, the funeral directors have much more experience at this than even veteran clergy, and they are capable of keeping the funeral moving along smoothly. At a deeper level, though, the role of the funeral staff in this service raises a concern. We will have more to say about the specific role of funeral directors in chapter 8, but at this point it is important to say that the strong and active presence of the funeral professionals, almost "standing guard" over the coffin, treaded perilously close to communicating that the funeral was a production of the funeral home, rather than a worship service of the church.

Note also that the family of the deceased was segregated from the rest of the community. They entered at a different time, sat in a separate seating area, and departed by a different route. Who knows the reasons? To give them a place of honor? To allow them a sense of privacy in their grief? Whatever the motive, the unhappy result of setting these people apart was a set of dramatic actions that run counter to the Christian affirmation that these grieving people are—and need to be—part of the community of faith, accompanied by the faithful and surrounded by the church's prayers as they travel with their loved one.

And what do we make of the rolling of the coffin from a side door to the center of the church and then out the other side door to the hearse? The meaning of this action within the drama of the funeral is, at best, confused. Death changes, but does not destroy, our relationship to the deceased, and in a Christian funeral, the deceased is still a member of the community of faith. The church walks along the pilgrim way and worships with the person who has died. The best way to represent this in the funeral is for the coffin to enter the church in the same way as all of the other worshipers, through the main door. The coffin is then taken down the aisle and placed in the position of worship, facing the east wall, pulpit, altar, or Communion table. But in the example funeral, the people were already in place, and the coffin rather mysteriously emerged from the wings ("Heeerrre's Johnny!") and, like a bird flying through a barn, sailed across the chapel and disappeared out the other side. The body of the deceased, rather than being honored and carried with thanksgiving to the place of farewell, became, in this case, more like a theatrical prop.

D. Theology. As is the case in too many contemporary funerals, our example funeral was muddled theologically. Often today two rival theological understandings battle it out for the soul of the funeral. To put it starkly, on the one hand, there is the gospel. The one who has died is an embodied person, a saint "traveling on" to God, continuing the baptismal journey toward the hope of the resurrection of the body and God's promise to make all things new. On the other hand, there is a more "spiritualized," perhaps even gnostic, understanding of death. The body is "just a shell," and the immortal soul of the deceased has now been released to become a spiritual presence among us, available through inspiration and active memory. In this view, the body, no longer of any use, is disposed of, but the "real person" is now a disembodied spirit. It is therefore not the deceased who is traveling, but the mourners, on an intrapsychic journey from sorrow to stability.

A funeral governed by the gospel is built upon the eschatological hope that the deceased is not a static corpse or a gaseous and disembodied spirit, but an embodied child of God moving toward the communion of the saints. Thus, in the drama of the funeral, the whole congregation follows the deceased from the church to the cemetery or crematorium, traveling with the deceased all the way to the end and completing the dramatic action. By contrast, in a funeral governed by the more spiritualized understanding of death, the congregation sits still and reflects about the life of the deceased, seeking comfort in the claim that, though the body is dead, the soul lives on. Many contemporary funerals limp haltingly between these two theologies, sometimes the official liturgy trumpeting the first view and the improvised remarks of the clergy and other participants expressing the second.

Our example funeral cannot seem to make up its theological mind. On the one hand, the body of the deceased is present, but as we noted above, its symbolic role is unclear. In many ways, the casketed body seems to make an odd and sudden appearance, mainly as a prompt to thought. The homily wavers back and forth between the gospel and a more spiritualized understanding of death. On the one hand, God as affirmed is the one who shepherds "through the valley of the shadow of death," but on the other hand, one suspects that when the minister announced that the deceased is "with us too," this was meant in a spiritualized way and not as an embodied presence in that coffin over there.

The pastor's affirmation that the deceased would "never be forgotten," though commonly said at funerals, is also ambiguous. Probably he meant to offer comfort by implying that, even though the deceased is now dead and gone, not all is lost, because the memory of his life and good works will live among us always. If that is what he meant, his words have the disadvantage of not being true. Cemeteries are full of the graves of people no one remembers any longer. If the deceased are of value only if we the living can keep their memory alive, then we are to be pitied. As the psalmist truly says, "As for mortals, their days are like grass; they flourish like a flower of the field; for the wind passes over it, and it is gone, and its place knows it no more" (Ps. 103:15–16).

The gospel does not place the burden on the living to keep alive the spiritual flame of memory. Rather, it affirms that the deceased is now raised to new life and sings in the great choir of the communion of saints standing in the presence of God. Only in this way, only in the life of God, is the deceased "never forgotten."

3. The Christian funeral, as a sacred ritual, has the power to reaffirm and deepen the gospel vision of life and death. But much depends upon the participants' capacity to enter with awareness into the ritual arena.

Several years ago, one of the professional associations of funeral directors launched a public relations campaign with the theme "Ritual Heals." The main idea was that human beings are by nature ritual creatures, and when the trauma of death occurs, we need some kind of ritual event to commemorate the loss and to provide closure and healing. Ritual is normally the concern of anthropologists and social scientists. So why were professional funeral directors concerned about it? Mainly, they were worried about what they were seeing happen all around them, namely, the cultural trend to minimize funerals and memorial services. Many people have lost patience with what they see as the formal and heavy funeral liturgies of the churches and are seeking simpler, more festive, more personalized ceremonies. In fact, a surprising number of people, when a loved one dies, simply don't bother with the hassle at all, choosing to skip any service or act of commemoration whatsoever.

This tendency to downsize or eliminate death rituals is, of course, bad for business in the commercial funeral sector, and the funeral professionals, with their eye on the bottom line, can hardly be blamed for wanting to stem that tide. But financial self-interest was not the only motivation for the "Ritual Heals" campaign. The best funeral directors see themselves as helping professionals, public ministers of a sort; as such, they are concerned about the health of their clients and of society. They know through experience that the rituals around death—from caring for the dying person to gathering for a funeral to the marking of time after a funeral—deeply matter and can be powerful instruments of healing. They sensed rightly that a society that fails adequately to mark the passing of its dead is a society impoverished.

The main problem, however, with the "Ritual Heals" campaign is that, on the face of it, it was simply not true. Ritualistic behavior, by itself, has no healing power. Dancing the "Hokey Pokey" three times a day is, after all, a kind of ritual, but hardly a healing one. The bare enactment of some ritual, any ritual, does not by itself exert any restorative power. Funeral directors, most of whom try to serve a broad swath of our multicultural, pluralistic society, could hardly be expected to advocate for some particular or sectarian way of doing funerals, but the empty sign "Ritual Heals" carries the same bland message of civil religion expressed by President Eisenhower in the 1950s when he famously said, "Our government has no sense unless it is founded in a deeply felt religious faith, and I don't care what it is."[14]

The "Ritual Heals" message was not completely off the mark, though. Something important is at work in our ritual life, but to understand what this is and what is at stake for funerals, we need to take a closer look at the nature of rituals and how they work. Scholars hotly debate these matters, of course, but for our purposes in thinking about funerals, it is perhaps most helpful to think of rituals as social performances, ordered ceremonies of reenactment, formally patterned rites in which communities remember formative events, imagine alternative worlds, and appropriate those memories and worlds in new circumstances. Here are some of the key functions of rituals that play a role in funerals.

A. Rituals are ordered events, and they are often performed in times of upheaval and disorder so that order may be brought to chaos. Take weddings, for example. Although we often think of weddings as joyful occasions, they actually mask social circumstances fraught with uncertainty and even danger. Two people are in a sense wrenching themselves free from their families of origin in order to form a new family. Everyone involved—parents, siblings, bride, groom—is being asked to do the hard work of changing social roles and relationships, and the question of the day is, How can we possibly get from here to there? Into the breach comes the ordered process of the marriage ceremony, which allows people to walk the well-worn ritual path from one social status to another. It is as if society said, "All right, these are perilous waters for everyone to navigate, but fear not, we have crossed this lake before. Let's put on an ancient play, enact a drama full of wisdom acquired through the ages, in which families say to their children, 'Yes, you have my permission to leave your father and mother and to join yourself with another,' and a man and a woman vow to stay together and care for each other, come what may." So, in the midst of the stormy waters of changing roles and uncertain outcomes, people step into the boat of the marriage service; they enter this ritual process designated as parents, bride, and groom, and they safely emerge on the other shore as in-laws, husband, and wife.

The capacity of rituals to order the messy business of life is much of what gives them their character as social mandate. In other words, rituals are not just things we *choose* to do on certain occasions; they are things we feel we *ought* to do. Puritan Thomas Shepard, who worked to evangelize the Native population of New England in the early 1600s, records a tender scene in his journal. One of the Native people had died, and he was buried as the Puritans had taught them to do, simply and without any ceremony. But as they stood there at the grave, this ritual-less moment seemed insufficient and unsatisfying. The situation cried out for something more to be done. So the Native folk withdrew from their white evangelizers and gathered under a nearby tree. There they appointed one of their number, Tutaswampe, "a very hopefull Indian," to pray, which he did.[15] Small wonder that one useful definition of ritual is that which people sense ought to be done in a time of transition.

B. Rituals frame ordinary time as extraordinary time and, by doing so, reveal the extraordinary character of everyday existence. Apart from ritual, life can appear simply as "one damned thing after another," a bleak and unbroken landscape of ordinariness. Rituals lift up particular times and seasons as peak moments, as turning points, as extraordinary, even sacred, time.[16] Birthdays, baptisms, graduations, weddings, initiations, and other ritual occasions gather up the threads of ordinary life and weave them into a tapestry of the extraordinary. The value of this ritual framing of time is not that it establishes a firewall between ordinary and extraordinary time but, rather, that it discloses that what we can see as true in the clear light of ritual remains true in the shadows of ordinary experience. The ritual of baptism, for example, though experienced only once in a lifetime, shines a beacon on every passing moment. "The Christian life," said Martin Luther in his *Large Catechism*, is "nothing else than a daily baptism." When life becomes hard, Luther counseled, Christians are to remind themselves, "I am baptized. I am baptized."

C. Rituals reenact significant stories, and this reenactment involves past, present, and future. Because these reenacted stories were formed by powerful events in the past, reenacting them is the way these past events are most deeply remembered. By inviting people to participate

in the ritual reenactment, these events are brought into the present and made available to the participants as a living possibility. By living out an alternative reality in the ritual, participants are provided new ways of living toward the future. A married couple I know decided on the occasion of their fiftieth wedding anniversary to renew their wedding vows. They invited some friends to their home for an anniversary party, and in the middle of these festivities they gathered everybody into the living room. As they stood together in front of the fireplace, their pastor led them through the same vows they had pledged a half century before.

It is clear, of course, that this renewal ritual hearkens back to a formative event in the past, namely, the couple's wedding five decades earlier. But their first wedding is not the only past event being recalled. Built into the DNA of this renewal ceremony, and indeed into the marriage ritual generally, is the history of the mating and cohabitating patterns of the human species; further, in the Christian marriage ritual is encoded the specific memory of the covenant between God and God's people and the declaration that "a man leaves his father and his mother and clings to his wife, and they become one flesh" (Gen. 2:24).

As for the present, this couple's participation in the ritual of renewal brings the past event powerfully into the present. They could have merely gotten out the photo album and recalled their wedding day, but the act of standing up in the presence of pastor and friends and putting their voices and bodies into action in the ritual makes the event present in a palpable way. And by doing so, they strengthen their identity as husband and wife, providing a resource for them as they navigate the uncertain future of old age together. As theologian Tom Driver says of ritual, "Rituals are primarily instruments designed to change a situation: They are more like washing machines than books. A book may be *about* washing, but the machine takes in dirty clothes and, if all goes well, transforms them into cleaner ones."[17]

THE FUNERAL AS RITUAL

Pulling together these observations about ritual and applying them to funerals, we can see that a funeral is more than a service of noble words and fine remembrances of the deceased. At a funeral, the Christian community reenacts the past. What past? The exodus, when the people of God moved from bondage through the waters of the Red Sea to freedom in the promised land. The baptism of Jesus. The death and burial of Jesus. The baptism of the one who has died. All of these formative events, and more, are gathered into the funeral ritual. In reenacting these past events, a funeral takes the chaos and upheaval of death and gives it order and meaning. While death may feel and look like the world coming apart and life dissolving into meaninglessness, through the lens of the funeral ritual we can see it for what it truly is: a saint moving through the troubled waters into the promised land, a follower of Jesus traveling his same road, from death to resurrection life.

But merely performing a funeral ritual, even one that is right and true and faithful in every way, does not guarantee that participants will experience its power to transform, to generate meaning, and to strengthen faith. Some experts in ritual, perhaps infatuated with their own topic, declare with unjustified enthusiasm the nearly magical powers of ritual. William Harman, for example, crowed that even people who have no idea of the sacred story or myth that stands behind a religious ritual "may find that ritual just as meaningful as someone who claims to know the mythology which the ritual involves. Ritual, once enacted, has a life of its own."[18]

Harman has a point, of course. It is not as if people get their theology straight and then act this out in rituals. Performing a ritual is something like dancing; the meaning and rhythms are in the steps themselves, and you aren't really dancing if you're looking at your feet. But the problem—and it is a major one—is that rituals are like big, enacted texts. Yes, they have a meaning, but not just one; they have many possible readings, and how they are read and experienced depends greatly on what participants bring to them. Liturgical scholar Lawrence Hoffman is closer to the truth when he observes that Christians who participate in the ritual of Christmas worship don't always "read the text" rightly:

> It would be nice if Christians leaving their Christmas mass walk out on a world where the reality of the Christian promise makes them over into hopeful charitable Christians; where even the most mean-spirited Scrooge among them sees the light, as we say. But as often as not, it is any one of the other meanings that carry the day.[19]

Hoffman is saying, in other words, that the ritual of the Christmas Mass has the possibility to open up a world of generosity for the participants, but that many of the participants decipher their experience in another way, that they have been among believers over against the heathen, for instance, or that they have had some warm experiences with "people like themselves."

What we are developing is a picture of a ritual, such as the funeral liturgy, in a mediating role, bringing together the power of the sacred story that gave birth to the ritual with the current circumstances, attitudes, and aptitudes of the participants. If a Christian funeral is to accomplish the transformative work it has the potential to perform, two realities must be in place: the funeral itself must be faithful to the gospel narrative that undergirds it, and the participants must be prepared to enact the ritual. This latter need involves education, of course, but more than just schooling. The funeral, as we have been insisting, is a drama, and the participants best serve their neighbors, nourish their own faith, and act out the gospel in the world when they rehearse their roles and learn their parts.

What it looks like to bring the gospel story and the people of God together at the meeting place of a funeral drama involves scores of practical choices and decisions. It is to those practicalities that we turn in the following chapters.

PART TWO

The Church's Ministry
in Death

6

In the Hour of Our Death

THE TIME OF IN-BETWEEN

There is life and there is death, but there is also the time of dying—the in-between season when the reality that a person will soon die looms large and becomes a magnetic pole around which the thoughts and actions of others are organized. "My sister is dying," we say, meaning that her life is ebbing, that time is now short, the moment of her death drawing near. The statement "His body is simply failing; the end is in sight," whether made by a physician or a family member, has the quality of a pronouncement, a declaration that signals a reshaping of expectations and obligations. The currents of social relationships around the dying person subtly change direction, the wind begins to shift, perhaps gradually at first, but everyone around the dying person perceives the signs in the sky and sea, adjusts the rigging, sets the heading for the harbor, and prepares now for the end.

Sometimes, of course, death comes swiftly and unexpectedly, and there is no in-between time of dying. More often, however, there is at least an hour, or a day, or a year that is not yet death but not unshadowed life either, a transitional time of dying, when the journey continues but the compass needle points toward the end. The person who is dying is at home, in the hospital, or in a hospice—waiting.

In Tolstoy's *The Death of Ivan Illych*, the narrator speaks of the shift from tending to a person who is ill to preparing for a death, an absence:

It is impossible to say how it happened, for it came about gradually, imperceptibly, but in the third month of Ivan Illych's illness his wife, his daughter, his son, his acquaintances, the servants, the doctors, and—above all—he himself knew that the only interest he had for others was whether he would soon vacate his place, free the living at last from the constraint of his presence and himself from his sufferings.[1]

When the time of dying arrived for Ivan Illych, those around him prepared only for a death, a void, a wearied freedom from the dying one's presence. In contrast, Christian faith views this time in between not with resignation, not merely as a season of passing time before someone passes away, but as a period filled with meaning and opportunity for communion with the one who is dying.

REHEARSING FOR DEATH

Most of us do not think of ourselves as people who are dying. We tend to make a sharp distinction between "being alive" and the experience of dying; as a consequence, very little about our lives prepares us for death. When people sense, or are told, that they are dying, that they have crossed the invisible boundary that separates those who are "terminal" from those who are not, often frightening and sometimes very new feelings and questions arise: "I'm frightened." "What will happen to my family?" "I don't want to not *be*." "I don't know what lies ahead for me. I haven't been a good enough person. I haven't lived as I should."[2]

The Christian faith intends to blur the boundary between the dying and the living. From the vantage point of the gospel, we are all dying, and when we are in the presence of those whose days have grown short, we are not gazing in horror at those who reside in a strange and alien territory. Rather, we are viewing, with love and understanding, brothers and sisters with whom we share an experience.

The church, paradoxically, imagines death occurring not only at the end of life, but also at the beginning. In baptism, new Christians die with Christ, which is a sign of hope. We have already died, we have already experienced the worst that can happen to a human being, and by dying with Christ, we also participate in the promise that we will rise with Christ. But to place a symbol of death at the very beginning of the Christian journey is also a sign of realism. It reminds us that we are not permanent and immortal, that we are made of dust and to dust shall we return. We walk in faith in a world where sin and death still exert their powers, indeed, in a world where the more faithfully we live for Christ, the more aggressive become the forces of death. "For while we live," said Paul, "we are always being given up to death for Jesus' sake, so that the life of Jesus may be made visible in our mortal flesh" (2 Cor. 4:11).

Indeed, theologically, all of the Christian life can be seen as the in-between time, the time of dying. When the physician says, "The time is now short; death is at hand," this is undeniably a dramatic moment, but it is only an intensification of what is always true about us. We are under the shadow of death every day, which means more than saying merely, as did Seneca, "We die every day" or, as we put it in contemporary casual conversation, "We're not getting any younger, you know." Instead, it means that every day Christians battle death in one form or another, and therefore they need the same resources of support on the deathbed that they required in the struggles of life.

When Elisabeth Kübler-Ross wrote her famous book *On Death and Dying*,[3] she outlined a five-stage emotional process through which the dying characteristically move. The five stages—denial and isolation, anger, bargaining, depression, and acceptance—have entered the vocabulary of popular knowledge, and many people can recite them from memory. Despite the fact that Kübler-Ross tried later to insist that these stages were not fixed and sequential categories, *On Death and Dying* does little to dispel the impression that "normal" people, when they know they are dying, move step by step from denial of death to its "acceptance with peace and dignity."[4]

There are probably many aspects of Kübler-Ross's work that should be criticized, but two stand out prominently. First, the fact that acceptance of death was named as the last (and presumably the highest) stage owes more to Kübler-Ross's implicit Platonism than it does to any innate moral sense in dying people. Yes, Christians know we will die, and we frankly acknowledge this fact. This, however, is a far cry from embracing, welcoming, and accepting the power of death. As a force that destroys life and all that life holds dear, death is worthy only of our sneer.

In her book *Intensive Care*, Mary Lou Wiseman recounts the last days of her fifteen-year-old son, Peter, as he lay dying of muscular dystrophy. Mary Lou recorded that she and her husband, Larry, were beside Peter's bed, when, in a dying whisper that sounded "so far away, so lost," Peter called out to his father,

"Daddy? What does 'impudent' mean?"

Bewildered, frightened, I look to Larry. He answers matter-of-factly, while tears stream from his eyes, "Impudent. It means bold. Shamelessly bold."

"Then put me in an impudent position."[5]

Christians, it seems to me, spend a whole life preparing themselves to take an impudent position over against the powers of death.

Second, and more to the point here, the implication in Kübler-Ross's work that knowledge of impending death somehow drives people rapidly up the stairway of emotional and ethical development is a fiction of the therapeutic culture. The fact is that people die pretty much as they have lived.[6] If someone has been enraged throughout life, we can expect rage at the end. A person who tries to bargain with life, family, physicians, and God on death's door has probably tried to cut a few deals before. A person who blesses the world at death has not learned this in the last few hours of life but has been shaped to live a life of blessing. As one rabbi said, "A Jew is expected to die, as he has lived, with the name of God on his lips."[7]

The best preparation for dying a Christian death, then, is living a Christian life. There have been times in our history when Christians have made this truth explicit by helping each other, in the middle of life, to marshal the resources of the faith that will be needed at the end of life. In particular, I am thinking of the *Ars Moriendi* (the art of dying well) tradition, which consisted of very practical devotional resources, dating from the fifteenth century, that enabled Christians to "dress rehearse" the experience of dying.[8]

Typical of the *Ars Moriendi* literature is the depiction of a dying person, a faithful Christian, who is alone when Satan approaches to destroy all confidence and faith. A dialogue ensues in which Satan speaks like a pastoral counselor from hell, literally:

> *Satan*: You're frightened, aren't you?
>
> *Dying person*: Yes, I am frightened, but I am trusting my Savior who calms my fears.
>
> *Satan*: Oh really? You think you are going to be rewarded by this Jesus, don't you? You who have no righteousness.
>
> *Dying person*: Christ is my righteousness.

Satan: Oh ho, Christ is your righteousness? You think Christ will welcome you to the company of Peter and Paul and the apostles? You who have sinned over and over again?

Dying person: No, I am not going into the company of Peter and Paul. I am going into the company of the thief on the cross, who heard the promise, "To-day, you will be with me in paradise."

Satan: Why are you so confident? You who have done nothing good.

Dying person: I have God's forgiveness and mercy.

Satan: Legions of demons are salivating, waiting for your soul.

Dying person: And I would be hopeless and fearful before that, if the Lord had not already crushed your tyranny.

Satan: Your God is unjust! What kind of God would bring someone like you into a kingdom of righteousness?

Dying person: God keeps promises. That is what justice is, and I will call on his mercy.[9]

Virtually every fear, anxiety, and doubt in the human repertoire of facing death is put into the mouth of the tempter, of Satan, and the responses of faith are voiced, in an almost catechetical fashion, by the dying person. The *Ars Moriendi* literature was read not only by dying people but also by people very much alive. This was a dress rehearsal for dying as a Christian. When Christians got to their deathbeds and felt the fear and anxiety and unworthiness that almost every dying person feels, they had been there before. They possessed the language to describe the experience and to speak faithfully in the midst of it.

The *Ars Moriendi* devotional practices built upon, and helped to form, Christian virtues: faith in the teeth of the fear of death, hope in the face of despair, patience in the midst of the struggle, and enjoying this world and the life given by God without clinging desperately to it.

Martin Luther practiced a form of the *Ars Moriendi*, daily preparing himself for the ultimate struggle with the devil and death, equipping himself in the middle of life to be able at the end to "fool the devil, finding himself threshing empty straw":

For what are you fighting, devil? Are you trying to find good works, to find fault with my own holiness before God? Serves you right, for I have neither! The power which I have is not my own; the Lord is my strength. . . . I have no knowledge of either sin or holiness in me. I know nothing, nothing but God's power in me.[10]

While Christians today are probably not going to be attracted to the old practice of *Ars Moriendi* devotions, it is urgent that the core of that tradition be retrieved, if for no other reason than to break the code of silence about death. Robin Marantz Henig, writing in the *New York Times* about American attitudes toward death, said,

> Most of us will be old and sick when we die and will have had years to tell our loved ones just what it is about dying that most frightens us and, in broad brush strokes, just how we hope to die. The trouble is, most of us aren't talking. The silence is another example of our ambivalence about death, our unwillingness to look it straight in the face even as we make noises about accepting it.[11]

How can we interrupt this silence? How can we encourage the Christian art of dying well? Sermons about death, church school classes about death, church reading groups on death—all of these are helpful ways to bring the reality of death into the context of the life of faith. But perhaps the most powerful way to recover the *Ars Moriendi* heritage is to allow the wisdom of faithful Christians who are themselves near death to be shared with the rest of the community.

Jon Walton, a pastor in New York City, did just that, when he related in a sermon an experience he had visiting an older woman in his congregation who had been hospitalized with severe and undiagnosed stomach pain. Walton had been advised that this woman, a person of deep faith, might appreciate hearing some psalms read to her, so he took his prayer book with him and made his way to the hospital. In her room, she seemed happy to see him, though she was weak and faint in voice. They chatted for a while, and then Walton read some familiar psalms: "God is our refuge and strength . . . ," "I lift up mine eyes to the hills . . . ," "The LORD is my shepherd, I shall not want. . . ." Walton described for his congregation what happened next:

> She closed her eyes and allowed the words to seep into the familiar places of her soul. After I finished reading she told me that the doctor had visited her a little earlier and explained what her diagnosis

was. "Lymphoma," he said, "rather advanced." But she was feeling relieved because it meant that there would not need to be any surgery in her weakened condition and she was thankful for the good care that she was getting.

Clean sheets, nurses to attend her, food prepared and served, and the visits of her son and pastors. She hoped, she said, to go home soon and spend her last days there.

She smiled and went on, "I wish you'd been here earlier. The doctor came to see me with three handsome young interns in tow. They told me their names and each one checked me over, and then the doctor said to me, 'Maybe you would like to share with these young men something that they should know as doctors, especially in light of your faith, and what I've just told you.'"

She said, "I hardly knew what to say. It seemed like it was so important. Here I was in this bed and I was supposed to say something that these young doctors could remember. I didn't think I had anything to say, so I just said, 'Somehow I trust that whatever happens to me I will be in God's hands, and that gives me hope. Whatever happens, I will be all right.'"

And then she looked at me and said, "I wish you'd been here. You would have said it so much better than I could."

And I looked at her and I said, "No, I couldn't. I couldn't have said it any better at all."[12]

It may well be that those Christians who have traveled well the baptismal path and have learned how to live well the Christian life are our best guides to the art of dying well. When theologian Douglas John Hall entered his seventies and faced his mortality every day, he wrote some wisdom for dying well:

I entered my seventieth year not long ago—the biblical age, as they say. . . . I am in a position now that I did not occupy at age twenty-one: that is, I can say with a certain real confidence I *have* seen the goodness of the Lord in the land of the living—and quite specifically in my own life. . . . Even this wonderful (if rather small and problematic!) body I live in and *am*, even these (now somewhat arthritic) hands that love to play the piano and write little yellow words on a computer screen; even this mind full of its own unique memories . . . all of this that is me . . . must come to an end, and sooner rather than later, now. . . . Resurrection is the ultimate declaration of God's grace. It is not . . . natural. It is not . . . automatic. It is wholly dependent upon the faithfulness, forbearance, and love of God.

And just for that reason—only that!—I am able, usually, to sleep at night. . . . Because the only thing of which I can be at all confident when I think of my own "not being" is that God will be.[13]

CLOTHE YOURSELVES WITH COMPASSION

The biblical book of James has some extraordinary advice about how the church should care for the sick and the dying: "Are any among you sick? They should call for the elders of the church and have them pray over them, anointing them with oil in the name of the Lord" (Jas. 5:14).

Sadly, this piece of Christian wisdom contains in the span of a single verse most of the acts of compassion that today's Christians are *least* likely to do. To begin with, James thinks that Christians ought to go and be with other Christians who are sick and dying; but today, when the word goes out that someone is dying, this is often the signal for the rest of the community to stay away, to cordon off the dying person from the rest of life.

Why? Ethicist William F. May is convinced that one factor that makes Christians reluctant to be with the dying is the fear that dying people need something that we don't have to give. Because they are facing death, being in their presence somehow compels one to "be a God-producer, a Christ-dispenser, or a religious magician in the sickroom." Since we are none of these things, of course, we are strongly inclined "to shy away from the dying to avoid [our] own poverty."[14]

According to May, such feelings of inadequacy, which keep us away from the dying, are the product of a faulty theology. We think the room where a dying person lies is a temple of death, devoid of God's presence. But the resurrection means that Christ has invaded the regions of death and reclaimed the territory. "There is no need to produce Christ in the sickroom," May says, "when he is already there."

May's theological reason for our reluctance to be present with the dying has, I think, a practical side. Perhaps we have been seduced by contemporary medicine into thinking that the approach of death demands heroic intervention, that if we were to visit a dying person in the name of Christ, we would need to be prepared to perform some exotic form of ministry needed only at the point of death.

Nothing could be further from the truth. Christians know that because we are always facing death, the ministries needed by the dying are exactly the same ministries ordinarily provided by the church. If anything is different, it is only that the shortness of the time causes us to perform them in a more focused fashion.

What do the dying need? As James says, they need the community to gather around to pray with them. They need people to read Scripture and to sing with and for them. In the congregation where I worship, the whole choir has, on occasion, traveled to a hospital room to sing in the presence of the dying. Invariably the choir members report their own faith strengthened by the experience. When they sing with the sick, they do ministry, ministry is done to them, and both choir and dying person discover anew the presence of Christ.

James also calls on the church to anoint the sick with oil. This was not an extraordinary act for James's congregation. Oil is a symbol for the Holy Spirit, and every member of James's church would have been anointed at the time of baptism. To be anointed with oil at the time of sickness is to remember one's baptism and to remember that one ultimately belongs to God.

Of course, anointing with oil means touching the body of the sick person. Physician Lewis Thomas observed in his book about medicine, *The Youngest Science,* that young physicians often lack two things: they have never been sick, not really sick, and therefore, don't know what it feels like to be ill; and they have forgotten that all healing begins with touch. He writes,

> There, I think, is the most effective act of doctors, the touching. Some people don't like being handled by others, but not, or almost never, sick people. They *need* being touched, and part of the dismay in being very sick is the lack of human contact. Ordinary people, even close friends, even family members, tend to stay away from the very sick, touching them as infrequently as possible for fear of interfering, or catching the illness, or just for fear of bad luck. The doctor's oldest skill in trade was to place his hands on the patient.[15]

In an earlier chapter we saw how the willingness tenderly to touch the bodies of the dead was one characteristic that set the early Christians apart from their neighbors. "With willing hands [they] raised the bodies of the saints to their bosoms." Because they viewed the bodies of the saints as holy, they were willing to provide the blessing of touch, to the living and to the dead.

In his moving memoir *Cancer and Faith: Reflections on Living with a Terminal Illness,* the late theologian John Carmody told of a priest, wandering from hospital room to hospital room, who played a pastoral hunch and asked Carmody, a patient in the oncology area, if he would like to be anointed.

> With no thought, I said yes. So we went through a spare, adapted version of the church's ancient ritual that asks God's help for the seriously sick—begs God's support and comfort for both body and spirit. Although it began almost shamefully casually, this anointing proved to be the most moving moment in my month's stay in the hospital. Indeed, it has lodged itself among the half-dozen most moving religious experiences of my entire life.[16]

A pastor I know was in the hospital visiting a parishioner who was dying. At the end of the visit she made a surprising request. "I have been reading the book of James," she said, "and I want you to come back to my room with the officers of the church, and I would ask that you pray for me and anoint me with oil."

The pastor had never done anything like that and was reluctant. "No," he said, "I'm sorry. I will pray for you, but I do ministry, not magic."

The parishioner became angry. "Look," she said, "I am dying. I probably don't have a month left. I know I am going to die!"

"Then why do you want to be anointed with oil?"

"It will be a sign," she said, "that I am claimed by Jesus Christ. I am going to die, but death cannot have me. I belong to another."

Anointing with oil is associated, perhaps, with particular Christian traditions, but the willingness to touch the dying tenderly and to pray for them is shared by all Christians. A friend of mine had, by his own account, a terrible relationship with his father, who was cold and emotionally remote. My friend was the apple of his mother's eye, and that made his father resent him all the more. The distance between father and son endured for more than fifty years. But when his aged father came home at last from the hospital to die, to receive home hospice care, my friend was able for the first time to attend to his father, to be in his presence in a way that was not adversarial. He still counts as the most remarkable day in his life the time when his father, weak and vulnerable, allowed his son, my friend, to shave him. My friend was able to touch his father, to gently apply the warm lather, and to caress his face. The dying father opened himself to his son in a way he had never done before.

"Are any among you sick?" wrote James. "They should call for the elders of the church and have them pray over them, anointing them with oil in the name of the Lord." Maybe James never envisioned that oil could become shaving cream, but we can. When California United Methodist pastor John Fanestil was on a trip to New England, he stopped for a beer at a Hanover, New Hampshire, bar. In a conversation with a man at the bar, Fanestil revealed that he had an interest in death and dying, and the man asked if he had ever heard of Bathsheba Wallace. Fanestil writes,

> Wallace, who lived from 1752 to 1831, is a legendary figure in the history of East Thetford, New Hampshire, and neighboring towns. She is credited with attending some 1,666 births throughout 42 years of practice as a midwife. When Wallace was dying, the people in East Thetford shut down the shops and schools and gathered with their children around her bed to send her off with scripture, song and prayer. She died surrounded by a large gathering of people, the majority of whom she herself had ushered into the world.
>
> I love this story because it demonstrates that our ancestors knew intuitively that being born and dying are somehow related. None of us is alone in our being born. Neither are we alone in our dying; no matter how desperate the circumstances, God's spirit is always present. As the story of Bathsheba Wallace beautifully illustrates, and as every pastor knows, the presence of God is felt most powerfully when the whole company of disciples is gathered at the foot of the cross.[17]

THE RITUALS OF DYING AND DEATH

In addition to the informal ministries that occur in the time of dying, it is an important practice in some traditions to observe more formal rituals that mark the passing of a saint. These are generally of two sorts, services of worship as a person is dying and services after death has occurred.

As an example of the former, the Episcopal Church provides for "Ministration at the Time of Death," which takes place in the presence of the dying person. It is a simple prayer service that begins with a prayer for the dying person:

> Almighty God, look on this your servant, lying in great weakness, and comfort him with the promise of life everlasting, given in the resurrection of your Son Jesus Christ our Lord. *Amen.*[18]

After the person has died, the family and friends gather around for a litany. The service concludes with a commendation of the deceased:

> Into your hands, O merciful Savior, we commend your servant *N.* Acknowledge, we humbly beseech you, a sheep of your own fold, a lamb of your own flock, a sinner of your own redeeming. Receive *him* into the arms of your mercy, into the blessed rest of everlasting peace, and into the glorious company of the saints in light. *Amen.*

> May *his* soul and the souls of all the departed, through the mercy of God, rest in peace. *Amen.*[19]

An example of the second is the Roman Catholic "Vigil for the Deceased," which is normally celebrated at the home of the deceased, the funeral home, or wherever the body is. It emphasizes prayer and the reading and proclamation of the Word. The opening prayer is as follows:

> Lord our God,
> the death of our brother/sister N.
> recalls our human condition
> and the brevity of our lives on earth.
> But for those who believe in your love
> death is not the end,
> nor does it destroy the bonds
> that you forge in our lives.
> We share the faith of your Son's disciples
> and the hope of the children of God.
> Bring the light of Christ's resurrection
> to this time of testing and pain
> as we pray for N. and for those who love him/her,
> through Christ our Lord. **Amen.**[20]

This prayer is followed by the reading of Scripture (including a responsorial psalm and an unusual reading from Luke—"If the master of the house had known when the thief was coming, he would not have let his house be broken into. You also must be prepared, for at an hour you do not expect, the Son of Man will come," Luke 12:39–40 NAB), a homily, prayers of intercession, the Lord's Prayer, a concluding prayer, and a blessing.

If we keep in our minds the central motif of the days of the funeral, a saint is traveling on to be with God, this gives us a rule of thumb for the briefer rituals that occur outside of the funeral itself: whenever there is significant movement, physical or symbolic, it can become the occasion for prayer, lament, thanksgiving, and praise. Thus we find in various traditions brief services of worship when the family gathers at the funeral home, when guests and friends come for a time of visiting or a wake, when the coffin is closed, when the coffin arrives at the church, and so on.

Again, not every tradition will have established liturgical rites to mark all of the movements of dying and death. Nevertheless, it is important for the community to show up, to set aside all the clutter that threatens to overcome the death of a saint, and to clear out a space for prayer. As John Fanestil advises, "When someone asks me what they should do when they visit a dying friend, I offer simple instructions. 'Take your Bible and hymnal with you . . . and turn off the television.'"[21]

7

The Marks of a Good Funeral

During a break at a clergy seminar on funerals, one of the ministers approached me, coffee mug in hand. We chatted for a few minutes, swapping stories about our families and discovering people we knew in common. Then he talked about his congregation and his ministry. "I may not do everything well," he said, "but I'll tell you one thing. . . ." He paused a half beat for effect. "I do a *good* funeral."

It was not the first time I had heard something like that from a pastor, or the last. Many pastors are persuaded that they do their very best work at funerals, and they may well be right to think so. Death obviously brings silence to those who die, but it also stills the voices of those around the dead, and the pastor is there with needed wisdom, ancient words of comfort and hope, personal words of remembrance and love. Even people who are normally cold toward the church and indifferent to its worship can be so hungry for a steady hand and a good word in the face of loss that they become uncommonly grateful for what pastors say and do at funerals.

At weddings, pastors sometimes feel trampled by overenthusiastic couples and their "wedding handlers," who can on occasion treat pastors as props, ecclesiastical bling in a schmaltzy fairy tale scripted by *Brides Magazine*. The wildness of death, however, is not so easily managed. People stand back in voiceless awe over death's terror and mystery, and perhaps it is just their reticence that gives room for ministry. Whatever the case, the truth is that many pastors, as odd as this may seem, would far rather preside at a funeral than a wedding. It sometimes feels to them in their more cynical moments that what they do at a wedding could be done by a robot in a clerical collar. What they have to offer at a funeral is a priestly act and almost always received as welcome, helpful, and significant. It is not surprising, then, that many of the clergy would say, at least to themselves, "I do a *good* funeral."

But what is a "good" funeral? A service where the pastor says just the right things? Surely, when a pastor speaks powerful and comforting words at a funeral, that is a worthy contribution; but, as we argued in chapter 5, the notion that a Christian funeral ought to be only a time when people gather in the memory of the deceased to hear inspiring spiritual thoughts, while they reflect inwardly about loss and meaning, is a corruption of the genre and a diminishing of the intent of the Christian funeral. A Christian funeral is not purely meditation; it is dramatic action. It is a public performance, an event of sacred community theater in which the people of God act out the promises of the gospel about life and death in relation to *this* life and *this* death. A pastor, no matter how wise or pastorally sensitive, cannot alone make a "good" funeral. A good funeral is something that the people of God must do together. It is not a pastoral soliloquy; it is an ensemble performance.

The claim that a funeral is a piece of worshipful theater acted out by the church (and its friends) begins to suggest ways to determine whether a funeral is a "good" one or not. Now, if the funeral were *light* theater, a piece of entertaining fluff like, say, the musical *Cats*, then we could judge it on technical merits and audience response: Was the singing on key? Did the actors have a keen sense of timing? Were the parts well spoken? Did the audience enjoy the play? Were they moved? Did it lift their spirits? Did they laugh and cry in the right spots?

But in fact, a funeral is not light theater. It is more like an ancient morality play than like a Broadway show. It is not entertainment, not even mere inspiration, but a deep probing into the things that make us or break us as human beings, and it is not performed only *for* the community; it is performed *by* the community. Everybody present at the funeral has a role to play, and the purpose of a funeral is not to uplift the audience but to transform the cast.

The late Stella Adler, a celebrated teacher of acting whose students included the likes of Robert De Niro, Martin Sheen, and Marlon Brando, often reminded her students that the word "theater" did not always suggest entertainment and escape. The word comes from a Greek term meaning "the seeing place," and, at its most profound, the theater, she said, "is the place that people come to see the truth about life and the social situation."[1] Because the theater is about the truth, there is, Adler said, one inviolable rule that an actor must learn: "Life is not you. Life is outside you. If it is outside you, you must go toward it."[2]

There is good wisdom for the funeral. First, the funeral is a kind of "seeing place," and the initial measure of a good funeral is, how well does it enable people to see a truth worth seeing? And the second measure of a good funeral is, how powerfully does it beckon the actors to inhabit their roles in the play and therein to be changed, to go beyond preoccupations with self, and to move toward that larger, redemptive truth that lies outside of them? The temptation we face at funerals is to allow the gospel to be absorbed into the black hole of private grief and painful personal loss, because these realities are often so urgently demanding. But a good funeral works the other way, drawing private grief and personal loss so fully into the gospel that mourning becomes not only consoled but transformed.

The great plays, Adler claimed, "are almost always larger than the experiences of even the best actors."[3] When actors invest their bodies into the outward truthfulness of the drama, the inner life follows. "[W]hen the body is true," she says, "the soul reacts. When the body lies, the soul gets frightened."[4] So, what is the measure of a good funeral? How well do the people on the great stage of this drama see, remember, trust, love, embrace, and rest their hope in the truth that they have performed?

FOUR NECESSARY ELEMENTS

In order to stage the drama we call a Christian funeral, and to stage it well—in other words, to perform a good funeral—at least four elements are essential. We need a holy person, that is, a deceased person who is viewed as a saint. We need a holy place, a sense of the sacredness of the spaces in which we live and move and have our being. We need a holy people, a community of the faithful who see themselves as having a divine mission. And we need a holy script, a truthful gospel narrative about life and death that the community can perform. Unfortunately, these are the very realities that in many ways are most imperiled in our culture.

1. Holy Person

It has been veiled in many funerals today, but the deceased is the central human character in a Christian funeral. This is the person whose death is the reason for our gathering in worship, the person who has been on a journey of faith inaugurated at baptism and who is now traveling toward God in a new and different way. A good funeral makes it clear that the deceased is a saint, one created in God's own image, a prism through whom we have seen refracted the grace of God.

The deceased a saint? Francis of Assisi or Teresa of Avila may leap forward to claim our attention as saints, but things get a bit muddier when we consider the twice-divorced single mom who comes to worship a couple of times a month and who died after a recurrence of breast cancer, the retired auto mechanic in our congregation who fought alcoholism all his life and who died of sclerosis of the liver, or the man who died at age eighty-two estranged from his own children. Are the funerals for these people ceremonies for saints?

Yes, they are. It should be remembered, first of all, that even those who have been named among the "official" saints by various Christian groups reveal themselves to be flawed when placed under the moral microscope. The saints who make it on the church calendar are actually, as some have wryly pointed out, figures out of the *Christian* past whose lives have been *insufficiently researched.* Even dear Mother Teresa, the nun who for a half century moved the world by the way she unselfishly cared for the wretched of Calcutta and who is well on her way to Catholic canonization, had her deep broken places. Her letters, which came to light only after her death in 1997, reveal that she endured, almost the whole time of her service, a tumultuous dark night of the soul in which she doubted the love and even the existence of God. "I've never read a saint's life where the saint has such an intense spiritual darkness," said James Martin, who wrote a book on the saints. "No one knew she was that tormented."[5]

In the New Testament, "saint" is not a label reserved for the rare person whose life shines with extraordinary holiness; it is used to describe the ordinary, garden-variety Christian. Baptism is a call to set out on a moral adventure in the name of Christ, but all Christians travel this path of discipleship hobbling and stumbling. When the evangelist Billy Graham was asked by a television interviewer about then–Minnesota Governor Jesse Ventura's slam that "religion is a crutch," Graham responded, "Maybe, but who doesn't limp?"

Seeing the people around us as saints is an act of moral imagination guided by love. In Richard Nash's play *The Rainmaker*, Starbuck, a traveling self-promoter who promises to bring rain to drought-stricken communities but never seems to succeed, has arrived to hawk his services in yet another rain-deprived and desperate Western town. He begins to fall in love with Lizzie, a local woman whose best years are slipping by and whose family has begun to despair that she will ever find love. In a moment of candor, the normally swaggering Starbuck confesses to Lizzie his disappointment in life because reality always falls far short of vision. Tapping his forehead with his fingers, he tells her angrily that the world outside never lives up to the world one can imagine, and he demands to know why. Lizzie replies that maybe his frantic, rushing, and self-absorbed life keeps him from really seeing the world for what it is, keeps him from loving it. She tells him that on some nights when she's washing the dishes in the kitchen, she will look out to the other room and see her father, her Pops, playing poker with the boys. She will begin to watch him closely:

> [A]t first I'll just see an ordinary middle-aged man—not very interesting to look at. And then, minute-by-minute, I'll see little things in him I never saw before. Good things and bad things—queer little habits I never noticed he had—and ways of talking I never paid any mind to. And suddenly I know who he is and I love him so much I could cry! And I want to thank God I took the time to see him real.[6]

When Christians look at other people and "see for real," they do more than look for the lovable qualities that can be found, if we squint hard enough, in most people. They look at them, and at themselves, in the light of Jesus Christ. All of us in the faith, fragmented as we are, nevertheless belong to Jesus Christ. Seeing each other as saints is not finally about *our* virtues, but his. This is what Paul was talking about when he said that we no longer even look at people "from a human point of view." The reason? We look at people not only as they are to the naked eye, but as they are when illuminated by the love of Christ, "If anyone is in Christ, there is a new creation: everything old has passed away; see, everything has become new!" (2 Cor. 5:17).

At a funeral, everything is aimed at this kind of "seeing for real," at recovering and celebrating the true identity in Christ of the brother or sister who has died. We have already done this at baptism. There we insisted that despite all of the ways that the world may seek to distort this person's true identity, indeed despite all of the ways this person herself or himself may forget and waste this identity, nonetheless this is and will remain a child of heaven, a daughter or son of God. We do the same at a funeral. Those who have died are not essentially "divorced people," "alcoholics," "rich," "poor," "bank presidents," "AIDS victims," "golfers," "veterans," "secretaries," "children with Down syndrome," "people with Alzheimer's," or any of the other labels they may have borne; these people are first and foremost saints of the living God, made holy by Jesus Christ.

And so there we are, and there they are—the single mom, the auto mechanic, the man who cannot put things back together with his children—broken human beings and new creations, flawed people and fellow saints all, traveling companions on the way of Christ.

2. Holy Place

According to some of the old rabbis, the land of Israel was the first piece of the earth formed by God at the dawn of time. So deep was their love, so profound their reverence, for the land of God's promise that they described Israel as the foundation stone of creation, the seat of all joy, the home of all wisdom, and the place from which the world's music flows. Its very dust could draw people toward holiness. They even told tales of Diaspora Jews, buried in faraway lands, whose bodies tunneled under the earth to Israel so that their place of final rest could be in that holy land.[7]

In his important book *The Land*, Walter Brueggemann notes that in the Bible the symbol of "land" functioned in two main ways.[8] First, it was the soil of Israel, the actual land of God's promise, the land that must be physically tended, tilled, and protected. In this land Israel's sacred memory would be formed, and its life of obedience to God would be lived out. When children in future generations looked at their parents quizzically, or perhaps skeptically, and asked them why they bothered with all the laws and commandments of Judaism, the parents were not to scold them but were, instead, told to tell them a story, a story about the land. "We used to be slaves in Egypt," the story was to begin, but God delivered us out of there with a powerful hand in order "to give us the land that he promised on oath to our ancestors" (Deut. 6:23). The commandments are "for our lasting good, so as to keep us alive" in the land (Deut. 6:24).

But land in the Bible was not only the actual real estate of Israel; "land" was also, second, an eschatological symbol of God's promise to do a new thing and to renew creation. Here the land was a place of hope, a place toward which the people of God would always be traveling, a place where justice would be done, where human life would be refreshed, whole, secure, and free. When, for example, the people of God were in exile, deprived of their homeland, it was God's promise, to renew the land, to shower rain on the waterless earth, and to pour the Spirit on a parched people, that calmed their fears and provided hope: "Do not fear, O Jacob my servant, . . . whom I have chosen. . . . I will pour water on the thirsty land, and streams on the dry ground; I will pour my spirit upon your descendants, and my blessing on your offspring. They shall spring up like a green tamarisk, like willows by flowing streams" (Isa. 44:2–4).

The Christian funeral continues to tell the biblical story of the land, in both the earthy sense and the eschatological sense. It speaks of the soil of our lives. It tells the story of a person who, in a certain place and time, lived, loved, made choices, formed relationships, expended labor, felt joy and pain, and otherwise tended and tilled the earth of a life. But the funeral also tells of a promised land, a land toward which we are traveling, a land where the water of life flows and hunger and thirst are no more. The funeral talks of the distant shore to which many have gone before us, and even now one among us has come to the last mile of the way.

Keeping the biblical symbol of the land fresh in funeral liturgies is important for at least four reasons.

1. The first reason can be said quite briefly. To employ the symbol of the land gives a spatial quality to the drama of the funeral and helps overcome the notion that a funeral is simply a place for stillness and meditation. To speak of the land is to make it clear that a funeral is going somewhere, that we are going somewhere, that the deceased is going somewhere. This dramatic movement was discussed fully in chapters 5 and 6.

2. To emphasize the symbol of the "land" at a funeral has the potential to invigorate the present ethical life of the Christian community. At a funeral we are bidding farewell to a fellow saint who is traveling on to that "city of peace that brings joy evermore," as the funeral hymn says. But then the rest of us return to our work in cities, towns, and communities that are not filled with peace and joy. The biblical witness makes it clear that the heavenly "land" toward which we are traveling

is firmly grounded ethically to the land presently under our feet. The justice, peace, and well-being we are promised in that land ahead of us form our mission mandate in the land where we now reside. In the funeral, even as we entrust our friend to the "heavenly home in the company of all your saints," we also pray, "Grant to us who are still in our pilgrimage, and who walk as yet by faith, that where this world groans in grief and pain, your Holy Spirit may lead us to bear witness to your light and life."[9]

If at a funeral we refresh our memory with the image of "a new heaven and a new earth" where God dwells among human beings and where "there will be no more death or mourning or crying or pain, for the old order of things has passed away" (Rev. 21:4 NIV), that makes it quite clear that war, poverty, neglect of the sick, abandoning the elderly, and loss of faith are not just wrong; they're obsolete, doomed to pass away. Investing in war and greed is not simply unethical; it's a foolish land investment.

Scripture uses the symbol of "land" to imagine a world that is not yet, a world that God will bring into being, a land toward which our hopes yearn, but Scripture never overspiritualizes it, never allows the cord to be cut between the eschatological "land" and the "land" we must get up and plow on Monday morning. This underscores the fact, as Brueggemann says it, "that the yearning for a land is always a serious historical enterprise concerned with historical power and belonging."[10] Here, for instance, is a passage from the prophet Zechariah that would make a powerful reading at a funeral:

> Jerusalem shall be called the faithful city, and the mountain of the LORD of hosts shall be called the holy mountain. Thus says the LORD of hosts: Old men and old women shall again sit in the streets of Jerusalem, each with staff in hand because of their great age. And the streets of the city shall be full of boys and girls playing in its streets. Thus says the LORD of hosts: Even though it seems impossible to the remnant of this people in these days, should it also seem impossible to me, says the LORD of hosts?
>
> (Zech. 8:3–6)

To read this at a funeral—a text that imagines the glorious reign of God as a public park in Jerusalem—and not also to hear in it a mandate to pray and to work for the safety and well-being of the elderly and the children right around us would constitute a failure of moral imagination.

The classic film *Places in the Heart*, set in small-town Texas at the height of the Depression, is often admired for its surprising closing scene. Early in the film, a young black man accidentally shoots and kills the local sheriff, who is white. In retaliation, the young man is lynched by a mob of whites. In the ending scene of the movie, a little Texas congregation is pictured at worship on a Sunday morning. During the Lord's Supper, as the communion plate is passed down the pews, each worshiper hands the plate to the neighbor and says, "The peace of God." As the camera follows the plate, moving from person to person, the viewer begins to recognize faces from the film and realizes that this is no ordinary Eucharist. Gathered in the congregation are young and old, black and white, people who have done wrong and those to whom wrong has been done; even the dead are there, the young black man and the sheriff he has shot, sharing God's banquet and God's peace. Suddenly we know we are not just in a Texas church on a Sunday morning; we are in the kingdom of God.

What is sometimes forgotten about this movie, though, is an earlier scene involving two graveside funerals: that of the sheriff and that of the young black man. The two funerals are thoroughly segregated racially; there are no whites at the young man's funeral, no blacks at the sheriff's. The two funerals, though utterly separate, are being held at the same time. As the camera takes us first to the young man's funeral, we see the black community carrying his wooden coffin across a rough cemetery to an open grave. As they move toward the grave, they are singing an old hymn:

> There's a land that is fairer than day,
> And by faith we can see it afar;
> For the Father waits over the way
> To prepare us a dwelling place there.
> In the sweet by and by,
> We shall meet on that beautiful shore.

As the people sing, their voices seem to grow stronger and more full, other voices joining in. As this happens, the camera pulls back, and suddenly we are at the grave of the sheriff. Over the words of his funeral, we can still hear the fullness of the singing from the other funeral: "In the sweet by and by, we shall meet on that beautiful shore."

There is, of course, a long way to travel and much hard work to be done before people separated for so long can meet on that beautiful shore and speak words of the peace of God. But the funeral hymn reminds us that this is where we are indeed going, makes it clear which direction our feet must be headed, and refreshes our hope that one day we will, by the grace of God, get there.

3. Third, the symbol of the "land" in a funeral helps to address the wandering, homeless quality of contemporary life. In *The Land,* Brueggemann makes a fine distinction between "space" and "place." If I say, "I want my space," I am asking to be left alone, to have the personal freedom to make unimpeded and autonomous choices about my life. Space, says Brueggemann, is gathered up in such images as "weekend, holiday, avocation, and is characterized by a kind of neutrality or emptiness waiting to be filled by our own choosing."[11]

"Space" is important, but it can easily end up as vacant space. A life characterized only by unfettered personal freedom has no accountability, no cords of love and commitment that hold one to others, no shape. One can so often pull up roots and leave that, finally, there are no roots left.

"Place," on the other hand, "is space that has historical meanings." Places are spaces, writes Brueggemann, "where some things have happened that are now remembered and that provide continuity and identity across generations. Place is a space where vows have been exchanged, promises have been made, and demands have been issued. Place is indeed a protest against the unpromising pursuit of space."[12] Urban life dangles before us the promise of virtually boundless existential space, limitless choice, and no involuntary commitments, but for many people this has turned out to be an empty promise. So many of us demanded our space, when all along what we were yearning for was a sense of place.[13]

It is precisely this distinction between "space" and "place" that prompted us to say in chapter 5 that Christian funerals are usually (but not always) at their best when held in churches, rather than funeral homes or auditoriums. Vows have been exchanged there, promises have been made, and demands have been issued. The church provides a place to hold a funeral, and not just a space.

The idea of a funeral occurring in a "place," and not just a space, touches on the matter of cemeteries and columbaria. Maintaining church cemeteries is not practical for many congregations now, and a growing number have instead established columbaria, where cremated remains can be placed, and still others have set aside "memorial gardens," where cremated remains can be placed. None of these is absolutely essential to the funeral, but if they are present, they do have meaning in the life of the congregation. The careful tending of the land where the names and stories of the faithful dead are remembered is a tangible, "earthbound" moral act that signals a congregation's living connection to the communion of the saints.

4. Finally, the symbol of the "land," brought into a funeral carries with it the same interplay of history and eschatology that it has in the Bible. In Scripture, the "land" is both the land on which we are living *and* the land toward which we are traveling. We receive this land on which we stand as the good gift of God, and we work to see signs of the beloved community here and now. But we know that the reign of God is not a matter of mere progress; it is a matter of God's promise to make a new heaven and a new earth. This means that the land here and now is urgent and crucial, but our ultimate hopes do not reside here. "If for this life only we have hoped in Christ, we are of all people most to be pitied" (1 Cor. 15:19).

Christians have a paradoxical relationship to this life and to this land. It is this life and this land where, the best we are able, the sick are cared for, children protected, the elderly honored, and ministries of justice performed; but "our citizenship is in heaven" (Phil. 3:20). The writer of Hebrews beautifully describes this paradox in the picture he paints of Abraham. By faith, old Abraham set out when God called, not even knowing where he was going, only that God had promised "a place that he was to receive as an inheritance" (Heb. 11:8). Abraham eventually got to that land of promise, but strangely he never exactly settled down. He stayed there for a time, but as a nomad, "as in a foreign land, living in tents" (Heb. 11:9). Why? Because he was looking forward to a land that lay beyond even Canaan; he was looking for "the city that has foundations, whose architect and builder is God" (Heb. 11:10). Abraham wasn't the only one with his eyes on a distant horizon. All of our ancestors in the faith described themselves as "strangers and foreigners on the earth" (Heb. 11:13), and people don't talk about themselves that way, says Hebrews, unless it is "clear that they are seeking a homeland" (Heb. 11:14), and that "they desire a better country, that is, a heavenly one" (Heb. 11:16).

Many years ago, a decision was made to build a new freeway into Atlanta, the city where I live. A swath of houses was condemned, and eventually a whole neighborhood was torn down to make way for the highway. For a short time, though, families were still living in those houses, homes that many of them had lived in for generations, but they knew that soon the bulldozers would come and tear them down. The effects were demoralizing on the neighborhood, of course, and most of the residents stopped doing any maintenance at all. Paint peeled, wood rotted, doors fell off hinges, roofs caved in. There were, however, a few residents who, oddly, continued to care for their homes. They painted porches, planted flowers, and repaired window screens, knowing that their houses were slated for destruction. Somehow, even knowing that they were temporary, that the land on which they lived was not their dwelling place forever, did not destroy their desire to make life good and beautiful where they lived.

So it is with the gospel. We carry in our bodies death, and we will pass away. We know that. But the death we carry in us is not just our mortality, but the death of Jesus, so that as we live the Christian life in the here and now, "the life of Jesus may also be made visible in our bodies" (2 Cor. 4:10). The earthly tents are slated for the bulldozer, but "we know that if the earthly tent we live in is destroyed, we have a building from God, a house not made with hands, eternal in the heavens" (2 Cor. 5:1).

The biblical paradox brings a certain tension to the funeral and keeps us from performing a sweet and nostalgic ceremony—like, Annette has died, and we read Psalm 23 and Proverbs 31 ("A capable wife who can find?"), and we celebrate that Annette was a good woman, a good Christian, and then we go to the grave where Annette now lies next to her husband and her parents in the family plot in the cemetery, and it will forever be this way. "We will always remember her," we say.

But of course it's a white lie; we won't remember her always. All of the pieces of Annette's funeral were fine as far as they went, but the fact is, they were built on the illusion that this land is our permanent home. We get a completely new set of people every 100 years, and it will not be too many generations before no one living much remembers Annette at all. If history rolls on long enough, her church will disappear, the building will disintegrate, the congregation will be scattered, and the cemetery will be covered by the dust, the tombstones long disintegrated.

But if Annette will be forgotten to history, she will be remembered by God, and she worships now in a building not made with hands. The funeral, then, should honor *this* land—the person Annette has been, the things she has done, the relationships she formed—but the funeral should not be consumed with nostalgia for Annette's past nor ours, because our hope does not lie in this land alone, but in the city whose architect and builder is God.

3. Holy People

In her book *The Cloister Walk*, Kathleen Norris tells of her unusual religious quest. A married, Protestant woman, she decided to become, for a spell, a resident of a Benedictine monastery in Minnesota. One day, after she had been at the monastery for a while, the monk who was training her in spiritual discipline, said something odd. "It's time for you to meet the rest of the community," he said. He then took her out to the cemetery. "[A]s we passed each grave," Norris said, "the monk told me stories about the deceased. Having been at the monastery over sixty years, he'd known nearly everyone buried there."[14]

Later a friend at the monastery, another Protestant, told her, "Monastic funerals always blur the line between this world and the next; one feels that the present is just a moment in the continuum, between this community, and the community of the saints." Norris realized that, in such funerals, "the 'rest of the community' turns out to be very large indeed."[15]

What Norris's friend said about monastic funerals is true of all Christian funerals. A group of worshipers gathers at the funeral, but they are more than meets the eye. They are part of "the rest of the community," the great communion of saints that transcends time and place. Here then is the challenge. How can we enable the people who come to a funeral—people who are not monks and who spend their lives in the workaday world rather than the cloister—to see themselves not merely as individuals coming to pay their respects to the deceased and the family, but as holy people with a sacred task to perform as members in the communion of the saints?

Many commentators on the state of funerals in our culture are especially concerned about a general breakdown in the old infrastructure of community support at funerals. They bemoan that funerals once were about people gathering in strength around their neighbors at the time of death, but now the congregations at funerals are smaller, and mainly just a collection of individual mourners. For example, David Moller laments,

> As we have seen, American funerals have changed notably since Colonial days. Perhaps the most important of these changes is not the shift from simplicity to lavishness, or even the expansion of the role of the undertaker; rather it lies in the significance of the funeral. . . . [T]he funeral has lost its value as an established and prominent

community ritual. The funeral has become a rite of individual expression—a personalized response to the death of a significant other.[16]

There is truth here, to be sure. It is certainly important that funerals be community events, and not just private ceremonies, and there are signs that many people in our society, particularly younger adults, are reluctant to come to funerals unless they have been touched personally by the death. But there may also be some exaggeration in the alarm. Many who attend funerals do so not just for reasons of personal grief, but to help a friend or neighbor, to show support for those who have lost a loved one.

But debating people's motivations in coming to funerals in many ways misses the point. The real question in a Christian funeral is not whether people come to support their neighbors or come out of a sense of their own grief—they do both—but what role they are to play when they get there. Today, many people have difficulty imagining any meaningful role for themselves at a funeral, other than being a sympathetic and consoling presence to people who mourn. As we have seen, in our therapeutically inclined culture, funerals have shifted toward being defined as occasions of grief management, so quite naturally people begin to think of their main role as providing emotional comfort.

As important as consolation is in a time of loss, the role of the Christian community at a funeral is much larger than emotional care. People feel grief, of course, but death is also a crisis of meaning. What is death? What has happened to the one who has died? Why is life so fragile? What is our hope? These questions find their best response not in discussion groups but in worship. At a funeral, the church has come not to provide therapy but to worship, to enact the story of the gospel about life and death, which, of course, provides the deepest comfort of all.

It will take a process of education to shape the awareness of a congregation about the role of a holy community at a funeral, especially in larger congregations. At first, the notion of coming to sing and pray at a funeral as a sacred duty, even when the deceased is someone not known intimately well, will seem strange and perhaps an unreasonable burden to bear. Education about funerals is helpful here, but the best teacher is a good funeral itself. If instead of a service of inner reflection, the drama of the funeral is performed well, if the congregation sings a saint to the edge of mystery, people will eventually figure out their parts.

Funerals, as Kathleen Norris's friend suggested, "blur the line between this world and the next." Part of the power of a funeral is that we can see so clearly "the rest of the community," that we are connected in worship to the one who has died and to those who, having died before us, now worship God in that land toward which we are traveling. In other words, at a funeral we become sharply aware that this worship involves the whole communion of the saints. When the church affirms its belief in the communion of the saints, it means to say, as Elizabeth Johnson has said, that "[d]eath's destructive power cannot sever the bonds holding persons in communion, for these bonds are grace, love, and community of God's own being. In dying, one falls into the living God and is quickened by loving-kindness which is forever faithful."[17]

The communion of the saints is the confident affirmation that the church communes with the dead in Christ, not as if they were walking the earth as vaporous ghosts, as disembodied personalities moving among the living. We believe that the dead in Christ have crossed the border of a "time zone," from historical time to eternal line. Their life is different from ours, and yet we belong still to the same community, which belongs to God in Christ and which itself participates in both the historical and the eternal.

The transformation that occurs in death means that we should be modest in how we picture the dead in Christ at a funeral. It is generally not helpful to speak as if the dead have simply wandered off into the next room and could return at any moment unchanged, or that they are merely standing on the other side of a veil, or that their life is some idealized version of our own domesticity, the dead growing rose gardens and enjoying casual conversations with each other around the table of heaven. We do not know what their life is like; we only know that the life they have is life in God, and that life we share. We do not know what their bodies look like; we only know that they are like us embodied, but unlike us their bodies are glorified and imperishable. We assume that the people God has raised from death are both discontinuous and yet continuous with who they once were, that God has raised *them* and not some utterly new creatures. This may well mean that we will recognize them, but we do not know how or in what ways. Because they have bodies, they must also have "place," but all spatial language of "heaven," though it is the only satisfactory language we have, finally falls before the mystery of our unknowing.

What we do know is that death changes, but does not destroy, our relationship to the dead. We stand on a great continuum of worship with the saints who have gone before us. We pray, and so do they. We praise God, and so do they. Only the prayers and praises on our end of the continuum are appeals to God from the midst of historical, communal, and personal brokenness and incompletion, and as such our prayers are all set to the music of "*Maranatha!* Come, Lord Jesus!" (Rev. 22:20), which is the penultimate acclamation of the New Testament. The saints, however, stand day and night in the presence of God and the Lamb. For them, the victory has been won, not just their victory but God's victory over all that destroys creation. For them, history has already been gathered into the great Yes of God, and their song of prayer is that the "kingdom of the world has become the kingdom of our Lord and of his Messiah" (Rev. 11:15). Our earthly intercessions blend into their acclamations of pure praise and joy.

If "*Marantha!*" is the penultimate cry of the New Testament, there is yet one more word, the ultimate word, and it names a place where our worship merges with that of the saints: "The grace of the Lord Jesus be with all the saints. Amen" (Rev. 22:21).

4. Holy Script

The final of our four elements needed for a "good" funeral is the gospel story itself. The funeral wants to proclaim the gospel. Ironically, the strongest rival to the gospel at a funeral is the life story of the deceased. Bob's funeral can easily end up being a "monogrammed service," the "Bob Show." Properly framed, though, the story of the deceased need not be a threat to the gospel at all. The funeral invites the story of the deceased to be told and desires that the one who has died be remembered, fully and well. But the gospel reminds us that the story doesn't end there; it ends with God. The funeral is not about some friends of Bob going to the church to be with Bob's memory, but about Bob going to be with God.

However, in a day when many people have only a tentative grasp of the gospel, it is difficult for them to imagine the dead going anywhere, except perhaps into the land of spiritualized memory. Death is a fearsome reality; it seems to hold all the cards. The death of someone nearby is an event of mortality that brings people as close, frighteningly close, to a sacred story as they know how to tell. So they put on a brave face and show photos of the deceased, read poetry loved by the dead person, and have a few warm and sometimes lighthearted remembrances. The problem with this is that, for all its affection and sentiment, such a service moves the deceased from being a saint to being a celebrity given an hour of fame. At its deepest, this kind of funeral finally raises the white flag of surrender to death. If the biography of the deceased is the only sacred story we know how to tell, then death, who has brought this story to its sad end, wins again, and no measure of our remembering and comforting each other can push back that grim truth. Only the resurrection story unmasks death's fraud. Only the story of the resurrection stakes out a victory over death, and this holy script needs to be told and performed again and again at funerals.

THE EIGHT PURPOSES OF A GOOD FUNERAL

When the four needed elements—a holy person, a holy place, a holy people, and a holy script—are brought together and put into motion in the theater of the funeral, we have the makings of a "good" funeral. These four elements, working together, enable a good funeral to achieve eight key purposes:[18]

1. Kerygmatic. A good funeral, whatever else it may do, tells the kerygma, the gospel story. The funeral is bold to proclaim that, though it may appear that death has claimed yet another victim, the truth is that the one who has died has been raised to new life in Christ and is now gathered with the saints in communion with God.

The kerygma proclaimed at a funeral is, of course, the same gospel announced every Sunday. This gospel is the assurance that death has been destroyed by the death and resurrection of Jesus. But there is a very personal quality to the kerygma at a funeral. Here we are given the comforting news that the risen Christ stands with us and for us, the Christ who promises that persons and relationships will not be eradicated by death.[19]

2. Oblational. The meaning of "oblational" is connected to "offering." As is the case in all services of worship, an offering is received at a funeral, but here the offering is usually not about money. What do people bring to a funeral to offer God? Their grief, of course, and their memories. Sometimes they bring regret and guilt, perhaps simply over a word they failed to speak, a smile they did not smile. They may bring anger, a need to shake the fist at God. And they bring the deceased, the body, actual or remembered, of the one who has died; and one purpose of a good funeral is to enable people to give the deceased to God and, thereby, to give them up, to let them go. People bring many things to a funeral to offer to God. As Hoon says,

> What is offered? All things within the range of human experience. Pain, obviously. Brokenness. Tears. Sins. Regret, remorse, guilt, repentance. Fear. Anger. Unfaith mingled with Faith. Memories. Thanksgiving. Love. Joy. Hope. Vows. Human life and the human heart will write this part of the liturgy for us, and we should be quite concrete in naming these realities with their true names.[20]

A good funeral "takes up the collection" and pronounces a blessing over all that is given.

3. Ecclesial. A good funeral is a work of the whole church, the communion of the saints, and it announces that we do not pass through the valley of the shadow of death alone. People should sit together at a funeral, mourning families surrounded by the others, and a good funeral allows for the voices of the congregation to be heard in the service, in prayer, lesson, song, and creed.

4. Therapeutic. A good funeral is not about pastoral counseling, but it is about providing comfort to the afflicted and the grief-stricken. Some of this comfort comes through directly addressing sorrow through the prayers, sermon, hymns, and other elements of the service. Much comfort comes indirectly, through placing the bitter loss of death into the context of the community's praise and the larger resurrection story of victory over death.

5. Eucharistic. An old practice in the church involves the celebration of Holy Communion at a funeral, in the earliest traditions at the graveside. In the Lord's Supper, the church gives thanks for all of creation and anticipates that day when the whole family of God will be gathered at the heavenly banquet. Even when the Eucharist per se is not observed, the funeral still is an expression of thanksgiving. The church gives thanks to God for the many gifts of life, especially the gift of the life of the deceased. Even when the deceased was a "difficult" person and our experience was conflicted, we give thanks for this life, this sometimes inscrutable embodiment of God's image, and for the ways our faith has been tested and strengthened by being in relationship with her or him.

6. Commemorative. A brother or sister in Christ has died, and a good funeral actively remembers this person. The book of Acts reports that when Dorcas, a much-beloved Christian in the town of Joppa "who was devoted to good works and charity" died, they washed her body and laid her in an upstairs room. Some women stayed beside Dorcas's body "weeping and showing tunics and other clothing that Dorcas had made while she was with them" (Acts 9:36, 39). This act of touching the things that Dorcas had sewn was not, of course, to admire her textile craft; it was to remember Dorcas. In a funeral, the church carries a saint to the place of farewell, and a good funeral brings to our memory the reality of the one we are carrying.

7. Missional. The funeral is not a stopping place for God's people, but a way station on the journey of faith. We take a loved one to the place of departure and say farewell, and then we go back and get to work serving God's world. A good funeral prays, then, not just for ourselves in our loss, but also for the world in its sorrows and needs.

8. Educational. The funeral is educational in two directions. First, it allows the church to participate once again in the ancient Easter drama, and we learn the script and our roles all over again. We discover anew who we are as Christians, the nature of our hope, the destination of the dead, and the power of the resurrection. The funeral is also an occasion for education on behalf of the guests in the household of God. Many funeral congregations include those who are not Christians, or at least who are not usually a part of the worshiping community, and the funeral can be an occasion for the biblical practice of showing hospitality to the stranger. These visitors are invited to get up on stage and read parts in a play with which they are not familiar. Sometimes a pastor can welcome participation with a simple and brief word of explanation—"The reason why we pray this prayer is . . ."

It is now time to see what a good funeral would look like in actual practice.

8

Planning the Funeral: Practical Matters

STRONG, LOVING, AND WISE

Planning a funeral involves blending that which is very old, deeply tra-ditioned, and oft repeated with that which is entirely new, profoundly personal, and utterly unique. What is old . . . very old . . . of course, is the act of human memorializing of the dead and the Christian rites that have developed over the centuries around burial. What is new is *this* death at this moment in time and place, *this* family's grief, *this* community's desire for meaning in the face of death's latest assault, *this* congregation's need to state the gospel afresh. Good funerals, as the old wedding saying goes, incorporate "something old and something new," and performing these rituals well, Tom F. Driver has observed, is much like art. We should heed the wisdom of established forms while, at the same time, being prepared to improvise.[1] To put it another way, whenever we perform a funeral on the occasion of a person's death, we should be ready to do what we have done a thousand times before, but in a way we have never done it before.

It is not easy to walk the balance bar between tradition and impro-visation in funerals, and we constantly run the risk of falling off to one side or the other. On the side of tradition, every major Christian group and denomination has its time-tested funeral liturgy, and there is much wisdom in following these ancient road maps as we travel from life to death to life. For the most part, the prayers are beautiful, the struc-ture sturdy, and the theology sound. Even so, merely plugging the

141

name of the next person to die into a liturgical template finally ignores the distinctiveness of each person's life and creates a coldly impersonal effect.

On the other hand, many people today have a pretty keen and active sense of being a "self," a unique personality, but they are ritually homeless. Because of shifts in society, changes in the life of the church, confusions generally about worship, many who come to the church to plan a funeral have either lost, or never had, a deep and appreciative memory of the patterns and words of worship. So, when a death happens and they encounter one of life's most challenging moments of transition, they become lost and disoriented. Like mountain climbers who are unaware of a well-traveled, well-marked trail to the crest, they feel compelled to forge their own path, to follow their intuitions, to "make up something really personal," and they inevitably reach out to the only resources they know: vague sentiments and impressions drawn from cultural stereotypes, movies, television, fleeting experiences with other ceremonies, and nostalgia. When funerals are woven out of such straw, the result—as is so often the case when, say, a couple crafts a do-it-yourself wedding with homemade marriage vows—is shallow, unsatisfying, and ultimately a loss to the participants themselves and to the community.

A major fault line lies between funerals that are "personal," which is good, and those that are merely "personalized," which is a diminishment. In a funeral, the church gives thanks to God for the gift of a life, indeed, this very particular person's life, and for all the ways the grace and mercy of God have been seen and experienced in this life, conflicted as it may have been. If we are paying attention to the claims of the gospel in the face of death, we can do nothing else but fashion funerals that are deeply personal.

A "personalized" funeral, however, is one that is caught up in all of the current cultural anxieties about selfhood and identity, such that what constitutes a "self" is a set of lifestyle circumstances and consumer choices. I may be (let us engage in a flight of the imagination) a Prius-driving, Red Sox–loving, Harvard-educated, independent-voting, environmental attorney of Italian heritage with a membership in a Methodist church, an extroverted personality, a physician wife, three fine children in college, and a penchant for sipping single malt scotch, listening to the music of John Coltrane, and spending weekends hiking in the Berkshires. But the Christian faith never for a minute would let me get away with thinking that this collection of traits, preferences, and social placements somehow defines my deepest self. Who am I really? In the Christian faith, definitions of self do not begin with outer markings, such as job or education, and even with inner characteristics, like personality or family origin. In Christianity, the definition of self begins with baptism. As one of the biblical texts often cited at baptism puts it,

> You are a chosen race, a royal priesthood, a holy nation, God's own people, in order that you may proclaim the mighty acts of the One who called you out of darkness into God's marvelous light.
>
> (1 Pet. 2:9)

This is not mere piety. It is not as if, when I am church, I put on a choir robe, speak mysteries of liturgical language, and play the part of being a member of "a royal priesthood," but in the rest of my life I put on a Red Sox cap and head up the hiking trail with some Coltrane blowing through my earphones. The stuff about family and job and education and ethnicity is the way a person is embodied in the world, the palpable ways that a person moves forth in life, and these things matter. In fact, they matter spiritually. To be baptized is a sign that everything we are—work and play, personality and character, commitments and passions, family and ethnicity—is gathered up and given shape and definition by our identity as one of God's own children. Every person is complex, a prism with many facets, and the deepest question of personal identity is, how are the many colors of the bright light of God's image refracted through this life?

So at my funeral it will all be remembered. In the prayers and the sermon, the music and the testimony, the church will almost surely bring to memory that I was a husband and a father, a lover of baseball, one who cared for and enjoyed the environment, and a fan of jazz and that all of it gathered together was my attempt, sometimes successful and sometimes not, to be a good Methodist and a faithful follower of Christ. There may even be a little Coltrane music played. But if I leave behind a letter specifying that at my funeral my coffin should be emblazoned with the Red Sox logo, that the choir should sing the Harvard alma mater, that the bulletin cover should be a photo of Mount Greylock, and that the prelude should be a selection from Coltrane's "A Love Supreme," because this is *my* funeral, damn it, and this is what expresses the true *me*, then the Christian community would be right to arch an eyebrow in suspicion that I had perhaps misunderstood both the definition of "true me" and the meaning of a funeral, slipping over the fault line from "personal" to "personalized."

In our time, the impulse to overly personalize funerals, to "mono-gram" them so to speak, is in many ways a cultural given. People who are saturated daily by commercials urging them to choose personal-ized versions of everything from cars to credit cards, from clothing to fragrances—in short, to piece together "my very own way of life" out of disparate fragments—approach a funeral imagining that the same range of options is necessarily placed before them and that they need to make decisions. Funeral homes, as service businesses, quite natu-rally often reinforce the notion that a funeral too is a set of consumer choices: cremation or burial? this metal casket or that wooden one? a flag on the casket or a spray of flowers?

How should a pastor guide families in planning funerals? "Strong, loving, and wise," a phrase drawn from 2 Timothy 1:7, is the title that Catholic liturgical scholar Robert Hovda gave to his book on presiding in worship,[2] and these words point to the virtues needed by pastors who consult with grieving families. When someone dies, the mourn-ing family wants to make sure that this beloved person will be known, remembered, and honored, and that the personal wishes, actual or imagined, of the deceased will be carried out. Thus, they will often suggest readings, poetry, music, speeches, and actions for the funeral, some of them healthy and creative and some of them injudicious, self-referential, and perhaps even harmful.

A pastor needs the strength and love to guide people well. In many ways, the postmodern hunger to invent ourselves through our autono-mous choices, which seems like freedom, is actually a kind of imprison-ment. We are condemned to make ourselves up, as if there were no shared, hard-won wisdom available to us; when we are faced with a crisis of meaning, we turn inward, hoping to find in the gardens of our souls flowers of truth that, sadly, no one has planted or cultivated.

In Acts 16 there is a dramatic story of the religious conversion of the head jailer in the prison at Philippi. He happens to have on his roster of inmates Paul and Silas, whose missionary work in town has gotten them arrested for disturbing the peace, roughed up, and shoved rudely into a cell block. But instead of spitting, cursing, and hurling threats, as any self-respecting prisoners should do, Paul and Silas have been sit-ting in their cell praying and singing hymns. As unsettling as this may have been to the jailer, it is nothing compared to what happens next. In rapid succession, there is a violent earthquake, the prison walls tremble, handcuffs fall away, doors fall off their hinges, and the jailer, certain that the prisoners have escaped in the chaos and justifiably terrified over what will be done to him when his superiors find him presiding over an empty jailhouse, draws a sword to take his own life. But suddenly from the darkness and confusion of the ruined prison comes the loud voice of Paul: "Do not harm yourself, for we are all here" (Acts 16:28). The jailer is overwhelmed. Whatever God has hold of Paul and Silas, the jailer now wants that God too. Within seconds he is on his knees, trembling. "What must I do to be saved?" (Acts 16:30). Before the night is out, the jailer tenderly washes the wounds of Paul and Silas, and then Paul and Silas, in their way, wash his wounds too: he and his whole family are baptized. The story ends with the jailer and his family at table with his former captives, sharing a meal of joy over the fact that he has "become a believer in God" (Acts 16:34).

Now can we possibly imagine that Paul would have said to this jailer when the man was trembling on his knees and being swept up in a moment of profound personal revolution, "Look, before you shove on to the rest of your life, there is this matter of baptism. It's a little ceremony we do whenever somebody becomes a Christian, but I'm sure you'd like to personalize it. You don't want to do just the same old, same old. Here's a pad and a pen. Why don't you go back and consult with your family, scratch down a few ideas, maybe some jailer motifs, and we'll talk?"

Well, we should not imagine it for a funeral either. Baptism, marriage, funeral—these are not polite dinner parties needing good decorator ideas. These are sacred ceremonies of dramatic transformation, torches marking the perilous way between life and death. No pastor, out of a well-intentioned but ill-advised desire just to serve people where they are, should assume the posture, "Whatever you'd like at the funeral, whatever would be meaningful to you, will be fine." Pastors have a responsibility to help people in a season of loss receive not merely those things that they, in the terrible crush of mourning, most think they need, but the very best gifts and the most grace-filled vision the gospel has to offer.

Also, as compelling as the needs of the grief-stricken family may be, a funeral is an event larger than these immediate needs, more encompassing than this family. Part of the power of a Christian funeral is that we do not do this alone; the funeral is not just a ceremony for a single family, to which guests are invited. It is a service of worship involving the whole church—indeed, involving the entire communion of saints—and it is a joyful duty of the church to reenact the promises of the resurrection on the occasion of someone's death. One role of a pastor is to be sure that the witness of the gospel is not lost, this hopeful vision does not get whittled down to the small story of our private grief and mere personalism.

We can learn wisdom about the power that lies in the practice of Christian funerals by comparing it to a Jewish funeral practice: the custom of saying the "mourner's Kaddish." When a Jew dies, the children of the deceased are to go to synagogue every day for eleven months, to join with the others in worship and to pray the Kaddish, a prayer that gets its name from *Qodesh*, the Hebrew word for "holy." The words of the contemporary Kaddish in English are,

> May the great name of God be exalted and sanctified, throughout the world, which he has created according to his will. May his kingdom be established in your lifetime and in your days, and in the lifetime of the entire household of Israel, swiftly and in the near future; and say, Amen. May his great name be blessed, forever and ever.
>
> Blessed, praised, glorified, exalted, extolled, honored, elevated, and lauded be the Name of the holy one, Blessed is he above and beyond any blessings and hymns, Praises, and consolations which are uttered in the world; and say Amen. May there be abundant peace from Heaven, and life, upon us and upon all Israel; and say, Amen.
>
> He who makes peace in his high holy places, may he bring peace upon us, and upon all Israel; and say Amen.[3]

As a mourning ritual, saying the Kaddish seems somehow counterintuitive. No one, in the hour of grief, would design such an exercise. This mourner's prayer, strangely, contains no words that appear to touch tenderly on the depth of mourning. Other Jewish death rituals are explicit about grief, but not the Kaddish. There's nothing here about grief at all. In its cadences there is no turn inward, no mention of loss, no cry of pain, no appeal to be comforted. There is only the turn toward the Holy One, toward the praise and blessing of the God who gives and sustains life.

But, of course, that is its power. The Kaddish is not an expression of how a grieving Jew *feels* to have lost a parent; it is an affirmation of where he or she is *going* as a faithful Jew, toward the unfettered praise of the holiness of God, a holiness that even the powers of death cannot destroy. The Kaddish is an opportunity for a mourning Jew, struggling with all the centripetal force that grief can bring, to move from the isolation of self to the giving of the self utterly to gaze upon the majesty of God, finally to be able to say, as does a character in one of Robinson Jeffers's poems, "I have fallen in love outward."[4]

When Leon Wieseltier, the literary editor of the *New Republic*, lost his father in 1996, he decided to comply with the custom of saying Kaddish, even though he had not been a ritually observant Jew for more than twenty years. Three times a day, during the morning, afternoon, and evening services, he would say the mourner's prayer, either in his home synagogue in Washington, DC, or, if he was traveling, in any synagogue he could find. A friend asked him why he, as one who had not followed Jewish law for two decades, had now chosen to participate in this strange and unfashionable practice. Wieseltier reflected on his reasons. There was duty, duty to his father, which left "thoughts about my father unimpeded by regret and undistorted by guilt,"[5] and also, in an odd way, duty to his religion. But there was yet one more reason: "It looks after the externalities," Wieseltier wrote, "and so it saves me from the task of improvising the rituals of my bereavement, which is a lot to ask."[6]

As is always the case when people engage in the exercise of any traditional ritual, there were good moments and bad. Sometimes the act of saying the Kaddish was full of meaning for Wieseltier, but at other times it felt like going through the motions, following by rote an empty ceremony. Gradually, however, the daily praying of the Kaddish began to gain in power. One day, just after dawn, Wieseltier was preparing to pray at an early service, and he had wrapped the cords of his phylacteries around his arm. Phylacteries, leather boxes containing passages from the Torah, are sometimes tied on the head and around the arms during morning prayer, symbolizing God's charge not to forget the commandments but to "bind them as a sign on your hand, fix them as an emblem on your forehead" (Deut. 6:8). As Wieseltier stood there in the dim daylight, he realized that these ancient prayer symbols, wrapped so tightly on his body, suddenly felt different. "They do not bind me," he said. "They gird me. . . . The arm on which they are wrapped feels strong."

A year after his father's death, Wieseltier, along with his family and friends and their rabbi, gathered in a bitter March wind at the cemetery for the unveiling of his father's gravestone. After the reading of some psalms, a few words from the rabbi about his father, and a memorial prayer, Wieseltier was asked by the rabbi to read one more psalm. Instead of reading, Wieseltier decided to sing. "The Lord is my shepherd, I shall not want . . . ," he began, singing the familiar psalm in "the sweet sepulchral manner in which it is sung on Sabbath afternoons." He sang all the way to the closing words of the psalm, "Surely goodness and mercy shall follow me all the days of my life, and I will dwell in the house of the LORD forever." Then Wieseltier, whose many grieving days of saying the mourner's Kaddish had prepared him for this moment, said Kaddish one more time:

> I stood in the ashes of fury and spoke the sentences of praise. Was that voice my voice? It was no longer the effusion of woe. Magnified, I said. Sanctified, I said. I looked above me, I looked below me, I looked around me, With my own eyes, I saw magnificence.[7]

Like the practice of saying of the mourner's Kaddish, the Christian funeral embodies more wisdom than we at first can see or know. The words, patterns, and meanings of the funeral service transcend grief's desire to curve in on itself. They allow us to journey outward and beyond with our dead to the place of farewell, bearing witness to the gospel and singing words of praise as we go. They do not bind us; they gird us. Pastors should be strong enough, loving enough, to do all they can, not to let their people miss these deep waters of healing by spending their energies languishing only in the shallows.

But if a pastor needs strength and love, a pastor also needs discerning wisdom to know where to improvise in funerals. Worship services, including funerals, involve real people and are therefore messy affairs. While worship includes words of truth, moments of awe, and experiences of the holy, it also includes people with mixed motives, confused purposes, wandering minds, halfheartedness, who lack even a thimbleful of understanding about what is taking place—and this sometimes includes the clergy. Anyone who has ever invited the congregation to shout out whatever comes to mind as "joys and concerns" or presided over a service on Mother's Day or preached on Stewardship Sunday or tried to figure out what to do about a national flag displayed in the house of God knows full well that the waters of worship do not always run pure and clear.

At a funeral, we do not bury the dead in general; we bury this very particular dead person, who was herself or himself a mixture of the well-being and woe, the commonplaces and eccentricities that make up any human life. And we do so with prayers and songs not preserved on unsullied pages in a divine liturgy but, rather, said and sung in the mouths and hearts of people who are themselves composed of the same admixture. As pastors, to complain in principle about fleshly contaminants intruding into Christian funerals is like griping about the weather. More significant, to yearn deeply for it to be otherwise is finally a misunderstanding of Christ's incarnation and a failure to love the real world—the one full of people whom God loves, not the uncompromised world we adore in our imaginations. Jane Doe's funeral will inevitably be Jane Doe's funeral, and who she actually was will make a difference in the rhythms and sounds of the ritual. We will sing the hymns, pray the great prayers, and read holy wisdom from the Scriptures, but it will all necessarily make luminous the life of this flawed but blessed saint who has died, producing unexpected hues and tones.

So there will be hard decisions involved in the planning of most funerals. As the joke goes, many people want both "Amazing Grace" and "I Did It My Way" sung at their funeral. Should the basketball coach be given the microphone to speak a eulogy? What if the soloist croons a syrupy, sentimental ditty? What about showing during the funeral service a continuous video of the frolicking dog of the deceased? What about permitting a military guard to fire guns in salute at graveside? Helping to decide whether such elements are simply a little spice thrown into the standard recipe of good worship or are impermissible flat contradictions of the gospel being proclaimed, will require nimbleness, sound judgment, empathy, and wisdom. Many congregations have rules and policies about funerals to step around common problems and to help keep funerals liturgically sound and theologically responsible. But as helpful as these can be, no policy manual can anticipate every circumstance, and no set of rules can substitute for good pastoral judgment and the need to improvise in every worthy act of living worship.

One truth about worship should be reassuring to pastors: worship that is essentially sound in structure and content can absorb and overcome elements that are less worthy. A good funeral is like a fine and large chorus singing Vivaldi's *Gloria*. While we could hope that every voice would be on pitch, a single tenor who is a bit flat cannot overcome the power and grandeur of the music. While we hope, for example, that the uncle of the deceased will not, "speaking a word of remembrance," perform a corny and inappropriate stand-up comedy routine, a funeral with a steady beat and a sense of gospel pitch can keep the resurrection song going and can absorb this false note into the richer music of hospitality and understanding.

Church contexts vary widely, of course, but most pastors find it useful to go to the family immediately upon receiving the news of a death, not to do planning but to establish a pastoral presence. Then there will be another meeting with the family to plan the service. These are often powerful times of pastoral care and fertile moments for the pastor to learn more about the deceased and how the person should be commemorated.

OF CHOREOGRAPHY, LITURGIES, AND CULTURES

We now turn to the details of planning a Christian funeral, to the specifics of arranging the choreography of the drama of death and life played out in the funeral. We will use, as primary reference points, two state-of-the-art funeral liturgies: first, *The Order of Christian Funerals* (1989; hereafter called *OCF*),[8] which is the currently approved Roman Catholic rite used in the United States and which is derived from the Latin edition of *Ordo Exsequiarum*, the funeral rituals developed as a part of the liturgical reforms of Vatican II; second, one of the most recent and best crafted of the Protestant rites, the funeral service in *Evangelical Lutheran Worship* (2006; hereafter called *ELW*).[9] In order to provide a wider sense of the ecumenical options, these two basic funeral orders will be supplemented with material from other Protestant sources, such as the Episcopal *Book of Common Prayer* (1979)[10] and the Presbyterian *Book of Common Worship* (1993),[11] and with material from an Eastern Orthodox rite for laypeople (1998), part of a recent translation of *The Great Book of Needs*.[12]

Even as we use these established funeral liturgies as benchmarks, we should heed two cautions. First, not every pastor or congregation looks to published liturgies for guidance on funerals. There are many pastors who use no prayer books in funerals, who do not pray printed prayers, who follow no prescribed patterns, who wear dark suits and not clerical vestments, who fashion funerals more in response to the immediate circumstances of a particular death than according to ancient custom, and who, when planning a funeral, in no sense imagine themselves to be choreographing a liturgical ritual.

However, the difference between the free-church traditions and the prayer-book traditions regarding funerals may not be as great as it seems. Pastors leading funerals in the more liturgical traditions rarely go completely by the book and so-called free-church funerals are in their own way still ritualistic events with repeated and predictable patterns (indeed, wearing dark suits and praying from the heart, rather than from a book, are vital ritual acts). Even though the emphasis appears in the free church to fall more heavily on the side of improvisation, most such funerals nevertheless are assembled on the same metaphorical chassis as their prayer-book cousins, namely, that the funeral is the enactment of the conviction that the deceased is a saint traveling on to be with God, surrounded by the songs and prayers of the church. In the same sense that an Episcopal priest, in order to conduct a good funeral, will need to develop the gift of ad lib and a dash of skill at improvisation, just so, by doing a little translation, the free-church pastor can gain much from tracing the maps of the prayer-book traditions. What one tradition does with holy water and the rhythmic chanting of psalms another tradition accomplishes through extemporaneous prayer and freewheeling gospel songs.

A second caution about using standard prayer-book services as reference points rises when we recognize that there are many local and ethnic customs not incorporated into these broadly ecumenical liturgies. But to say that a certain liturgy does not specify a practice does not mean that it doesn't allow it, that its branches cannot provide a welcome roosting space for many local customs. *Romeo and Juliet* can be reimagined as *West Side Story*, the same basic narrative retold in a different cultural setting and patois; and the basic pattern outlined in the *Book of Common Prayer* can take root in Appalachian or Caribbean soil. A nimble pastor can take the basic funeral structure described here and refashion it into a hospitable space for all sorts of customs that make good sense in some locations but would be unimaginable in others—from opening a previously closed coffin at graveside for a "last look," to taking time to speak words of farewell to the corpse, to delaying the "funeralizing" days or weeks waiting for ice to thaw or for the funeral home bill to be paid.

This is not to say there will not be some tough decisions and judgment calls to be made about local and cultural customs. While it may be attractive to assume the posture of an easy multiculturalism, welcoming every idea and practice in the name of generosity and inclusion, the specifically Christian character of a funeral matters. As our society, and to some extent our churches, become increasingly multicultural, and as worship continues to draw deeply from many sources, Christian pastors and their congregations will more and more have to pull out surveying instruments to assess where the real boundaries of the Christian tradition lie.

A good example is the funeral held in the First Covenant Church of St. Paul, Minnesota, for Nhia Her Lo, who died at age 93, a revered leader of St. Paul's Hmong community. The roots of the Hmong are in the mountains of southern China, but the St. Paul area is now the home to the world's largest concentration of Hmong people, more than 60,000 residents. Funerals, very important in Hmong culture, are traditionally elaborate shamanistic ceremonies designed to transport the souls of the deceased to their ancestors. They typically last for several days and include such elements as animal sacrifice and offerings made to the spirit of the departed.

Nhia Her, a Hmong Christian, had requested that his funeral be religiously Christian and culturally Hmong. So the pastors and family began a careful and challenging sifting and comparing of practices to create a service that faithfully reflected both traditions. Tough calls had to be made. Would animal sacrifice, the ancient custom, be allowed? Yes. The decision was made to include in the ceremony meat from several cows, prepared at a local slaughterhouse. But would it be permissible to include the ritual of feeding this meat to the spirits? No. It was decided to make clear in the ceremony that this meat was provided to feed the people present and not the departed spirits.

Another crucial question was whether to include a traditional "blessing table." Near the close of many Hmong funeral rituals, a table is set up in the middle of the room, and all who wish can come forward to "settle accounts" with the person who has died. Speaking to the dead person, people express complaints, voice old grudges, and make financial claims; then the shaman makes a long speech on behalf of, in fact in the voice of, the deceased. When the air has been cleared, the shaman turns the table upside down and hands out glasses of an alcoholic beverage to the participants. People drink the beverage, a sign of blessing and confidence that, with all accounts now settled, the dead person will never trouble them again.

As he was dying, however, Nhia Her had been eager to speak not of retribution but of forgiveness. "I have no grudges against anyone," he repeated to all who would listen. There would be no need to "settle accounts." But Nhia Her's family knew that many of those coming to the funeral from a distance were coming to do just that, and they would expect and desire the ritual of the "blessing table." So the clergy and family decided to keep it in the funeral but to modify its practice and thus redefine some of its meaning. At the funeral, after everyone had come to the blessing table and spoken his or her mind, the table was not turned over but left standing upright. The congregation was then told about how Jesus gathered with those he loved at tables and that this table was a symbol of Christ among them. "The blessing may not have been what most had expected or wanted," one of the participants said, "but this was not your typical Hmong funeral. This was a Christian funeral for a beloved Hmong man, and we were doing our best to honor his wishes and to honor the God he served."[13]

Such interfaith, intercultural decisions are tricky and controversial, and other pastors may well have drawn different boundaries from those marked out by the leadership at First Covenant. But two false alternatives here must be challenged. On the one hand, pretending that religious customs do not ever conflict and that choices need not be made is neither helpful nor true. On the other hand, attempts to seal off a tradition and keep it sterile are not possible either (from baptism to Christmas, Christian practice is full of ceremonies and symbols borrowed from other religions and reinterpreted). But if an actor knows his part by heart and loves it, then he can improvise if something unexpected should happen on stage—if, for example, another actor should forget her lines or a phone that is supposed to ring, doesn't. Just so, pastors who know the gospel and love the ancient texts by which Christians have buried their dead can with boldness perform improvisations of those texts and traditions in the shifting and unpredictable mix of contemporary cultures.

Before I examine the details of the structure of funerals, a word about terminology. For the sake of simplicity (and as has been the case throughout this book), we will speak mainly about "funerals" and "burials." Obviously, these terms do not cover the full range of possibilities, but much of what follows can apply equally to "memorial services," the term commonly used for rituals where the body of the deceased is absent and for situations where other dispositions of the body, such as cremation or bodily donation, are performed. There are exceptions and special cases, of course, and these will be noted and discussed. Also, the focus in this book is on what we have been calling "the Christian funeral," meaning the death ritual for a baptized Christian. However, many Christian groups make ample and hospitable room in their life for funerals for those who are outside of the faith or alienated from the church. This issue will be discussed in a separate section.

DRAMATIC STRUCTURE OF THE
CENTRAL FUNERAL RITE

We have been making the case that the Christian funeral embraces the whole ensemble of acts and rituals around death, but in this section we will narrow the scope somewhat, focusing on the central funeral rite. What I mean by the "central rite" is what people generally mean when they say they are going to a funeral. It is the portion of the overall funeral process that is patterned as a formal order of worship, and because the vast majority of these services take place in a church or a chapel, this setting will be assumed.

The central funeral rite is composed of the following sequential movements: gathering, procession, service of prayer and word, Holy Communion, and sending.

1. The Gathering

All Christian public worship begins when the people gather. Most congregations gather for worship every Sunday at the same hour, but this is not merely keeping an appointment on the calendar, as with the hairdresser or the dentist. It is instead an act of memory, faith, and hope. We remember that God has called us to worship in the past, we have faith that God is calling us even now, and we have hope that God will meet us in the Spirit when we gather. The God who appeared to Moses in the burning bush, to Isaiah in the temple, to Paul on the Damascus road, to John on the Lord's Day, evoking worship, is calling us to worship once again, and so we go. Summoned by God, people come from east, west, north, and south to assemble as a congregation for the praise of God. Funerals are no exception; at a funeral, just as it is for a service on the Lord's Day, the congregation gathers for worship.

What sets a funeral apart, though, is that among the faithful who gather is the one who has just died. This saint, though deceased, is still joined to the congregation and is coming in the body to this place one last time for worship. It is difficult to underestimate either the importance of this truth or how deeply it is misunderstood and neglected today. Sometimes people say, "Funerals are for the living," usually meaning that the content of a funeral should be shaped entirely around the needs of the mourners and not at all focused on the person who has died, but this is a simplistic view. As we have said, in the Christian faith, death changes, but does not destroy, the relationship between the community of faith and the deceased. Certainly at a funeral the living do not worship God on *behalf* of the dead in the sense that we would be so arrogant as to try to strike a bargain with God, but the living also do not worship in spite of the dead or in the absence of the dead. They worship *with* the dead.

It is not far-fetched to say that the deceased saint has a role in a funeral similar to that of the bride and groom in a wedding or the one being baptized in a baptismal service. In each case, the church has gathered in prayer to mark a transition in the life of a Christian. A wedding, as worship, is about the adoration of God by the community of faith, but it is worship being entered into on the occasion of a marriage, and we couldn't perform this act of worship without the bride and groom. A funeral is also about the adoration of God, but the occasion is the death of a saint, and we could not engage in this act of worship without the presence of the one who has died.

This is represented in the funeral by giving dramatic emphasis to the arrival of the body of the deceased. When the congregation has gathered and the time for the funeral is at hand, the coffin bearing the body is brought to the entrance of the church. Usually the coffin is carried by pallbearers (or, if borne on a cart, escorted by them) and accompanied by the family. There are two good options for the presiding clergy at this point: they can go to the family home, or wherever it is that they are, and accompany them and the deceased to the church; or they can wait for them at the church and meet them with a greeting at the entrance when they arrive.

One good option (*ELW*) is for the minister(s) to meet the coffin and the mourners at the church entrance, while the congregation stands and faces them as they arrive. Then, from the door of the church, the minister does three things. First, the minister turns toward the congregation and welcomes them. Second, the minister tells them what the funeral is about:

> Welcome in the name of Jesus, the Savior of the world.
> We are gathered to worship, to proclaim Christ crucified and risen,
> to remember before God our sister/brother _____,
> to give thanks for her/his life,
> to commend her/him to our merciful redeemer,
> and to comfort one another in our grief.[14]

Third, the minister looks at the coffin, perhaps gesturing toward it, and names the deceased as one who belongs to Christ in baptism:

All who are baptized into Christ have put on Christ.
In her/his baptism _____ was clothed with Christ.
In the day of Christ's coming, she/he shall be clothed with glory.[15]

The *OCF* calls on the priest to go to the church entrance, to greet the family and others who have accompanied the deceased, and then to perform certain actions pointing to the baptismal nature of the funeral. These can include sprinkling holy water on the coffin (symbolizing the water of baptism) and placing a funeral pall over the coffin (usually white, symbolizing the garments of baptism).

In the Orthodox tradition, the priest leads a candlelit procession to the church, accompanying the deceased in an open coffin. The coffin is brought down the aisle and to the front of the church as they together sing from Psalm 91 ("You who live in the shelter of the Most High, who abide in the shadow of the Almighty, will say to the LORD, 'My refuge and my fortress; my God, in whom I trust'") and Psalm 119 ("Happy are those whose way is blameless, who walk in the law of the LORD. Happy are those who keep his decrees, who seek him with their whole heart, who also do no wrong, but walk in his ways").

Another option is for the minister to meet the deceased at the entrance to the place of worship with words like these: "We greet our brother/sister _____, a sheep of God's own fold, a lamb of God's own flock, a sinner of God's own redeeming." These words have the advantage of anticipating similar language in a prayer of commendation often used at the end of the funeral:

Into your hands, O merciful Savior, we commend your servant *N.* Acknowledge, we humbly beseech you, a sheep of your own fold, a lamb of your own flock, a sinner of your own redeeming. Receive *him* into the arms of your mercy, into the blessed rest of everlasting peace, and into the glorious company of the saints in light. *Amen.*[16]

In less formal traditions, the minister may wish simply to enter with the coffin and the family and pause for a moment at the door, a prelude to walking with them down the aisle as the whole congregation sings a hymn. However it is done, the main symbolic import of the gathering movement is to signify that the community of faith (including the deceased) is present, assembled in response to the call of God, and that worship has begun.

2. The Procession to the Front of the Church

In a funeral, the deceased is, in a sense, one of the worshipers, a member of the praying congregation in the way that he or she has always been. In another sense, though, the deceased person is obviously not just another worshiper. The death of this Christian is a main reason and context for this service. This is the last time this saint will be present in the body in this place of worship, and this is in part a service of farewell. God will be worshiped here and the gospel proclaimed as always, but today this worship and proclamation will be done in the light of this particular person's life and death. Taken together, this means that the deceased should assume a both/and position—both as one among the congregation, and also as one this day prominent and visible. So, in the next movement of the funeral, the coffin is taken down the aisle to its proper place of worship: at the front of the church but still in the midst of the gathered congregation.

The movement is essentially simple: the coffin is carried or rolled from the door to the front of the church. What happens while this is taking place? Sometimes the visible action of the deceased moving into place is accompanied by other things to see. In some traditions, the coffin is preceded by people carrying symbols of the Christian life, such as a cross and a paschal candle. If this is done, the usual order for this procession is shown in figure 1.

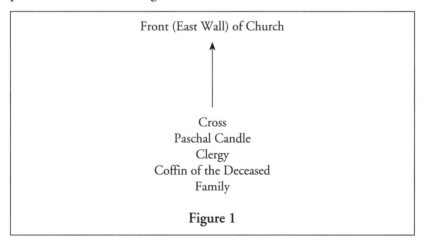

Front (East Wall) of Church

Cross
Paschal Candle
Clergy
Coffin of the Deceased
Family

Figure 1

Sometimes there are things to hear. For example, as the coffin is moved, the ministers may speak words about the resurrection and Christian hope, such as,

I am Resurrection and I am Life, says the Lord.
Whoever has faith in me shall have life,
even though he die.
And everyone who has life,
and has committed himself to me in faith,
shall not die for ever.[17]

Or perhaps the congregation sounds out the faith here, singing or
chanting a psalm, spiritual, or hymn such as "Abide with Me," "For
All the Saints," or "Precious Lord, Take My Hand." Congregational
singing during this movement hearkens back to the early Jewish and
Christian precedent of chanting psalms as the body was carried to the
grave. One eleventh-century hymn sung in funeral processions, "*Media
Vita*," continues in use in various translations and hymns and prayer
settings today. Here is a contemporary translation from *BCP:*

In the midst of life we are in death;
from whom can we seek help?
From you alone, O Lord,
who by our sins are justly angered.
Holy God, Holy and Mighty,
Holy and merciful Savior,
deliver us not into the bitterness of eternal death.
Lord, you know the secrets of our hearts;
shut not your ears to our prayers,
but spare us, O Lord.
Holy God, Holy and Mighty,
Holy and merciful Savior,
deliver us not into the bitterness of eternal death.
O worthy and eternal Judge,
do not let the pains of death
turn us away from you at our last hour.
Holy God, Holy and Mighty,
Holy and merciful Savior,
deliver us not into the bitterness of eternal death.[18]

Because this procession of the coffin from the door to the front of
the church symbolizes the deceased taking his or her place in the assembly for worship, there is an old tradition that laypeople are carried feetfirst toward the altar/table (i.e., facing the front, as they did in Sunday
worship) and clergy are carried in headfirst (i.e., facing the people, as
they did when they presided). Whether carried in headfirst or feetfirst,
the coffin is best placed as pictured in figure 2, because this position

most clearly symbolizes that the deceased has arrived at the place of worship. Here the deceased is both in a prominent place and yet is still a part of the congregation:

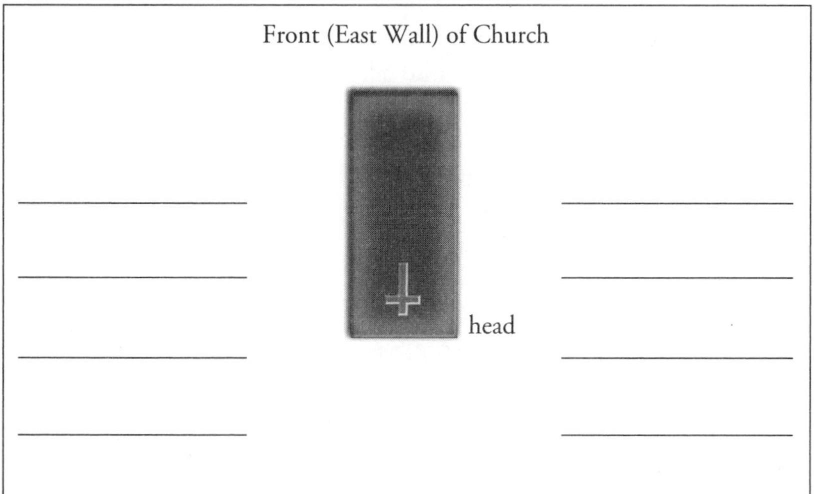

Front (East Wall) of Church

head

Figure 2

Placing the coffin in this way is not always possible or desirable. Sometimes the body is placed in the church earlier for a viewing; sometimes the room doesn't have a wide, central aisle or the necessary space to place the coffin perpendicular to the altar/table. A common alternative placement of the coffin is shown in figure 3:

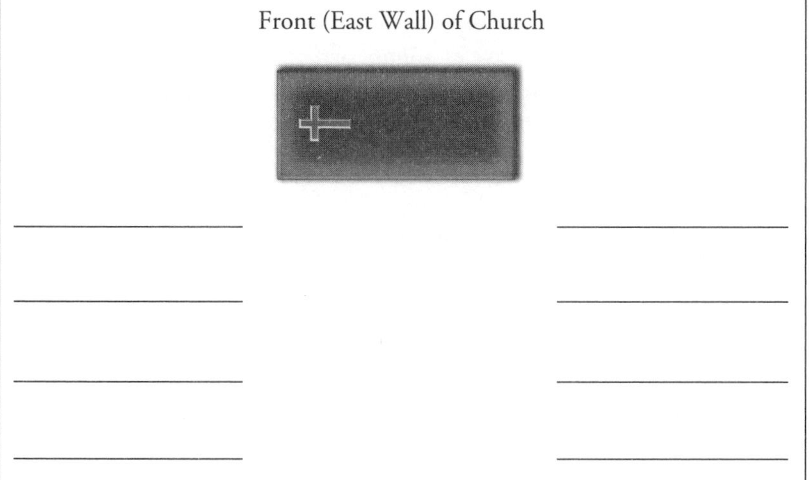

Front (East Wall) of Church

Figure 3

While this placement may be serviceable, it has the disadvantage of muting the imagery of the processional and making the coffin more an object to be viewed (and perhaps revered) than a symbol of the presence of the deceased in the worshiping community. If architecture or circumstance call for this arrangement, an emphasis upon the deceased as a participant in the assembly and as one who is on a baptismal journey should be made a part of the service elsewhere.

The family members, following behind the coffin, take their places in seats near the front, but still among the congregation. The custom, practiced in some funeral home chapels, of seating the family in an area separated, sometimes even screened off, from the rest of the congregation, is unjustified and significantly undermines the communal character of worship.

3. Service of Prayer and Word

Now that all are in place for worship, the funeral proceeds with prayers and Scripture:

1. Collect. The first element is usually a "prayer for the day" or a collect. The purpose of this prayer is to catch up in a stitch or two the fact of death and the prayer expressions of the congregation in this moment. In some ways, this opening prayer is like passing an offering plate, collecting thoughts, feelings, and hopes from those present, and placing all of them before God. Therefore, in the prayer-book traditions, this prayer usually assumes the form of an expanded "collect" form, adding to the usual five elements of a collect (name of God, attribute of God, petition, reason, and closing), other petitions or thanksgivings. Representative of these prayers is one found in *ELW*:[19]

(N)ame of God: O God
(A)ttribute of God: of grace and glory,
(T)hanksgiving: we remember before you today our sister/brother,
        _____. We thank you for giving her/him to know us
        and to love as a companion in our pilgrimage on earth.
(P)etition: In your . compassion, console us who mourn. Give us the
        faith to see that death has been swallowed up in the victory
        of our Lord Jesus Christ,
(R)eason: so that we may live in confidence and hope until, by your

call, we are gathered to our heavenly home in the company
of all your saints;
(C)losing: through Jesus Christ, our Savior and Lord. **Amen.**

Here is an example from the Roman Catholic tradition:

(N): O God
(A): in whom sinners find mercy and the saints find joy,
(P): we pray to you for our brother/sister _____, whose
body we honor with Christian burial,
(R): that he/she may be delivered from the bonds of death.
(P2): Admit him/her to the joyful company of your saints and
raise him on the last day
(R2): to rejoice in your presence for ever.
(C): We ask this through our Lord Jesus Christ, your Son, who
lives and reigns with you and the Holy Spirit, one God,
for ever and ever. **Amen.**[20]

Another example comes from the Presbyterian tradition:

(N): O God
(A): who gave us birth, you are ever more ready to hear than we
are to pray. You know our needs before we ask, and our
ignorance in asking.
(P): Show us now your grace,
(R): that as we face the mystery of death, we may see the light
of eternity.
(P2): Speak to us once more your solemn message of life and
death. And when our days here are ended, enable us to die
as those who go forth to live,
(R2): so that living or dying, our life may be in Jesus Christ
(C): our risen Lord. **Amen.**[21]

2. Prayer of Confession. Some traditions (e.g., United Methodist,
Presbyterian, United Church of Canada) add a prayer of confession
after the prayer of the day. While it may seem unusual to ask the congregation to confess their sins at a funeral, the inclusion of this prayer is
actually a mark of the pastoral care and therapeutic concerns inherent
in a funeral. A death often stirs up feelings of anger and guilt, regret
and remorse, and a prayer of confession provides the means for these

feelings and experiences to be offered to God. One woman, for example, reported that she entered the church for her father's funeral with deeply conflicted feelings. She had loved her father, but their relationship had been damaged, mostly, as she saw it, by his desire to continue controlling and scolding her well into her adult years. They had clashed many times over this and never arrived at a place of reconciliation, and now he was dead. But when, in the prayer of confession, the minister prayed this phrase, "and redeem, O God, even our memories," she reported feeling a deep wave of peacefulness pass over her, a gratitude that memories that neither she nor her father had been able to repair could now be given in trust to the mercy of God.

The prayer of confession from the United Church of Canada is particularly apt for a funeral:

> God of the living and the dead,
> we are burdened by the things we have done
> and by the things we have not done.
> We remember our broken promises
> and missed opportunities;
> the gifts we have taken for granted,
> the love we have not shown or returned.
> Forgive us, comfort and heal us.
> Lift our guilt from us,
> that we may walk in freedom and grace. **Amen.**[22]

Here is another fine funeral prayer of confession from the United Methodist tradition:

> Holy God, before you our hearts are open
> And from you no secrets are hidden.
> We bring to you now our shame and sorrow for our sins.
> We have forgotten that our life is from you and unto you.
> We have neither sought nor done your will.
> We have not been truthful in our hearts,
> in our speech, in our lives.
> We have not loved as we ought to love.
> Help us and heal us, we pray.
> Raise us from our sin into a better life,
> that we may end our days in peace
> trusting in your kindness unto the end;
> through Jesus Christ our Lord,
> who lives and reigns with you in the unity of the Holy Spirit,
> one God, now and forever. **Amen.**[23]

If a prayer of confession is used, it should, of course, be followed by an announcement of pardon.

3. Scripture. Generally two or three passages of Scripture are read, and in most traditions at least one of these should be from the Gospels. Though it is fitting to read "favorite passages" of the deceased or the family members, the main purpose of these readings is for the whole congregation to be reminded, through Scripture, of the promises of God in the face of death and loss.

4. Sermon or Homily. Not every funeral includes a sermon or homily, though some traditions stipulate that one be given. A detailed discussion of the place of preaching at a funeral is given in chapter 9.

5. Naming and Witness.[24] Here is a controversial element in a funeral, the time when the community explicitly evokes the biography and memory of the deceased. This can be done in a variety of ways. A memorial statement describing the life of the one who has died can be read by the pastor or someone else. Something created by the deceased (music, poetry, art, etc.) can be offered. People who were close to the deceased—neighbors, friends, relatives—can make short speeches, giving remembrance. Inspirational readings from sources other than Scripture can be included here.

What makes this element controversial is that there are so many ways it can go off the rails. It can drift into an inauthentic form of eulogizing, in which the deceased is romanticized and, thus, misremembered. It can lapse into sentimentality, pomposity, frivolity, pedantry, or just sheer tedium. So many and so great are the risks that some pastors and congregations forbid this sort of activity in funerals altogether, which is probably an overreaction. It is better to think of this, like the collect, as a kind of offering of the people. At this point in the service, what they have brought to give to God—their memories, their sense of sorrow, their words of thanksgiving for the life of the person they have lost—is now received and blessed. Of course, it can help if the coaches, cousins, and coworkers who plan to speak at the funeral are told in advance that they are actually crafting offerings, not roasts and after-dinner speeches.

6. Creed. If a creed is recited by the congregation, this is the location for it. Placed here, the creed serves three purposes. First, it is one of those moments when the voice of the community at worship is heard, an audible sign that those who mourn are not alone but surrounded in prayer. Second, coming close after the sermon, it ritually reenacts the creation of the church: the Word evokes faith. Third, it serves as yet another reminder of the connection between the funeral and baptism, especially if the creed used is the one most associated with baptism, the Apostles' Creed. The *BCP* makes this baptismal linkage specific by introducing the creed with these words: "In the assurance of eternal life given at Baptism, let us proclaim our faith and say . . ."[25]

7. **Prayers of Intercession.** Although several different kinds of prayers are rightly included here—thanksgiving, adoration, petition, intercession—the main theme of this prayer section is pleading with God, praying for the mourners that they will be consoled, for the church that it will continue along the path of discipleship, and for the deceased that she or he will be received into the mercy of God.

These prayers of intercession, placed as they are at the end of this section, are "traveling prayers." In fact, assuming that the funeral is taking place inside a church, these prayers are joined with the symbolic sound of the people of God getting to their feet and heading out, resuming the journey with the deceased toward the place of farewell. As the congregation travels, it begins to call toward heaven, as it were, telling God to get ready for the new saint's arrival. Let the angels of light walk before him. Let the gate of righteousness be opened to him. "Let him join the heavenly choir," say the words of the old Coptic prayer noted in an earlier chapter. "Bring him into the paradise of delight."

This kind of intercessory prayer at a funeral, in effect praying *for* the deceased, makes many Christians, maybe especially Protestants, nervous. By the time of the Reformation, these intercessory funeral prayers for the dead had become firmly connected to the concept of purgatory, particularly the idea that the living could somehow help pray people out of their time of purgation and into paradise. Such prayers, the Reformers claimed, were anathema, vain attempts to save people by works instead of through faith. As such, the prayers of intercession were banished from funerals, and once people had died, the church's voice of prayer on their behalf, at least among most Protestants, grew silent.

The fact that certain types of intercessions for the dead have reappeared in contemporary funeral services, even among Protestants, is by no means a sign of amnesia, a theological misstep, or a reversion to medieval views. It is a sign, rather, that these intercessions have taken on a different character and are understood by the church, Catholic and Protestant, to have different meanings from their sixteenth-century counterparts.

Put briefly, today's prayers of intercession grow out of an understanding of the Christian funeral as a rite of passage,[26] as a ritual act marking an event of human transformation that has been enacted by the grace of God. A person who was alive and with us in this earthly life has now died and, through God's mercy, has been raised to new life and joined to the communion of the saints. Precise language is not possible for us, but the deceased has moved from this world to the next; someone who was "this" is now "that," who was "here" is now "there," and the funeral, as a rite of passage, ritually marks this change and bridges this distance.

In rites of passage, even nonreligious ones, "real" time and ritual time are two different realities. Take, for example, the graduation ceremonies that are held every year on the campus where I teach. The soon-to-be graduates put on funny-looking academic regalia, march to the ceremony, and when the officials pronounce the magic words, everybody flips a tassel from one side of the cap to the other, and . . . Voila! People who were students one minute have become degree-holding graduates the next.

Now all of us on the faculty know that this is not really the magic moment. These students actually became graduates, in a legal sense anyway, several days before when the faculty voted to grant them their degrees. The ritual simply acts out in ceremonial fashion what is already true about them, that they have made the transition from being not-graduates to being graduates. But even though the ceremony itself does not actually *cause* them to change status and to be graduates, this does not mean that it amounts to nothing. Something actually happens when they flip those tassels and clutch the sheepskins. Even though nobody absolutely requires our students to show up for the ceremony, few miss it. It would hardly do to send out a mass e-mail saying, "We voted. You're a grad!" Walking ritually through the process of moving from one status to another is important to humans; it is the way that we participate in a reality that has changed around us.

In Christian worship, the issue of ritual time is even more complex, because all worship is an enactment of eschatological time, that is, God's time. Our worship, measured by the ticking of the clock, is gathered into eternity. If, for example, on Sunday we pray the prayer of confession pleading for forgiveness at 11:06 a.m., and we announce the assurance of pardon at 11:08, does that mean we were unforgiven at 11:06 and forgiven two minutes later? Of course not. In the economy of God we were, are, and will be forgiven. But this doesn't mean that the prayer asking for forgiveness is irrelevant. What it says is that the confession and forgiveness sequence that we marched through in clock time is our way of participating in and experiencing that which is eternally true in God's time.

To get us a bit closer to funeral intercessions, consider this prayer of the psalmist, "Remember how short my life is; remember that you created all of us mortal!" (Ps. 89:47 TEV). Does this prayer imply that it has somehow slipped God's mind that the life of the human creature is brief and fleeting, but that after the prayer, because of the prayer, God remembers it all over again? Taken literally, that is silly, of course. We are the time-bound creatures, not God. We are the ones who are locked into "before" and "after," and our prayer "Remember me!" is our cry to be gathered up once more into the eternal remembrance of God. It is a little time-bound boat launched into an everlasting sea.

So when we pray for ourselves and for our departed loved ones at a funeral, we are neither bargaining with God nor performing some meritorious good work to polish the apple with God. We are doing what we always do in prayer: crying out in the midst of time to be gathered body and soul into God's eternal love. We are, as we pray on earth, gathered into the life of the Trinity, even, as the *OCF* suggests, praying "in the voice of Christ," "who is at the right hand of God, who indeed intercedes for us" (Rom. 8:34). When a Christian sister dies, we believe that she has been raised, imperishable, and that it happened, as Paul says "in the twinkling of an eye." One moment she was an alto in the choir of First Baptist on Main Street, and then, faster than light can travel, she was singing in the great chorus of the saints singing "day and night without ceasing . . . , 'Holy, holy, holy, the Lord God the Almighty, who was and is and is to come'" (Rev. 4:8).

But that is in God's time, which is not yet our time. And so at the funeral we walk step by step over the pathway from here to there. We lovingly carry the body of the sister who is already with God, walking toward eternity, but walking—as we must, one step in front of the other through time and space—singing, and praying as we go, that both our sister and we ourselves will be welcomed into the open arms of God. All of this is getting around to the point that, properly understood theologically, the old fights about purgatory are long past, and it makes perfect sense for the church to pray, "You raised the dead to life; give to our sister eternal life. . . . You promised paradise to the repentant thief; bring her to the joys of heaven." A prayer of intercession used in the Orthodox liturgy acknowledges that the prayer is bridging two temporal realms:

> With the saints, give rest, O Christ, to the soul of Thy servant, where sickness is no more, neither sorrowing nor sighing, but life everlasting. Thou only art immortal, who hast created and fashioned [human beings]. For out of the earth were we [mortals] made, and unto earth we shall return . . . we [mortals] all shall go, making as our funeral dirge the song: Alleluia, Alleluia, Alleluia.[27]

Here, from *The Book of Common Worship*, is another fine example of a contemporary funeral intercession:

> For our *brother/sister* N.,
> let us pray to our Lord Jesus Christ
> who said, "I am the resurrection and the life."
> Lord, you consoled Martha and Mary in their distress;
> draw near to us who mourn for N.,
> and dry the tears of those who weep.
> **Hear us, Lord.**
> You wept at the grave of Lazarus, your friend;
> comfort us in our sorrow.
> **Hear us, Lord.**
> You raised the dead to life;
> give to our *brother/sister* eternal life.
> **Hear us, Lord.**
> You promised paradise to the repentant thief;
> bring N. to the joys of heaven.
> **Hear us, Lord.**
> Our *brother/sister* was washed in baptism
> and anointed with the Holy Spirit;
> give *him/her* fellowship with all your saints.
> **Hear us, Lord.**
> *He/she* was nourished at your table on earth;
> welcome *him/her* at your table in the heavenly kingdom.
> **Hear us, Lord.**
> Comfort us in our sorrows at the death of N.;
> let our faith be our consolation,
> and eternal life our hope.
> **Amen.**[28]

4. Holy Communion

As early as the fourth century, there is explicit mention of celebrating the Lord's Supper, the Eucharist, at graveside. Most contemporary prayer book funeral services place Holy Communion right at this point in the funeral. Some traditions expect the meal to be observed; others make it optional.

When the Lord's Supper is observed at a funeral, it is the kind of farewell meal with the deceased observed in many human burial practices. Even more, though, it is the paschal, Easter meal which remembers the death of Jesus, presents the resurrection of Christ, and anticipates the heavenly banquet when all the saints will gather at table.

Most funerals in our society now involve people who are not members of a church, and presiders should weigh, as a practical and pastoral matter, whether observing the Supper at a given funeral would serve as a sign of hope or mainly as a reminder of division and separation. If the meal is observed, the usual manner is followed, but the suggestion that family members and friends of the deceased be invited to bring the bread and wine forward is good.[29]

Several of the prayer book services specify that, if the Eucharist is not observed, the service include the Lord's Prayer at this point. This prayer, which would normally be a part of Holy Communion, is particularly fitting, both because of its connection to Holy Communion and because, as familiar as it is to most people, it provides one more place for the voice of the congregation to be heard.

5. Sending[30]

The drama of the funeral has now arrived at its climax: the community of faith carries the deceased to the grave and bids farewell, entrusting her or him to God. It then goes forth with God's blessing to live and serve in the world, its grief tempered by hope. As Dennis Bushkofsky and Craig Satterlee comment:

> If we understand that different parts of the pattern of worship are more prominent in some services than others, we might think of the Sending as especially prominent in the funeral liturgy. Everything the assembly has done in the service to this point—giving thanks for the baptism, proclaiming and hearing the gospel, and receiving

Christ's body and blood—prepares the assembly to be sent to live in the hope and peace of Christ, even as they symbolically take leave of the deceased and "send" her or him into God's all-embracing hands.[31]

The sending movement of the funeral consists of two parts: the Commendation and the Committal:

1. Commendation. In the Commendation, the presider prays on behalf of the deceased and in the spirit of Jesus' own prayer on the cross, "Father, into your hands I commend my spirit" (Luke 23:46). This is done most powerfully when the spoken words are accompanied by visible action. The minister comes to the side of the coffin, and family members and others may join the minister around the coffin. The pastor then speaks a preface to the prayer.

ELW's preface is simple, calling for the pastor to say, "Let us commend __name__ to the mercy of God, our maker and redeemer."[32]

The *OCF* is more elaborate, providing for a statement like the following to be said, after which holy water, as a sign of baptism, may be sprinkled on the coffin:

> Before we go our separate ways, let us take leave of our brother/sister. May our farewell express our affection for him/her; may it ease our sadness and strengthen our hope. One day we shall joyfully greet him/her again when the love of Christ, which conquers all things, destroys even death itself.

The Book of Common Prayer includes a preface in the form of a prayer that employs the biblical imagery, so familiar from Ash Wednesday, of dust:

> Give rest, O Christ, to your servant(s) with your saints,
> *where sorrow and pain are no more,*
> *neither sighing, but life everlasting.*

> You only are immortal, the creator and maker of mankind; and we are mortal, formed of the earth, and to earth shall we return. For so did you ordain when you created me, saying, "You are dust, and to dust you shall return." All of us go down to the dust; yet even at the grave we make our song: Alleluia, alleluia, alleluia.

> *Give rest, O Christ, to your servant(s) with your saints,*
> *where sorrow and pain are no more,*
> *neither sighing, but life everlasting.*

Then the pastor, and perhaps the others near the coffin, places a hand on the coffin and prays a prayer similar to this:

> Into your hands, O merciful Savior, we commend your servant *N.* Acknowledge, we humbly beseech you, a sheep of your own fold, a lamb of your own flock, a sinner of your own redeeming. Receive *him* into the arms of your mercy, into the blessed rest of everlasting peace, and into the glorious company of the saints in light. *Amen.*[33]

2. Committal. The whole community of faith now processes again, this time to the grave to commit the body of the deceased to the place of burial. The order of procession is essentially the same as was used to process to the front of the church: crossbearer (if there is one), clergy, coffin of the deceased, and family. The paschal candle, if used, remains in the place of worship. The main difference in this processional is that the rest of the congregation is invited to follow.

The procession proceeds to the grave. If this is some distance from the church, the minister (and crossbearer) stands by the hearse as the coffin is loaded. At the cemetery, the minister (and crossbearer) again stands by the hearse until the coffin is unloaded, then leads the procession to the grave site. When all are in place, the presider begins with a greeting from Scripture, such as one of these:

> Grace and peace from our Savior Jesus Christ be with you all.

> Do not be afraid; I am the first and the last, and the living one.
> I was dead, and behold, I am alive for forever and ever. Because I live, you also will live.

One or two Scripture lessons may be read, and then the words of committal are said toward the coffin, preferably as it is actually being lowered into the grave:

> In sure and certain hope of the resurrection to eternal life through our Lord Jesus Christ, we commend to Almighty God our *brother N.*, and we commit *his* body to the ground (or to the deep, or the elements, or its resting place); earth to earth, ashes to ashes, dust to dust. The Lord bless *him* and keep *him*, the Lord make his face to shine upon *him* and be gracious to *him*, the Lord lift up his countenance upon *him* and give *him* peace. *Amen.*[34]

If the coffin is lowered into the grave as the people are still present, some dirt may be placed by hand or shovel on the coffin. Then the following may be said or sung:

> Rest eternal grant to *him*, O Lord;
> *And let light perpetual shine upon* him.
> May *his* soul, and the souls of all the departed,
> through the mercy of God, rest in peace. *Amen.*[35]

The committal and the funeral close with a prayer and a blessing.

O Lord, support us all the day long until the shadows lengthen and the evening comes and the busy world is hushed, and the fever of life is over, and our work is done. Then, in your mercy, grant us a safe lodging, and a holy rest, and peace at the last; through Jesus Christ our Lord. *Amen.*[36]

> Go in peace,
> and may the God of peace,
> who brought back from the dead our Lord Jesus,
> make you complete in everything good
> so that you may do God's will,
> working among us that which is pleasing in God's sight,
> through Jesus Christ,
> to whom be the glory forever and ever!
> **Amen.**

OTHER ISSUES OF PRACTICE

In addition to the main structure and elements of central funeral rites, there are also other recurring practical issues that need to be considered:

1. Music

The movement-by-movement analysis of the funeral above made no mention of music. This is not because music is unimportant in the funeral, but because it is so important that it is not possible to put one's finger on the order of worship and say, "There! *That's* where the music goes." There are obvious places for hymns, spirituals, or psalms—during the procession to the front of the church and after the sermon, for example—but hypothetically almost every element of the service could be sung.

The service should have lots of music, and most of it, if not all of it, should be congregational song. Accompany them with singing! It is good for the voices of the community singing praise to be heard above the noisy clamor of death. If there is a soloist or a choir, don't allow them to serenade the congregation. The experience of death cancels all concerts. We have holy work to do, to carry a brother or sister to the grave; so let the choir and the soloists walk along with us. Let them sing *with* the people and on their behalf.

People will often request quiet, meditative hymns like "Abide with Me" and "Near to the Heart of God." The static inwardness of such hymns is fine, but the funeral is a confident procession of the faithful to the place of departure to hand our loved one into the arms of God. The best funeral hymns are traveling music, pilgrim songs. It is better to sing "I Want Jesus to Walk with Me" than "In the Garden."

I am not particularly a fan of the militaristic "Onward, Christian Soldiers"; I wouldn't want it sung on a regular Sunday, much less on the Sunday nearest Memorial Day. But it was used powerfully in the funeral of a young man who died of AIDS. When the commendation was said and the funeral was to proceed to the cemetery for the committal, a crossbearer lifted up the cross and led the coffin and the community in procession to the grave as they sang, "Onward, Christian soldiers, marching as to war, with the cross of Jesus going on before: Christ the royal Master leads against the foe." When it is clear who the foe is— namely, that scurrilous destroyer of all that gives life, that author of AIDS and cancer, the one who takes delight in inflicting pain and abandoning children to starvation, old Death itself—and that we cannot on our own strength defeat it, we need Christ to lead against the foe.

The "funeral" sections of many denominational hymnals simply have not caught up theologically, preferring a quasi-gnostic, we-will-always-remember-Harriet theology to the Easter kerygma. A popular funeral hymn from the 1960s, "Lord of the Living," gets a bit coy when it affirms, "You gave us Jesus to defeat our sadness with Easter gladness" and "Lord, You can lift us from the grave of sorrow." It's hard to quibble with that. The resurrection does generate joy, and God can surely lift our hearts from grief; but there is some unmistakable downsizing here. With all due respect to the pain of grief, the notion that God gave Jesus to defeat *our* sadness, while perhaps technically true, is like saying that God gave Jesus to defeat the flu, which is also true, I suppose, but seems way too small for a hymn. I know we are mournful at a funeral, but why not stand up in the midst of our tears and shake a fist at the old Enemy and say, "In Jesus, God defeated the powers of death." Why not shout out, "Joyful, Joyful, We Adore Thee":

> Mortals, join the happy chorus
> Which the morning stars began;
> Love divine is reigning o'er us,
> Joining all in heaven's plan.
> Ever singing, march we onward,
> Victors in the midst of strife,
> Joyful music leads us sunward
> In the triumph song of life.
> (Henry van Dyke, alt.)

2. Cremation and Bodies

Some readers will wonder if this book has been written oblivious to the fact that the practice of cremation is now, for a rapidly growing number of people, the method of preference for the disposition of the body. True, I have only rarely spoken of cremated remains and urns, sticking mainly to the language of bodies and coffins. This does not imply that I am opposed to cremation; I am not. With only a few exceptions, most Christian groups now accept cremation as a perfectly acceptable alternative to earth burial, and I am with them. The old superstitions that the fires of cremation are symbolic of the fires of hell or that cremation makes it somehow impossible for God to raise a person bodily are just that, superstitions, and are based on serious misunderstandings of both cremation and of bodily resurrection. Burning a body subjects it to no more hellish form of indignity than burial, given what water and worms will eventually do to a corpse, and no embalming or rubber sealed vaults will keep them at bay forever. And while the bodily resurrection, as an exasperated Paul explained to the Corinthians, is a bodily resurrection, it is not a mere revivification of *that* body. Our bodies are transformed, glorified. "It is sown a physical body, it is raised a spiritual body," said Paul (1 Cor. 15:44).

In the second century, the Romans burned at the stake the venerable Bishop Polycarp, student of the apostle John, because he would not deny his Lord, whom he said he had served for eighty-six years. The Christians who witnessed the execution said they did not smell the odor of burning flesh but something more like gold and silver being refined in a furnace or the fragrant aroma of frankincense. Cremated by the Romans though his earthly body was, I am confident that a fully embodied Polycarp is now singing the alleluias in the presence of God.

If there is a problem with cremation in regard to a funeral, it is that the cremated remains are required to stand in for the whole body of the deceased, which at its worst could be like asking Ralph Fiennes's hat to play *Hamlet*. We have experienced and known the deceased as an embodied person who speaks with a mouth, touches with hands, caresses with arms, and walks with feet this way or that. Commitments are made with the body, not the spirit, and the embodiment of the person *is* the person we have known and loved. The thought of substituting a container of bone and ashes for a human body puts me in mind of what Frederick Buechner once said of using grape juice instead of wine at holy communion:

> Unfermented grape juice is a bland and pleasant drink, especially on a warm afternoon mixed half and half with ginger ale. But it is a ghastly symbol of the life blood of Jesus Christ, especially when served in individual antiseptic, thimble-sized glasses.
>
> Wine is booze, which means it is dangerous and drunk-making. It makes the timid brave and the reserved amorous. It loosens the tongue and breaks the ice especially when served in a loving cup. It kills germs. As symbols go, it is a rather splendid one.[37]

If the deceased is to be cremated, then the best option is for the funeral to be held before the cremation and for the body to be present at the funeral. Most funeral homes are adjusting to this option and can provide a temporary (rental) coffin or a sturdy cardboard coffin that can be used instead of a more expensive permanent coffin. If the funeral is held reasonably soon after death, in most cases embalming is not required.

Second best, but definitely second best, is for the deceased to be cremated immediately and for the cremated remains, in an urn or other container, to be treated in a funeral just like the body in other funerals. Some congregations have commissioned the crafting of a small, coffin-like box of wood, metal, or stone, that holds the urn and can be carried or wheeled into a funeral, with or without a pall, just like a regular coffin.

There are some funerals where, for good reasons, the body cannot be present. The body was lost and could not be recovered, or the body was donated to medical science, or the funeral is being held miles away from the place of interment, or the family simply insisted uncompromisingly that the body be buried or burned in advance. In proper hands, these funerals are not lesser services in any respect, but they should not be services where the body is ignored.

During the time of slavery in the southern United States, slave owners were known to take Bibles away from slave preachers, fearful that the biblical message was stirring up insurrection. There are moving accounts of these preachers standing beside open graves and leading funerals, reciting Scripture from memory while holding open folded hands as if they were cradling a Bible.

Just so, funerals without the body present should open hands and arms as if the body were in fact there. The leaders of these funerals should do everything in their power, in prayers and in sermons, to evoke the bodily presence of the one who has died and who is now being offered back to God, embodied and with gratitude and in hope that God will raise this body from the dead.

One additional issue about cremation needs to be addressed: what to do with the remains. In addition to the usual repertoire of possibilities—burying them, putting them in a "niche" in a columbarium, or scattering them on the earth—people today are exploring a whole new host of choices, from dividing them among the surviving relatives to having the ashes swirled into lamps, furniture, and jewelry.

The Catholic *Order of Christian Funerals* takes a firm stand here. The only acceptable practices are burial or entombment in a mausoleum or columbarium. "The practice of scattering cremated remains on the sea, from the air, or on the ground, or keeping cremated remains in the home of a relative or friend of the deceased is not the reverent disposition that the church requires."[38]

This position grows out of a commitment to keeping the symbolism straight, that the cremated remains represent the body. Although the rubrics do not say so, there may also be concern about the inherent meanings of the alternative practices. Keeping a vase of the deceased ashes on the mantle may be a psychological refusal, perhaps temporary, to let the dead go. As for scattering ashes, if we pushed hard enough, we might discover that where people choose to scatter ashes reveals something of their eschatology, their view of the afterlife. Scattering Pop's ashes "in the woods where he loved to hunt" may be an overdomestication of the concept of eternal life.

Personally, though, I don't try to push these images quite so far, and I think we can help people think through these choices in wise and practical ways. I like the advice of one cemetery director, who suggested that a good test of what is done with cremated remains is to ask if there is any parallel with what we would sense as proper to do with a body.[39] Would we commit Pop's body to the earth in the woods he cherished? Probably. Would we divide Pop's body and send pieces to the children so that they could encase them in jewelry and lamps? Probably not. But some Catholics have defended the practice of dividing the cremated remains, arguing that this is precisely what the church has done with the bodily relics of the saints. So stay tuned.

3. Coffins Open or Closed

A good many contemporary funeral liturgies put a foot down when it comes to open coffins. They allow them at the viewing or the wake, but they want that coffin snapped shut at the funeral. I can think of no good theological reason why this should be done, and I suspect that the preference for a closed coffin has more to do with class consciousness and squeamishness than with gospel sensibilities. A fine counterwitness was offered in the last days and the funeral of Pope John Paul II. As he was dying, he did not try to hide the ravages on his body of Parkinson's disease, and when he died, his body, not in a coffin but exposed on a cot, was carried in full view to his grave.

Perhaps the best way to think of the open-or-closed coffin issue is to consider it as adiaphora, a wonderful liturgical term meaning "either way is fine" or, more precisely, those things that are neither morally prohibited nor morally commanded. Some ethnic groups make much of having the coffin open; some others are bothered and distracted by an exposed body. So, adiaphora. Open it if you will; close it if you prefer. There is simply no way that a coffin, open or closed, does not convey the presence of the dead body, and *that* is the main point.

4. Going All the Way to the End

If a funeral is a piece of community theater, one noble goal is to keep people from yawning and exiting the stage in the second act, never carrying the performance all the way through to the end. It has become commonplace to consider the church funeral service as a self-contained service. When that's done, the funeral is over, and the family can take care of the disposal of the body in private. But in a funeral we are carrying the body of a saint to the place of farewell.

As a practical matter, people will peel away at various points along the way, but we should strive to make it clear that we are not done here until we have handed our loved one over to the earth and to God. In short, we are carrying a loved one to the edge of mystery, and people should be encouraged to stick around to the end, to book passage all the way. If the body is to be buried, go to the grave and stay there until the body is in the ground. If the body is to be burned, go to the crematorium and witness the burning.

Resistance to going the full distance with the dead will occasionally be encountered from some crematoriums, which are not accustomed to people who want to stay for the firing up of the retort, and some cemeteries, which view trudging to the grave as an inefficient use of employee time or don't like the idea of families being present for the dirt being placed on the coffin in the grave. These cemeteries much prefer for funeral processions to end not at graveside but in some plastic pseudochapel where the ceremonies can be peremptorily put to an end and the worshipers dispatched without delay, thus freeing up the burial crew to get on with their business unimpeded. These so-called chapels are—why mince words?—Chapels of Convenience and Cathedrals of *Funeralia Interruptus*. Tell the cemetery owner or the crematorium manager, kindly of course, to step out of the way, that they are impeding the flow of traffic. You have been walking with this saint since the day of baptism; the least you can do is go all the way to the grave, to the end, with this child of God. They may refuse, but if enough clergy demand to be able to go the last few yards with the dead, change will happen.

5. The Graveside Service

Many funerals are held entirely at the grave. They are usually smaller gatherings, and the service is abbreviated. Pastors should think creatively about how to preserve, even in graveside ceremonies, the symbol of the church processing with the body of the deceased to the place of farewell. Two ways to do this are, first, to be sure that, even when shortened, the service still retains the basic movements outlined above, and second, to invite the worshipers, rather than going directly to the grave, to gather by the hearse. The opening statements of the service can be made there; then the group can follow in procession behind the coffin to the grave, perhaps singing a familiar hymn as they go.

6. The Funeral Director

A great irony hangs over the relationship between clergy and funeral directors. In the literature, they are often portrayed as adversaries and competitors, with colliding values and goals. I do not want to minimize the frictions that can result when trying to work together to serve families at a difficult time, but relationships in practice tend to be better than they are pictured in theory. Clergy will often say, "You know, you have to watch funeral directors like hawks; they're just out for the dollar. But, now, Ralph down at Kilpatrick's, he's different; he's great."

The real stress points emerge when unstated and incompatible images of a funeral clash in the planning process. At the time of death, Christian families who use the services of a funeral home do some planning with the staff of that home, and they do some planning with their pastor, but hardly anyone is completely clear where the division of labor lies. When families arrive at the funeral home with the idea that for the funeral to be meaningful they have to monogram the service in some way to "make it more personal," then the funeral director can be placed in a difficult situation. He or she may not agree with the family's request to, say, stencil "Go Cowboys!" on the side of the coffin or to hire a sad-faced clown to hand out programs, and may gently try to guide the family in another direction. But funeral homes don't stay in business long if they sternly resist the desires of their customers. After all, from the funeral director's perspective, it's *the family's* funeral. If Pastor Kate should say to the funeral director, "A clown handing out bulletins? Not in *my* church, we don't!" then an impression is created that Pastor Kate has *her* way of doing funerals, and the family has *its* way of doing this funeral, and the funeral director is caught in the middle, just hoping to do something dignified and professional, and not get sued.

Actually, most thoughtful funeral directors are as worried as are pastors about the loss of public and cultural value in funerals. They are concerned as business people, of course, but they are also concerned as citizens and sometimes even as people of faith. Every week they see people choosing the trivial over the profound, and they sense that our society is the poorer for it.

If the church and its clergy can recover for themselves the character of the Christian funeral, the kind of public community theater that it is, the power of its script, the sacred nature of its cast, then this vision needs to be shared with the local funeral director. Most good funeral directors would welcome a conference with a pastor with whom they will be working. Such meetings allow for relationships to build, for frank conversation about mutual concerns, and for the pastor to say, "When I am working with my families, I am trying to help them to participate in a Christian ritual of long-standing and great power. Here is how I understand it." The point is, this is not Pastor Kate's funeral, shaped by her personal peeves and preferences; this is the church's worship. It is to everyone's benefit to help faith communities retrieve and then to perform their sacred funeral rituals.

For the time being, anyway, funeral directors have settled on calling themselves just that: funeral *directors*. But it is, or should be, a misnomer. We would be puzzled and wary if someone should build a lovely, white-columned establishment down the block from the church and put out a tasteful sign reading "Sullivan and Sons, Baptism Directors." When it comes to the Christian funeral, this is a liturgy that is a part of the church's heritage, a ritual the church has been enacting for two millennia. We need plenty of help to do it, but we should not be so indifferent to our own gospel, our own traditions, and our own worship that we hand these treasures over to others.

Although I am not optimistic that it will happen, I would like to see the recovery of an older designation for funeral directors, namely, *undertaker*. Most funeral directors will probably not take kindly to this suggestion, since it seems like a demotion from the so-called ranks of the professions. But I mean to honor their work, not diminish it. There are scores of tasks that need to be done, and done quickly, to carry out the drama of a funeral. The staff of a funeral home are those who *undertake* some of the tasks that we are no longer able or willing to do. This kind of "undertaking" is a solemn responsibility, and a faithful stewardship of it is a sacred work.

There is a small trend to bypass the funeral home altogether, to go back to the practices of an earlier time, and for families to bury (or cremate) our own dead. For the most part I find this movement interesting and praiseworthy, as I do the accompanying trend toward "green" funerals in which non-embalmed bodies are placed in the earth either directly or in a biodegradable coffin. I hope both trends gain strength. But in a complex, fast-paced urban society where we don't make our own candles, shoe our own horses, or even fry our own chicken any more, realistically most people need the help of others to prepare the bodies of their dead and transport them to the cemetery or crematorium. They need people with the equipment and expertise to *undertake* these important responsibilities and to perform them in ways that enhance the worship of the faith community.

Who does what in all this has to be figured out locally. I know of one congregation that has a rule: the funeral home can bring the coffin to the front door of the church, but the church takes it from there. This rule gladdens my heart. Here is a congregation that wants to reclaim its sacred responsibility and to conduct its own ritual. However, a funeral director in that town makes a good point when he notes that most of the members of this congregation are on the elderly side and to watch them try to navigate a coffin down a narrow center aisle without banging into the pews is an anxiety-making experience. Maybe someone else could be allowed to perform that task—not to change the ritual, but to *undertake* the job of helping us enact it.

7. Leadership and Community Involvement

One advantage of the village funerals of two centuries ago is that everybody had a job to do. There was a grave to be dug, a coffin to be made, food to be prepared, the body to be washed and dressed. Once again we can see how the Christian funeral was built on the chassis of necessity. These tasks had to be done, and doing them was the human thing to do. Doing them in ways that disclose the gospel is what makes them the Christian thing to do.

Now many of these tasks are done by others; about the only job left for people is psychological consolation, a daunting task. Churches are beginning to recognize the value of weaving back into the funeral ritual the labor of our hands. For example, some congregations have rotating groups of members who volunteer to participate in the whole funeral process. They see that phone calls are made, programs prepared, and that food is available. The ideas for gathering in more of the community to help perform the drama of a Christian funeral are many and depend upon local circumstances, but the goal is worthy.

It is also helpful to see the funeral service itself as a drama with several parts, and not just a monologue by the pastor. To ask people to read Scripture, pray, and, as fitting, perform other parts in the service, makes the dramatic character of the funeral richer and more evident.

8. Military and Other Civil Ceremonies

Sometimes the family of the deceased will desire to have the funeral include a military ceremony or a civil ritual, such as the Elks fraternal ceremony. In some ways, doing one of these rituals in the midst of a Christian service is like performing two plays on the same stage at the same time. The best solution is to keep the two rituals completely separate, but this is usually unrealistic. The best acceptable compromise, in my view, is to do the civic ritual first, then perform the full Christian ritual. However, some of these civic ceremonies are designed to be done at graveside, which creates a problem. Either the civic ceremony takes place as soon as the funeral group arrives at the grave, which interrupts the logical dramatic movement of the funeral, or it is done as the final event, which means that the last word of a funeral is not the blessing of the committal but a secular ceremony. Given the choice, I go with having the ceremony as soon as the group arrives at the grave so that the last word spoken will be the gospel. But pastors will simply have to work out their own salvation here, with fear and trembling.

9. Preplanning

The preplanning of funerals normally occurs in two ways. The first is the purchasing of a preneed contract with a local funeral home, which allows one to pay in advance for a funeral at a locked-in price. Frankly, many of these contracts are really just overpriced insurance policies, and people should investigate carefully before purchasing them.

The other kind of preplanning is deciding in advance what one's wishes are for the funeral: what hymns, what Scripture, whether to be buried or cremated, and so on. Sometimes this is done in a letter to one's children or even more formally in a will. Some congregations, as a part of a program of end-of-life planning, provide forms for people to describe their specific desires.

All preplanning, though, should be held like a thistle, very gently. We have already pointed to the questionable value of preneed contracts, and we should also question the desire to pin down the details of one's own funeral. Why would we want to do that? Either we don't want our families making those decisions, so we decide to stay in control from beyond the grave (a person with no heirs is, of course, an exception). More commonly, we don't want to be a burden on our family. Truthfully, though, bearing one another's burdens makes us human and brings us closer to the spirit of Christ. We may feel the weight of trying to figure out the best hymns and so on for mother's funeral, but it is a good weight, much like the good weight of putting our muscles to work in carrying her to the arms of God. We have the duty and the delight to carry one who has, in times before, carried us. Some broad-brush preplanning may be helpful, but we don't want to deprive our loved ones of the soul-making labor of fulfilling the law of Christ by bearing our burdens in a time of need.

9

Telling the Truth about Life and Death: Preaching at Funerals

SERMON OR EULOGY?

When it comes to the idea of sermons at funerals, much confusion has raged. Is a sermon at a funeral necessary? Desirable? If so, what is it supposed to be and do? What should be its basic content and aim? These questions have proved vexing and difficult to answer, and what are deemed to be the "correct" responses depend in large part upon where one stands in the stream of church history. As an example of how the funeral sermon has been something of a wax nose—bent first this way and then that way by the tides of history and fashion—consider Jacques Bénigne Bossuet (1627–1704), possibly the most celebrated Christian funeral sermonizer in history.

Bossuet's ornate, polished funeral orations are still admired and studied as fine rhetoric in French schools. Well-born, classically educated, and possessed of a rich, sonorous voice and theatrical pulpit manner, Bossuet quite naturally made his way rapidly through the clerical ranks of French Catholicism, climbing finally to be chaplain to the court of the "Sun King," Louis XIV. Bossuet clearly had what it takes to be a royal chaplain—polish, grace, charm, a gift for flattery—but mainly the man could preach a good funeral. What that meant at Versailles was, among other things, that Bossuet could sprinkle the fancy perfume of his oratory over the fetid moral lives of various deceased royals and cause them to smell like roses at their own funerals.

A particularly challenging example was the funeral of one Princess Anne of Gonzaga, a conniving schemer whose back-stabbing tactics, hateful personality, and very public transgressions were the talk of Paris. Finding something good to say at her funeral would be, to put it mildly, difficult. To make matters worse, Anne had, just prior to her death, foolishly and vainly published a ghost-written memoir confessing all in shocking detail. How could even the redoubtable Bossuet handle this one?

He rose to the occasion, however, first describing a Damascus-road conversion experience that had overtaken her highness late in life, a remarkable tale of personal transformation that had strangely gone unnoticed among her compatriots. It was, trumpeted Bossuet, "a miracle as astonishing as that where Jesus Christ caused to fall in an instant from the eyes of converted Saul the scales with which they had been covered. Who then would not cry out at such a sudden change, 'The finger of God is here!'"

Having thus, with a waggle of his tongue, turned the princess from reprobate to righteous, Bossuet could then give the congregation what they really wanted, extensive and titillating passages from her majesty's own confessional, but now they served as evidence of the power of grace to provoke so dramatic a change. He ended with an evangelical flourish imitated by many subsequent funeral preachers, "I wish all souls who are far from God . . . were present here today. You, then, who gather in this holy place, and chiefly you, O sinners, whose conversion He awaits with such long patience, harden not your hearts."[1]

By all reports, Bossuet's congregation at the funeral was moved by his oratory, but a bit dubious of his facts. The notion of the poison princess as a sudden hot gospeler was a bit much, and a skeptical Voltaire had a little sport with Bossuet's account of her deathbed flight to Jesus. "Bossuet told this as true," he said, tongue in cheek, "therefore he must have believed it. Let us join him in his belief, in spite of the raillery which it has occasioned."[2]

The point, however, is that Bossuet was not alone by any means in what he took to be the basic purposes of a funeral sermon. He was merely the most accomplished of a legion of clergy engaging in this sort of funeral preaching, namely, rhetorically polished eulogies flattering the dead (and, generally speaking, the wealthier or more well-placed the deceased, the finer the eloquence and the more glowing the eulogy), with a moral twist at the end designed to summon the living to higher Christian obedience.

It was almost inevitable that a reaction would set in, and sure enough, one Christian reform movement after another began to condemn these class-based and flowery funeral eulogies. Perhaps the earliest, and certainly the most extreme, reaction came from the Calvinists at the Westminster Assembly. Having had quite enough of precious liturgies and windy, high-blown eulogies, the Westminster divines decided that the less said and done over the deceased, the better. Since funerals, they said in the *Directory for the Publick Worship of God* (1644), "are no way beneficial to the dead, and have proved many ways hurtful to the living," they and their apple-polishing eulogies should be avoided altogether. If a minister happened to be present and a sermon was desired, then the people could leave the graveyard after the burial and go to the meeting-house for preaching. But the preacher should keep it simple, not singing the praises of the deceased, but instead doing only what a sermon always should do: put the hearers "in remembrance of their duty."

Stern stuff there, and while no major Christian denomination today takes such an austere view of funerals and funeral sermons, the antipathy toward eulogies endures. The rubrics for the current Roman Catholic funeral mass, for example, expressly forbid eulogies: "A brief homily based on the readings is always given after the gospel reading at the funeral liturgy and may also be given after the readings at the vigil service; *but there is never to be a eulogy.*"[3] In the Protestant world, the command of the Lutheran *Manual on the Liturgy* is typical: "The sermon may include a recognition of the life of the deceased, *but its purpose is not eulogy but a proclamation of hope and comfort in Christ.*"[4]

We know what these rubrics are after—preach the gospel, don't preach the life of the deceased. Drawing on the image, often attributed to Karl Barth, that a preacher ought to preach with the Bible in one hand and the newspaper in the other, Episcopal priest Charles Hoffacker says that "a eulogy is *not* a funeral sermon. . . . The eulogy is what happens when one hand raises the obituary notice and the other hand does not raise the Bible."[5]

If zero tolerance on eulogies seems a tad strict, it comes not just out of theological principle but also out of much bad experience. To some degree, the stop sign thrown up on eulogies is, like the allergic reaction of the Westminster divines, a response to real abuses. Over time the church has learned that the minute we take our hands off the steering wheel of funerals, they veer off the road in the direction of sentiment and overpersonalization, and the sermon is often the guiltiest of parties. The gospel of Jesus Christ gets replaced by the gospel of Al. In his provocative antieulogy essay "Homily or Eulogy? The Dilemma of Funeral Preaching," Catholic priest John Allyn Melloh argues that the tendency to hijack the larger purposes of congregational worship and replace them with individualistic concerns is a problem not only in funeral sermons but in preaching at all "occasional" services. Thus, for example, wedding sermons also have a propensity to bite through the homiletical leash and run off toward personalization, turning into special instructions to the bride and groom, instead of a word for the whole congregation.[6]

The eulogistic abuses come not just from the clergy, of course. Given the contemporary trend toward open-mike sessions at funerals, the heartfelt speeches of kith and kin, flooding the room with stories and jokes about the deceased, can descend rapidly into bathos. Even the advocates of secular memorial services are beginning to sound the alarm. A New York event planner, who professionally organizes high-end public events such as museum openings and social soirees, has recently added "society funerals" to his portfolio. He acknowledges that his biggest headache at funerals is not wilting flowers or a tardy caterer but those vexingly long eulogies from friends. So he has laid down a rule: after three minutes, stick a sock in it. "I have a pet peeve," he said. "It doesn't matter how much you loved someone, after you've heard someone drone on for five minutes you're annoyed. It's about poignant moments. Maudlin is not poignant."[7]

So it is hard for the eulogy to find a thoughtful friend, but what seems liturgically objectionable is often pastorally necessary. Most funerals include at least some reminiscences about the deceased that would fall within the range of the definition of a eulogy (literally, a "good word"), and it would seem cold and sterile not to include them. What, after all, is a sermon that includes "a recognition of the life of the deceased" but is in no way a eulogy? Surely it *doesn't* mean that one may speak of the dead, as long as it is *not* positive. A funeral preacher should be warned away from raising up the obituary without also raising the Bible, but, says Hoffacker, it is equally unsatisfactory to lift up "the Bible but not the obituary."[8] Strange indeed would be the contemporary funeral in which mention of the life of the deceased is altogether omitted. Small wonder pastors are unclear about the shape and aim of a funeral sermon.

There are many wise manuals about funeral sermons, guides that advise us on how to use images and narratives and good, psychologically congruent structures, but long before the technical aspects of funeral preaching come into view, a more basic question should be asked: What in the name of God are we trying to do in a funeral sermon anyway? What, exactly, is the purpose of a funeral sermon? Toward what goals are our words flung? Before we can know what to say and how to say it, we must face the question of why we are up there trying to say anything at all.

Most ministers who have conducted many funerals over the years recognize that, in practice, funeral sermons and homilies are so varied as to defy categorization. Sometimes in a funeral sermon we tell gentle stories we have heard from the family, and sometimes we explore an image from Scripture, and sometimes we state as clearly and simply as we can the promises of God, and sometimes we search for the words that name what everyone is thinking and feeling, and sometimes we just stand there and give voice to the sorrow or the anger or the perplexity or the relief or the gratitude. But, drawing back to gain some wider perspective, underneath these mixed genres and varied themes, what are we trying to do?

The picture gets a bit clearer when we get back to basics and remember both what a Christian sermon is and what a Christian funeral is. A Christian sermon is built on the conviction that when we take what is happening in our lives and in our world to a biblical text and honestly and prayerfully listen, a word from God may be heard there. The sermon happens when the preacher, who has gone to the Bible from the people and on behalf of the people, now turns and goes back to the people and is a faithful witness, telling them courageously and truthfully what has been heard. A Christian funeral, as we have emphasized, is a piece of drama in which the church reenacts the gospel by symbolically walking with the deceased on the pilgrim path toward resurrection, singing and praying as they go.

Putting these two things together, we can describe more fully a Christian funeral sermon. First, like all Christian sermons, it is both biblical and contextual. Funeral preachers go to Scripture to hear the word of life and hope, but they do not go as blank tablets. They take with them the circumstances of the funeral—*this* death, *these* people, *this* loss, *these* needs. Second, funeral sermons are preached "on the road," so to speak. Because the funeral is essentially a processional, funeral sermons are preached figuratively as the church walks to the grave. They are proclamations of what the gospel has to say about *these* people walking along *this* path carrying the body of *this* brother or sister in sorrow over *this* loss and in joyful hope of the resurrection.

This means that funeral sermons will all be biblical and will all be gospel, but they will not all be the same. The interaction of ancient text and specific context will yield, as it always does in preaching, sermons that arc out in varied ways across the occasion. Perhaps the best way to talk about this in practical terms is to see how the funeral sermon can participate in the eight purposes of a good funeral, discussed in chapter 7.

THE EIGHT PURPOSES OF
A GOOD FUNERAL SERMON

1. Kerygmatic: "In the valley of the shadow of death, you are there." Of all the purposes of a funeral sermon, the need to proclaim the gospel, the kerygma, is possibly the only one that constitutes a genuine sine qua non. The indispensability of shouting out the good news of Easter at a funeral gets highlighted when we realize that there are actually two preachers at every funeral. Death—capital-D Death—loves to preach and never misses a funeral. Death's sermon is powerful and always the same: "Damn you! Damn all of you! I win every time. I destroy all loving relationships. I shatter all community. I dash all hope. I have claimed another victim. Look at the corpse; look at the open grave. There is your evidence. I always win!"

Funeral sermons that spend all of their time on gentle themes of comfort and pastoral care miss both an opportunity and the point. Death is running after the pilgrim throng, pointing gleefully at the lifeless body and trying to drown out the songs of resurrection. It is the great privilege of the funeral preacher to shake a fist in the face of Death, to proclaim again the vow of baptism and the cry of Easter triumph: "O Death, we reject all your lies! O Death, where is your sting? Thanks be to God, who gives us the victory in Jesus Christ!"

As an example of a kerygmatic section in a funeral sermon, consider this from Lutheran Bishop Stephen Paul Bouman's homily at the funeral of theologian Walter Bouman, in which he tells about the day when he helped Walter teach a seminary class, which turned out to be the last time Stephen saw Walter alive:

> He asked me to teach his class with him. With pj's, robe and slippers he held forth surrounded by his students in his living room. When I had to leave he asked me to bless him. He wanted his students to see that a bishop is a pastor at heart. I put my hands on his head, and gave a blessing. He was weak and ready to complete the baptismal adventure. It was the last time I saw him in this world. So now, come to the table, where the end of the story is enacted once more.

Walter is here, along with all of our loved ones whose baptism has carried them safely to the one who holds the future in his living hands. Christ has died. Christ is risen. Christ will come again. In a moment we will sing a hymn which always tears at my heart. "Lord let at last thine angels come." At the table they are already here.[9]

2. Oblational: "Bring an offering and come into God's courts." Someone driving by the cemetery or columbarium at the time of a funeral would see only a group walking with a burden, a coffin or an urn. Viewed through the lens of Scripture, though, the body of a saint is not just a burden to be borne but an offering to be made. The church is bearing the body of a saint and in effect shouting out a prayerful petition, "God, get ready! Here comes Elizabeth! Here comes Roberto! A sinner of your redeeming, and a lamb of your own flock. You have given her, given him, to us, and now with gratitude for that gift of life, we are returning them to you." A funeral sermon can bring this offertory aspect of the funeral to light, and when it does, it is like the prayer after the offering, "We give thee but thine own," except in this case the offering is not money but the brother or sister we have loved.

I once attended a funeral in a country church. The deceased was a man who had, years before, left for the big city and had lived there a life out of accord with the moral expectations of the folk back home Everyone wondered what the preacher would say. The preacher that day made no moral judgments; what he did was to make an offering. In the sermon, he moved figuratively from the pulpit to the pews and said, in essence, "God gave us _____, and we loved him, even when it was hard to do so. And now we give him back to God, back to the God who loves him too, and who can be trusted."

The oblational character of funeral preaching also allows the preacher to name as sacred the sacrifices and offerings that have been made during the time of dying. As a hospice nurse, Carolyn Burns has had many experiences with dying people and their families. "I had a man who put on his wife's makeup every morning," she said. In the initial stages of the wife's illness, Burns reported, the woman had been very concerned about her appearance, and she never got out of the bed without putting on her makeup. Then, as her illness progressed, she needed help, and her husband, though clumsy at it, would assist her. As she moved closer to death, she slipped into unconsciousness, but "even when she was in a coma, every morning he would comb her hair, put on her eyeliner and powder and lipstick and all that stuff. It was such an act of love. And bless his heart, it looked horrible. . . . He said, 'Well, it's important to her.'"[10]

From the perspective of the gospel, these tokens of love, passed from one human being to another, are also holy offerings given in the courts of God.

3. Ecclesial: "Such is the company of those who seek God." One of the sinister lies of Death is that we are finally alone: the dead are abandoned and the grief-stricken are left to be alone. One morning, a young woman named Lynn Caine received the telephone call no one wants to receive. A physician, phoning from the hospital where Lynn's husband had been in a coma for two weeks, said simply, "Mrs. Caine. Your husband died this morning." Writing about that awful moment, she said, "Funny, but I can't remember anything beyond those five words. I can't remember what I said, what I did, or whom I called— nothing." A few years later, trying to form some memory of what happened, she asked her son Jon if she had cried. "No," he said, "you were acting brave."[11] She soon discovered the terrible isolation of grief. "Being a widow," she said, "is like living in a country where no one speaks your language."[12]

But a Christian funeral is a visible enactment of the gospel claim that death cannot finally sever the ties that bind, that the feeling of isolation and abandonment that death brings is, in the deepest sense, an illusion. The funeral sermon can lift up the truth that not only is the Christian community gathered around the mournful, praying for them, singing with them; the deceased is being offered into the great communion of the saints. As Elizabeth A. Johnson reminds us, the biblical witness about heaven is not of some abstract and static reality, but instead,

> the scriptural images of final fulfillment are corporate, cosmic, and filled with joy. The vision of God itself entails "knowing" in the biblical, experiential sense, relating intimately to the unfathomable mystery of another in deeply mutual regard. And analogues in the human experience of loving in freedom, enjoying beauty, pursuing truth, and interacting in community have an absorbing and life-giving character that is the opposite of stasis. At root, heaven is the symbol of a community of love sharing the life of God.[13]

Here is a portion of a funeral sermon preached by biblical scholar Patrick D. Miller, one that shines a light on the communion of the saints:

[H]eaven is . . . a highly relational symbol, and this is a part of the Christian hope and confidence about the future that seems to mean more and more to me as the years go by. It is what the church means by the communion of saints. That is a way of speaking about the fellowship of all who have lived as a part of the community of faith. It is also a way of saying that as our lives have been lived together, whatever is beyond that continues that relationship. The image that is most helpful to me and comes to mind again and again is the picture at the beginning of Hebrews 12: "Since we are surrounded by so great a cloud of witnesses . . ." I see in my mind that cloud of witnesses every time I sing "The Church's One Foundation" and come to that verse: "Yet she on earth hath union with God the three in one; and mystic sweet communion with those whose rest is won."

I really do believe that in some way, George, and our fathers and mothers, our grandfathers and grandmothers, and all those who have gone before surround us even now and keep us and bear witness to us beyond their life. And whatever we have known of loving relationships is not lost. How we shall experience that relationship beyond our death, we do not know. But it belongs to whatever future with God we have. I know that the climax of 1 Corinthians 13 is meant to be the final verse. For me, however, it comes at the end of Paul's characterization of love and all that it means with those concluding three words: "Love never ends."[14]

4. Therapeutic: "In the day of my trouble, I seek the Lord." The funeral sermon can be an expression of Jesus' promise, "Blessed are those who mourn, for they will be comforted" (Matt. 5:4). The healing offered by the gospel includes, but is larger than, psychologically coming to terms with grief. In fact, the word "therapy," long before it was something done on a psychiatrist's couch, was a biblical term, *therapeia,* meaning healing in the deepest and fullest sense. Luke, for example, uses this word to describe the ministry of Jesus: "When the crowds found out [that Jesus was in Bethsaida], they followed him; and he welcomed them, and spoke to them about the kingdom of God, and healed those who needed *therapeia*" (Luke 9:11).

Sermons with the goal of providing *therapeia* will be filled with understanding and compassion, and they will also be filled, as was Jesus' *therapeia,* with the good news of God, who alone can heal. The therapeutic dimension of funeral preaching, however, is a caution to preachers not to forget that the truths of the gospel can sometimes sound in the ear of the mournful as empty promises. Preachers should not preach the gospel victory in such a way that it implies that hope and joy are qualities that the mournful somehow lack and that everybody else, including the preacher, possesses.[15]

William Sloane Coffin, in a sermon preached only a few days after the death of his son Alex, spoke eloquently about the need of the grieving for support and compassion and not just empty-sounding biblical "truths":

> I mentioned the healing flood of letters. Some of the very best, and easily the worst, came from fellow reverends, a few of whom proved they knew their Bibles better than the human condition. I know all the "right" biblical passages, including "Blessed are those who mourn," and my faith is no house of cards; these passages are true, I know. But the point is this. While the words of the Bible are true, grief renders them unreal. The reality of grief is the absence of God—"My God, my God, why hast thou forsaken me?" The reality of grief is the solitude of pain, the feeling that your heart is in pieces, your mind's a blank, that "there is no joy the world can give like that it takes away" (Lord Byron).
>
> That's why immediately after such a tragedy people must come to your rescue, people who only want to hold your hand, not to quote anybody or even say anything, people who simply bring food and flowers—the basics of beauty and life—people who sign letters simply, "Your brokenhearted sister." In other words, in my intense grief I felt some of my fellow reverends—not many, and none of you, thank God—were using comforting words of Scripture for self-protection, to pretty up a situation whose bleakness they simply couldn't face. But like God herself, Scripture is not around for anyone's protection, just for everyone's unending support.[16]

Coffin's warning does not mean that preachers should be silent about the promises of the gospel. It means, rather, that when those promises of victory and joy are directed to those in the pain of grief, they should have the tone of words being held in trust for them until they can claim them for themselves, rather than obligations of the present moment.

5. Eucharistic: "O give thanks to the Lord." Every human life, no matter how short or long, complicated or simple, sorrowful or joyful, is nevertheless a text that can be read in the light of God's image and grace. The words may catch in the throat for some, but "Thank you, O God, for this life" is one of the refrains we sing as we process to the grave.

John Killinger tells in a sermon about a couple who made great sac-rifices to raise a child with severe birth defects. The child even slept in a bed in his parents' room so that they could hear if he stopped breathing in the night. When the boy died, his parents stood at his bedside and, even as they wept, sang the doxology. "He taught us how to love," his mother said.[17]

When we give our dead back to God, we do so with the recognition and gratitude that, because of this life, we have learned truth, experi-enced growth, received gifts, and felt blessings. The sermon can give voice to our gratitude.

6. Missional: "That I may walk before God in the light of life." The funeral sermon that lifts up the missional theme shines a light on the truth that the procession of faith does not end at the grave. Even as our eyes are downcast in grief, the missional sermon reminds us that baptism defines us more lastingly than grief and calls us to "keep our eyes on the prize" of the kingdom of God and our call to be about the work of God in the world.

The theme of mission, though it may seem to be at odds with the therapeutic purposes of the sermon, may in fact be deeply healing. It signals that today is not the end of meaningful life, that tomorrow there will be a world to serve and that the labors of our hands will be needed.

7. Commemorative: "Lord, you have been our dwelling place in all generations." In a sermon I heard years ago at the Cathedral of St. John the Divine in New York City, the poet Wendell Berry described the tobacco harvest in Kentucky. When the tobacco is ready to glean, he said, the harvest must be done quickly, and there is an air of urgency, even emergency, about getting the crop out of the field and into the barn. Everyone, young and old, is summoned to the labor, and as chil-dren play around the edges, the rest of the community is at work, mov-ing methodically across the field. As they work, there is plenty of time for storytelling, and many of the stories, Berry said, are about those who once worked the harvest but who have now passed away. Then, as I recall it, Berry paused dramatically, and said, "The problem with most of the jobs that people have today, working at computers and telephones, is that they cut us off from children and the dead."

The funeral liturgy, and with it the funeral sermon, refuses to cut us off from the dead. As we walk to the cemetery with the one who has died, we remember and tell stories of this person. We tell them because Christians believe that death changes, but does not destroy, the communion with this saint. We tell stories of the one who has died because we can see through the prism of this life, both in glad and sorrowful memories, refractions of the grace and love of God. We tell stories of the deceased while carrying, at least symbolically, their body, because the Christian faith is not just an idea or a sentiment; it is a Way, an embodied form of living, and what we do with our bodies counts. What the deceased did in the embodiment of his or her life matters. We remember the deceased because the resurrection is not a promise to raise some disembodied spirit, but the real, full persons that God knew, loved, and saved.[18]

John Fanestil was eighteen years old when his grandfather, who worked for forty years at a small-town Kansas Texaco station, died. At the funeral, the preacher told a story about his grandfather that Fanestil remembers to this day. One Sunday, his grandfather, as he left church, mentioned to the pastor that he had noticed that the license plate frame on the pastor's car was loose. The pastor laughed and said he'd been meaning to take care of that problem for a long time, but that he didn't have the right screw to repair it. That very afternoon, the pastor was eating his Sunday dinner when he heard a noise outside. He looked out the window and saw Fanestil's grandfather on his knees in the driveway holding a screwdriver, repairing the frame.

The picture of his grandfather doing this deed of service so captured the man's character, and so captured something about the nature of Christian service, that years later, Fanesil revisits the memory. He writes, "I cherish the image, and bled it routinely with other images I hold dear. As I close my eyes I see my grandfather kneeling in a driveway turning a screw with a screwdriver. I also see my wife as a young mother, bending over to pick up our fallen child. I see Jesus, squatting and washing his disciples' feet. I see a pastor at the altar clasping the hands of two people who have just exchanged wedding vows."[19]

It is this kind of faithful storytelling that the contemporary liturgical books have in mind, I believe, when they say things like, "The sermon may include a recognition of the life of the deceased, but its purpose is not eulogy but a proclamation of hope and comfort in Christ." We walk to the grave and we walk toward the resurrection remembering the one with whom we are traveling.

8. Educational: "Teach us to number our days." Though education may be the least prominent of the purposes of the funeral sermon, it should not be overlooked. Sometimes funeral sermons are used for crass and manipulative evangelistic goals ("James is dead now. Friday night he was at the senior prom; by morning he was gone, killed in a collision. We never know when our hour will come, so young people, before it's too late . . ."). But the gospel does not play on people's emotions or take advantage of the vulnerable. Instead it welcomes people into the place of worship. Often a Christian funeral involves language, actions, and symbols that are strange, even potentially divisive, for those who are not Christians. People who come to Christian funerals sometimes find themselves on stage in a play they neither recognize nor understand. The preacher, like the stage manager in Thornton Wilder's *Our Town,* can momentarily step away from the play and explain what is happening so that people can be drawn in more deeply.

I quoted above a few words from the sermon preached at the funeral of theologian Walter Bouman. When Bouman knew that he had only a few weeks to live, he was invited to preach one more time in the chapel of Trinity Lutheran Seminary in Ohio, where he had been a professor. In his sermon he spoke honestly about his cancer and that he was now "counting his days." The sermon closed this way:

> I am being readied for my final baptism, my last dying and rising with Christ. All my baptisms of dying and rising with Christ, from July 28, 1929, to the present moment, have prepared me for this time. I turn often to the hymn-prayer with which J. S. Bach concludes his magnificent *Passion according to St. John.* It is the final stanza of a hymn. . . . I ask you to join me in praying/singing that final stanza.
>
> > Lord, let at last thine angels come,
> > To Abr'ham's bosom bear me home,
> > That I may die unfearing.[20]

Appendix: Difficult Funerals

Almost every funeral presents distinct pastoral and liturgical challenges, but some funerals are more difficult than others. The circumstances that generate special demands vary widely. Perhaps the deceased took his own life, died estranged from her family, was murdered, or died lacking any evident faith or connection to the church. Maybe the funeral is for a stillborn infant, or a young child, or someone who died a particularly painful death. Perhaps several members of a family have been killed in an automobile accident, or perhaps two parents have died, leaving children orphaned. Each of these cases, and others like them, places pastoral care and theological weight on the funeral that can often seem like more than even a funeral can bear.

While pastors will certainly want to lift up and address in funerals the specific concerns and needs of the mourners, especially in such acute situations, it is important to remember and to reaffirm the power and meaning that are already present in the Christian funeral. To enact the drama of the funeral, to sing the psalms and hymns, to speak the prayers, to read the Scriptures, to announce the gospel—these are the touchstones that we need over and over again in every hour of need, the ancient sources of meaning and comfort that we desire, even in the face of a severe pastoral crisis caused by death.

Most of the time, the very same planning process and issues that were presented in detail in chapter 8 will accommodate even the unusually difficult cases. As in any other funeral, Scripture readings and prayers are chosen partly in response to the circumstances. There are, however, several kinds of difficult funerals that occur often enough to justify some special attention, specifically, the funeral of a person "outside" the faith, the funeral for a person who committed suicide, and the funeral of a child (including children who died in utero or at birth).

1. Funerals for People outside the Faith. The primary emphasis of this book has been on the Christian funeral as an expression of baptism, a dramatic event performed by the faithful community on the occasion of the death of a baptized Christian. In our society, however, often the church is asked to provide a funeral or memorial service for people with little or no connection to the church and to the Christian faith. Funeral directors are often asked by families to "find a pastor or priest" who will preside at the service, and in some communities pastors are asked to participate in far more of these "outside" funerals than funerals for members of the church.

In the past, some Christian traditions made sharp inside-outside distinctions, sometimes refusing to provide funerals or burials in church cemeteries to those who were not active in the life of faith. Sometimes the distinction was made on sacramental grounds (whether or not the deceased was baptized), and sometimes it was made on moral grounds (could the village atheist or the town reprobate have a church funeral?). Today, most Christians are unwilling to draw the lines so crisply between insiders and outsiders. There are many baptized people in our culture who do not participate meaningfully in any Christian community of faith; conversely, there are people active in church life who have never been baptized and who have never officially "joined" the church. Also, even for the most devout Christians, there are always doubts and moral failures. We are all sinners, and the territory between "I believe" and "Help my unbelief" is very gray and highly populated.

The question of what sort of funeral service should be provided for those "outside" the faith is shifting, I think, away from sharply defined sacramental or moral divisions, to issues of truthfulness and integrity in worship. Suppose that a family in the church has an adult son, Jonathan, who has consistently and publicly rejected the Christian faith. Jonathan dies as a relatively young man, and his family desires that a funeral for him be held at the church. Simply to insert Jonathan into the regular funeral liturgy and to pray petitions like, "Into your hands, O merciful Savior, we commend your servant Jonathan. Acknowledge, we humbly beseech you, a sheep of your own fold, a lamb of your own flock,"[1] is not so much a moral outrage as it is just plain untrue. It does not do justice to Jonathan to pretend at death he was someone he freely chose not to be in life, and it undermines the integrity of the language of worship.

On the other hand, there is much about the customary funeral service that can be said with honesty about Jonathan and about our relationship with him. Consider, for example, this funeral prayer from *The Book of Common Prayer*:

O God of grace and glory, we remember before you this day our brother [Jonathan]. We thank you for giving him to us, his family and friends, to know and to love as a companion on our earthly pilgrimage.[2]

Jonathan himself may not have chosen to give thanks to God, at least in formal prayer language, but that does not undermine the truthfulness of our doing so.

How much of the language of a Christian funeral can be honestly said about one who had an ambiguous or even adversarial relationship to the faith is, of course, a matter of discernment for a pastor, and much depends upon the pastor's own theological tradition and convictions. My own theological understanding includes the view that all human beings will, in some way, stand before the living God and that they will encounter there a God whose judgment, grace, mercy, and transforming love I have experienced in Jesus Christ—in short, a God who can be trusted. This view encourages me to be more expansive in the ways that the language of a gospel-centered funeral can be spoken at the death of one who was disconnected or estranged from the church. Other pastors, however, in their own wisdom would make different decisions about which words can be honestly spoken and which words cannot.

Some ready-made funeral liturgies for those outside the faith are available, but most traditions leave the decisions about the language of such funerals to the pastors who will be presiding at those services. Typical is the instruction in the Presbyterian (USA) and Cumberland Presbyterian *Book of Common Worship*: "When the deceased was not known to be a believer or had no connection with a church, then it is appropriate to hold the funeral elsewhere [than in the church building] and to omit or adapt portions of it as seems fitting."[3] While I do not agree with the implication that it is somehow always "inappropriate" to hold these funerals in the church building, I do think it is wise for pastors to craft funeral services for those outside the faith. Indeed, it can be very clarifying theologically and pastorally for a pastor to craft a funeral service that can be employed for a person with a distant relationship to the church.

The text of such a funeral can be divided into three broad categories: (1) affirmations voiced (by the church, by the Scriptures) about the meaning of life and death, (2) prayers, responses, statements, and affirmations spoken by those in attendance at the funeral, and (3) words spoken about the deceased. The language of all three categories should be truthful, but this does not mean that the categories operate at the same level of faith articulation. It is fitting, for example, to speak clearly of the church's faith in category #1 even on those occasions when such faithful language cannot be honestly spoken in category #2 or claimed for the deceased in category #3.

2. Funerals for Those Who Have Committed Suicide. Suicide is the eleventh leading cause of death among Americans, and a high proportion of deaths by suicide occur among males (four times more than among females) and among teenagers and people more than sixty-five years old.[4] When people take their own lives, this clearly creates an extraordinary occasion of pastoral care, but several factors render the funerals in these cases worthy of special consideration:

First, there once was a time when a number of Christian traditions considered the act of suicide to be a sin so grievous and damnable that a Christian funeral and burial were not allowed. Almost every Christian group has changed on this point, recognizing now with more pastoral compassion the many causes, reasons, and emotional stresses that can lead a person to commit suicide. However, the stigma and shame around suicide linger, and it is likely that some people who come to the funeral of a person who has taken his or her life will assume that this person is condemned by God, the church, or both. Thus, it is usually beneficial and redemptive for the pastor to reassure the family and the other worshipers that neither God's love nor the care and compassion of the church are diminished by the act of suicide.

Second, because it is often the case that a suicide generates among those left behind guilt, anger, recriminations, and second-guessing about what might have been done to prevent this, it is important for these funerals to afford the opportunity for these feelings and thoughts to be expressed in the context of God's forgiveness and healing. This can be done in prayers of confession and lament and in wisely chosen remarks, as the pastor deems fitting, during the homily or sermon about how such responses to a suicide are to be expected and can be offered to a merciful God. Again with good pastoral judgment, it can be helpful at funerals of persons who have committed suicide to allow the closest family, as a part of the oblation or naming sections of the funeral, to speak about their experiences or even to read letters written to the deceased.[5]

Third, suicide, because of the social stigma that often accompanies it, is one example of the kind of deaths that some call "disenfranchised losses,"[6] losses that carry a large measure of social disapproval. Depending upon the social location, they include the deaths of people who die in certain lifestyles (e.g., convicted criminals, drug users) or of certain diseases (e.g., alcoholism, AIDS). What is important at all funerals—the active, visible, and vocal participation by the community—becomes even more urgent in these circumstances. Just the sounds of prayer and of the congregation singing hymns become a welcome and needed sign of support, encouragement, and healing.

3. Funerals for Children. There is probably no loss more wrenching than the death of a child, increasingly so in a time when infant mortality is relatively rare. Until the middle of the twentieth century, it was not uncommon for families to experience the loss of one or more children. This fact did not diminish the pain of such losses, but the death of a child was an experience shared by many. Now, parents who lose a child cannot help but feel that they have been singled out for a catastrophic blow.

The best witness to the gospel when a child has died is not to somehow fashion a "child's funeral," whatever that might be, but to gather the emotions and concerns surrounding the death of a child into the fullness of the Christian funeral. There can be an impulse to become overly sentimental at a child's funeral, and while most good pastors are wise enough to resist the maudlin "God wanted a little angel" language, all temptations to make the funeral "sweet" should be avoided. The sturdy and confident language of the gospel, spoken at every Christian funeral, is the best and most redemptive form of ministry, even here in the death of a little child. The Christian community should carry this child to God, as we would carry any other person, singing as we go.

There are, of course, unusually intense emotions and needs surrounding a child's death, and these are most often best acknowledged in the including of prayers that gather up these concerns. Consider, for example, the following prayers for the occasion of a child's funeral from *The Book of Common Prayer:*

> O God, whose beloved Son took children into his arms and blessed them: Give us grace to entrust *N.* to your never-failing care and love, and bring us all to your heavenly kingdom; through Jesus Christ our Lord, who lives and reigns with you and the Holy Spirit, one God, now and for ever. *Amen.*

The Celebrant may add the following prayer:

Most merciful God, whose wisdom is beyond our understanding:
Deal graciously with *NN.* in *their* grief. Surround *them* with your
love, that *they* may not be overwhelmed by *their* loss, but have confidence in your goodness, and strength to meet the days to come;
through Jesus Christ our Lord. *Amen.*[7]

These prayers have the virtues of connecting the child to the story of
Jesus and in particular the accounts of Jesus' care for and blessing of
children, of affirming God's continuing love, of making it clear that
this saint too is traveling on toward the communion of saints, and of
giving voice to the support of the gathered community of faith.

Here, as another example, is a prayer of committal for a child's
funeral from the *Book of Common Worship:*

Loving God, give us faith to believe, though this child has died, that
you welcome *him/her* and will care for *him/her,* until, by your mercy,
we are together again in the joy of your promised kingdom; through
Jesus Christ our Lord. **Amen.**

In its frank "though this child has died" language, this prayer honestly recognizes the challenge to faith and trust that can be caused by a
child's death, and, without being overly specific, touches on the anxiety
of separation and loss by affirming that we will be "together again in
the joy of your promised kingdom."

One other matter regarding the death of children needs to be
addressed: stillborn children and fetal deaths. As a pastoral matter, this
issue of what sort of funeral to provide for children who are not born
alive presents itself frequently. Currently in the United States, women
have, on average, slightly over three pregnancies in their childbearing
years, and about one-third of these do not result in a live birth (because
of abortions, miscarriages, and stillbirths).[8]

While it was once the custom not to provide funerals for stillborns or
infants who died in utero (in fact, some hospitals would simply inciner-
ate the bodies of stillborns immediately after delivery), this practice is
rapidly changing. A stillborn child is a child to the parents and, theologically, a child of God. It is quite fitting, under most circumstances,
to have a funeral when a child is stillborn. Circumstances vary, and
pastors will, as always, have to make decisions related to those circumstances, but generally speaking, funerals are not held on the occasion of
miscarriages.[9] A ritual of loss and prayers for healing and hope are often
a more suitable response to a miscarriage than is a full funeral service.

Notes

Introduction

1. The details of John XXIII's death have been compiled from Lawrence Elliott, *I Will Be Called John: A Biography of Pope John XXIII* (London: Collins, 1974), 320, and "Vatican Revolutionary," *Time*, June 7, 1963, www.time.com/time/magazine/article/0,9171,874758,00.html.

2. *The Book of Common Prayer* (New York: Church Hymnal Corp., 1979), 499.

3. Robert W. Hovda, "The Amen Corner: Reclaiming for the Church the Death of a Christian, II" *Worship* 59/3 (May 1985): 251.

4. Ibid.

5. Herbert Anderson and Edward Foley, *Mighty Stories, Dangerous Rituals* (San Francisco: Jossey-Bass, 1998), 115. For another contemporary statement on Christian funerals narrowed by its more or less exclusive focus on the funeral as an instrument of consolation, see Gene Fowler, *Caring through the Funeral: A Pastor's Guide* (St. Louis: Chalice Press, 2004). The pioneering effort in this direction was the enormously influential Paul E. Irion, *The Funeral and the Mourners: Pastoral Care of the Bereaved* (New York and Nashville: Abingdon Press, 1954). Irion understood funerals to have two main aspects: "divine worship" and what Irion termed the "personal function," which was "to enable individuals to engage in the therapeutic process of mourning" (8) and to employ the Christian faith as a resource for that therapeutic process. Irion focused in this volume almost entirely on the personal aspect, confident that he could attend to the therapeutic dimensions of funerals "without in any sense distracting from the objective validity of the worship of God" (8). This emphasis on the therapeutic and personal dimensions of the funeral has continued to be a strong theme in works of practical and pastoral theology about funerals published in the last half century, which is both their main strength and their most glaring weakness.

6. Daniel Callahan, *The Troubled Dream of Life: In Search of a Peaceful Death* (New York: Simon & Schuster/Touchstone, 1993), 15.

Chapter 1: Marking Death

1. Kodo Matsunami, *International Handbook of Funeral Customs* (Westport, CT: Greenwood Press, 1998), xv.

2. Constance Jones, *R.I.P.: The Complete Book of Death and Dying* (New York: HarperCollins, 1997), 3.

3. Richard Rutherford, *The Death of a Christian: The Order of Christian Funerals* (Collegeville, MN: Liturgical Press, 1990), 116.

4. Robert J. Hoeffner, "A Pastoral Evaluation of the Rite of Funerals," *Worship* 55/6 (Nov. 1981): 482.

5. Michelle Cromer, *Exit Strategy: Thinking Outside the Box* (New York: Jeremy Tarcher/Penguin, 2006), xiv.

6. Funeral director Lou Stellato, as quoted in Lisa Takeuchi Cullen, *Remember Me: A Lively Tour of the New American Way of Death* (New York: Collins, 2006), 27.

7. Ibid., 208–9.

8. Ibid., 208.

9. Thomas Lynch, *The Undertaking: Life Studies from a Dismal Trade* (New York: W. W. Norton, 1997), 157.

10. *Alternative Services, Second Series* (London: Church of England Liturgical Commission, 1965), 105–6.

11. Robert Pogue Harrison, *The Dominion of the Dead* (Chicago: University of Chicago Press, 2003), xi.

12. Throughout this book, preference is given to the term "coffin" rather than "casket." Although some argument can be made that the difference between the two is a matter of shape (i.e., coffins, viewed from above, have six-sided shapes while caskets are four-sided, rectangular boxes), the real distinction between the two is one of marketing. Since "coffin" is negatively associated with death, the term "casket," or "jewel box," was borrowed to make the concept more commercially appealing.

13. Yasuhiko Richard Kuyama and Keith P. Inouye, "Japanese-American Worship Practices," in Kathy Black, *Worship across Cultures: A Handbook* (Nashville: Abingdon Press, 1998), 147.

14. Elaine Nichols, ed., *The Last Miles of the Way: African American Homegoing Traditions, 1890–Present* (Columbia: South Carolina State Museum, 1989), 16.

15. See David Sudnow, *Passing On* (Englewood Cliffs, NJ: Prentice-Hall, 1967), esp, chap. 7.

16. A. B. Hudson, "Death Ceremonies of the Padju Epat Ma'anyan Dayaks," *Sarawak Museum Journal* 13 (1966): 361–98.

17. Anscar J. Chupungco, *Worship: Beyond Inculturation* (Washington, DC: Pastoral Press, 1994), 1.

18. Ibid., 2, emphasis added.

19. The "land flowing with milk and honey" phrase, taken from the third century rite known as *The Apostolic Tradition*, is cited in Chupungco, 11.

20. Dennis L. Bushkofsky and Craig A. Satterlee, *The Christian Life: Baptism and Life Passages, Using Evangelical Worship,* vol. 2 (Minneapolis: Augsburg Fortress, 2008), 167–68.

21. H. Richard Niebuhr, *The Responsible Self: An Essay in Christian Moral Philosophy* (New York: Harper & Row, 1963), 60, 67.

22. Alasdair MacIntyre, "A Partial Response to My Critics," in John Horton and Susan Mendus, eds., *After MacIntyre* (Notre Dame, IN: University of Notre Dame Press, 1994), 303.

23. Chupungco, *Worship: Beyond Inculturation*, 11–12.

24. Richard Lischer, *Open Secrets: A Spiritual Journey through a Country Church* (New York: Doubleday, 2001), 81.

25. Ibid.

26. Annie Dillard, *Teaching a Stone to Talk* (New York: HarperCollins, 1982), 32.

Chapter 2. On Bodies Shunned and Bodies Raised

1. See Geoffrey Gorer, "The Pornography of Death," in *Death, Grief and Mourning* (Garden City, NY: Doubleday, 1965), 192–99.

2. Plato speaking in the voice of Socrates in *Phaedo,* in *The Dialogues of Plato translated into English with Analyses and Introductions, in Five Volumes.* 3rd ed., trans. Benjamin Jowett (London: Oxford University Press, 1892), 36.

3. Emile Durkheim, "The Dualism of Human Nature and Its Social Conditions," in *Essays on Sociology and Philosophy*, ed. K. Wolff (New York: Harper & Row, 1960), 326.

4. John Leland, "It's My Funeral and I'll Serve Ice Cream If I Want To," *New York Times*, July 20, 2006, E-2.

5. N. T. Wright, *Surprised by Hope: Rethinking Heaven, the Resurrection, and the Mission of the Church* (New York: HarperOne, 2008), 28.

6. Karl Barth, *Church Dogmatics*, *III/4* (Edinburgh: T.&T. Clark, 1960), 491.

7. See Paul Ramsey, "The Indignity of 'Death with Dignity,'" *The Hastings Center Studies* 2/2 (May 1974).

8. See Timothy P. Jackson, "A House Divided, Again: 'Sanctity' vs. 'Dignity' in the Induced Death Debates," in *In Defense of Human Dignity*, ed. Robert Kraynak and Glenn Tinder (Notre Dame, IN: University of Notre Dame Press, 2003).

9. Sherwin Nuland, *The Way We Die: Reflection on Life's Final Chapter* (New York: Alfred A. Knopf, 1994), xvi–xvii.

10. Catherine Madsen, "Love Songs to the Dead: The Liturgical Voice as Mentor and Reminder," *Cross Currents* 48/4 (Winter 1998/99): 458–59.

11. Nuland, *The Way We Die*, 164.

12. Madsen, "Love Songs to the Dead," 460.

13. Margaret R. Miles, *Bodies in Society: Essays on Christianity in Contemporary Culture* (Eugene, OR: Cascade Books, 2008), 13.

14. Ibid.

15. Ibid., 14.

16. Ibid.

17. Paul Waitman Hoon, "Theology, Death, and the Funeral Liturgy," *Union Seminary Quarterly Review* 31/3 (Spring 1976): 170.

18. Herbert Anderson and Edward Foley, *Mighty Stories, Dangerous Rituals: Weaving Together the Human and the Divine* (San Francisco: Jossey-Bass, 1998), 120.

19. Jessica Mitford, *The American Way of Death* (New York: Crest Books, 1963), 173.

20. Oscar Cullmann, *Immortality of the Soul or Resurrection of the Dead? The Witness of the New Testament* (New York: Macmillan, 1958), 27.

21. Thomas Lynch, *The Undertaking: Life Studies from a Dismal Trade* (New York: W. W. Norton, 1997), 20–21.

22. Ibid., 21

Chapter 3. The Future of the Dead in Christ

1. As reported in Langdon Gilkey, *On Niebuhr: A Theological Study* (Chicago: University of Chicago Press, 2001), 224.

2. See Lloyd R. Bailey Sr., *Biblical Perspectives on Death* (Philadelphia: Fortress Press, 1979), esp. 47–61.

3. The notions of death as "the final stage of growth" and "acceptance" as the highest form of human response to death's reality were introduced into popular consciousness by the work of Dr. Elizabeth Kübler-Ross. In her masterwork, *On Death and Dying* (New York: Macmillan, 1969), she implies that "acceptance" of death is the last and most advanced stage of response, but what makes it the best stage is that the self is finally able to cut loose from all of its encumbrances and ties with others. In the "acceptance" stage, the self regresses to "primary narcissism," and one experiences "the self as being all" (119–20). Your "circle of interests diminishes," and you want "to be left alone or at least not stirred by the news and problems of the outside world" (113). This is simply Platonism redux in psychological dress, the self breaking free from the

material world. For a somewhat more sympathetic reading of Kübler-Ross, see Bonnie J. Miller-McLemore, *Death, Sin, and the Moral Life* (Atlanta: Scholars Press, 1988), esp. 93–99.

4. Nancy Byrd Turner, "Death Is a Door," in Hazel Felleman, ed., *Best Loved Poems of the American People* (New York: Doubleday, 1936), 544.

5. From a study document drafted in 1972 by the Council for Christian Social Action of the United Church of Christ and cited in Paul Ramsey, "The Indignity of 'Death with Dignity,'" *The Hastings Center Studies* 2/2 (May 1974): 51.

6. William Stringfellow, *Free in Obedience* (New York: Seabury Press, 1964), 51–52.

7. Reinhold Niebuhr, *The Nature and Destiny of Man,* vol. 2: *Human Destiny* (New York: Scribner's, 1964), 308.

8. Arthur C. McGill, *Suffering: A Test of Theological Method* (Philadelphia: Westminster Press, 1982), 91–92.

9. Ibid., 295.

10. Eberhard Jüngel, *Death: The Riddle and the Mystery* (Philadelphia: Westminster Press, 1974), 98.

11. Rowan Williams, *Resurrection: Interpreting the Easter Gospel* (Cleveland: Pilgrim Press, 2002), 92–93.

12. Reinhold Niebuhr, *Beyond Tragedy: Essays on the Christian Interpretation of History* (New York: Scribner's, 1937), 289–91.

13. Jüngel, *Death,* 109.

14. Ibid., 110.

15. Jürgen Moltmann, *The Coming of God: Christian Eschatology* (Minneapolis: Fortress Press, 1996), 84.

16. "An Easter Sermon from St. John Chrysostom." Catholic Online, http://www.catholic.org/hf/faith/story.php?id=33126.

17. Niebuhr, *Nature and Destiny,* vol. 2, 312.

18. The Westminster Confession of Faith, XXXIV.1, in *The Book of Confessions* (Louisville, KY: Presbyterian Church (U.S.A.), 1999), 159.

19. John Baillie, *And the Life Everlasting* (London: Faber & Faber, 1933), 299.

20. James Barr, *The Garden of Eden and the Hope of Immortality* (Minneapolis: Fortress Press, 1992), 103.

21. N. T. Wright, *For All the Saints? Remembering the Christian Departed* (Harrisburg, PA: Morehouse Publishing, 2003).

22. N. T. Wright, *Surprised by Hope: Rethinking Heaven, the Resurrection, and the Mission of the Church* (New York: HarperOne, 2008).

23. Wright, *For All the Saints?* 36.

24. Wright, *Surprised by Hope,* 130.

25. Ibid., 158.

26. Bruce Gordon and Peter Marshall, *The Place of the Dead:Death and Remembrance in Late Medieval and Early Modern Europe* (Cambridge: Cambridge University Press, 2000), 2–6. Natalie Zemon Davis has argued that the dead in medieval Catholic society were much like an "age group," something like senior citizens in contemporary society, an identifiable social group with rights and responsibilities in relation to the younger generation. See N. Z. Davis, "Some Tasks and Themes in the Study of Popular Religion," in Charles E. Trinkaus and Heiko A. Oberman, eds., *The Pursuit of Holiness in Late Medieval and Renaissance Religion* (Leiden: Brill, 1974), 327–28.

27. Joseph Ratzinger, *Eschatology: Death, and Eternal Life,* 2nd ed. (Washington, DC: Catholic University of America Press, 1988), 230–31.

28. Moltmann, *The Coming of God,* 103.

29. See Barth's powerful discussion of time in *Church Dogmatics*, III/2, 417–640.

30. Moltmann, *The Coming of God*, 109.

31. Miroslav Volf, *Exclusion and Embrace: A Theological Exploration of Identity, Otherness, and Reconciliation* (Nashville: Abingdon Press, 1996), 303.

32. Ibid., 304.

33. Niebuhr, *The Nature and Destiny of Man*, vol. 2, 298.

Chapter 4. Whatever Happened to the Christian Funeral?

1. Tacitus, *Annals*, xvi, 6.

2. J. M. C. Toynbee, *Death and Burial in the Roman World* (Baltimore: Johns Hopkins University Press, 1971), 40. See also A. C. Rush, *Death and Burial in Christian Antiquity* (Washington, DC: Catholic University of America, 1941), 253, and A. Mau, "Bestattung," *Realencyclopädie der classischen Altertumswissenschaft*, vol. 3, ed. August Friedrich von Pauly (Stuttgart: J. B. Metzler, 1894–1963), 346–47.

3. Frederick S. Paxton, *Christianizing Death: The Creation of a Ritual Process in Early Medieval Europe* (Ithaca, NY: Cornell University Press, 1990), 20. See also *Inscriptiones latinae selectae*, ed. Herman Dessau (Berlin: Apud Weidmannos, 1892–1916), nos. 8162–66.

4. Paxton, *Christianizing Death*, 20.

5. Toynbee, *Death and Burial in the Roman World*, 41.

6. Byron R. McCane, *Jews, Christians, and Burial in Roman Palestine* (Ann Arbor, MI: UMI Dissertation Services, 1993), 66, 68.

7. Ibid., 66.

8. Paxton, *Christianizing Death*, 21.

9. McCane, *Jews, Christians, and Burial in Roman Palestine*, 68.

10. Geoffrey Rowell, *The Liturgy of Christian Burial* (London: SPCK, 1977), 4.

11. McCane, *Jews, Christians, and Burial in Roman Palestine*, 68–72.

12. Ibid., 70.

13. Paxton, *Christianizing Death*, 21.

14. Joachim Jeremias, *New Testament Theology* (New York: Scribner's, 1971), 198–99.

15. McCane, *Jews, Christians, and Burial in Roman Palestine*, 71–72. See also Eric M. Meyers, *Jewish Ossuaries: Reburial and Rebirth* (Rome: Biblical Institute Press, 1971).

16. *Semahot*, 12.6–7.

17. McCane, *Jews, Christians, and Burial in Roman Palestine*, 76.

18. Ibid., 57.

19. *Semahot*, 12.5.

20. Eusebius, *The History of the Church*, 7.22 (Baltimore: Penguin, 1965), 305–6.

21. *Apostolic Constitutions*, 6.27.

22. Ibid., 6.30.

23. Meyers, *Jewish Ossuaries: Reburial and Rebirth*, 72–77.

24. Augustine, *Confessions*, 9.11.27.

25. Toynbee, *Death and Burial in the Roman World*, 43–55.

26. The descriptions of the death practices of Roman Christians that follow are drawn mainly from Rush, *Death and Burial in Christian Antiquity*, 91–273.

27. Ambrose, *De Obitu Satyri*, I, 19.

28. *The Odes and Psalms of Solomon*, vol. 1, ed. J. Rendell Harris and A. Mingana (Manchester: Manchester University Press, 1916), 207. This is a Christian or Christian-redacted work dating from near the beginning of the second century.

29. Chrysostom, *Homily on John 11* (no. 42), lxxxv.

30. Tertullian, *Scorpiace 7.*

31. Augustine, *Confessions,* 9.12.28–29.

32. Chrysostom, *Homilia 44,* in *Hebraeos 5.*

33. Lactantius, *Divinae Institutiones,* VI. 2.5,7.

34. The kiss of peace at the point of burial was a practice widespread among Christian communities. Only in Gaul was it prohibited by church leaders, probably because locally it was too deeply associated with the pagan practice of the last kiss.

35. Drew Gilpin Faust, *This Republic of Suffering: Death and the American Civil War* (New York: Alfred A. Knopf, 2008), 210.

36. As cited in James H. Moorhead, *World without End: Mainstream American Protestant Visions of the Last Things, 1880–1925* (Bloomington: Indiana University Press, 1999), 60.

37. Ibid.

38. Susan J. White, *Christian Worship and Technological Change* (Nashville: Abingdon Press, 1994), 72–80.

39. Ibid., 77.

Chapter 5. The Funeral as Worshipful Drama

1. Shannon Craigo-Snell, "Command Performance: Rethinking Performance Interpretation in the Context of Divine Discourse," *Modern Theology* 16/4 (Oct. 2000): 481–82.

2. These baptismal customs of St. Paul's Baptist Church in Monroe, LA, are described in Annie Staten and Susan Roach, "Take Me to the Water: African American River Baptism," which originally was published in the booklet accompanying the 1996 Louisiana Folklife Festival and is now available online at www.louisianafolklife.org/LT/Articles_Essays/creole_art_river_baptism.html.

3. *The Book of Common Prayer* (New York: Church Hymnal Corp., 1979), 306.

4. *The Book of Common Worship* (Louisville, KY: Westminster John Knox Press, 1993), 406.

5. Martha Nussbaum, *Love's Knowledge: Essays on Philosophy and Literature* (Oxford and New York: Oxford University Press, 1990), 15–16.

6. Craigo-Snell, "Command Performance," 430.

7. Jessica Mitford, *The American Way of Death* (New York: Crest Books, 1963), 214. Mitford did not attend the service herself, but her husband did, and the description comes from him.

8. Craig M. Koslofsky, *The Reformation of the Dead: Death and Ritual in Early Modern Germany, 1450–1700* (New York: St. Martin's Press, 2000), 2–3.

9. See, for example, David Charles Sloane, *The Last Great Necessity: Cemeteries in American History* (Baltimore: Johns Hopkins University Press, 1991), esp. 44–64.

10. Susan J. White, *Christian Worship and Technological Change* (Nashville: Abingdon Press, 1994), 75–78.

11. Thomas Lynch, *The Undertaking: Life Studies from a Dismal Trade* (New York: W. W. Norton, 1997), 37.

12. Paul E. Irion, a professor of pastoral theology and a student of American funeral trends, commented on the pattern of reduced attendance at funerals as early as the mid-1960s. One consequence of this shift, noted Irion, is that funerals have become more private than public, more family affairs than events in the larger ecclesial or social communities. Paul E. Irion, *The Funeral: Vestige or Value* (Nashville: Abingdon Press, 1966), 18–19.

13. LeRoy Bowman, *The American Funeral: A Study in Guilt, Extravagance, and Sublimity* (Washington, DC: Public Affairs Press, 1959), vii.

14. Dwight D. Eisenhower, as quoted in the *New York Times*, Dec. 23, 1952, 16.

15. David E. Stannard, *The Puritan Way of Death: A Study in Religion, Culture, and Social Change* (Oxford: Oxford University Press, 1977), 109.

16. See Paul Connerton, *How Societies Remember* (Cambridge and New York: Cambridge University Press, 1989), 65–71.

17. Tom F. Driver, *The Magic of Ritual: Our Need for Liberating Rites That Transform Our Lives and Our Communities* (San Francisco: HarperSanFrancisco, 1991), 93.

18. William Harman, *The Sacred Marriage of a Hindu Goddess* (Bloomington: University of Indiana Press, 1989), 68.

19. Lawrence A. Hoffman, "How Ritual Means: Ritual Circumcision in Rabbinic Culture and Today," *Studia Liturgica* 23 (1993): 82.

Chapter 6. In the Hour of Our Death

1. Leo Tolstoy, *The Death of Ivan Illych,* trans. Lynn Solotaroff (New York: Bantam Books, 1981), 99.

2. See Robin Marantz Henig, "Will We Ever Arrive at the Good Death?" *The New York Times Magazine,* August 7, 2005.

3. Elisabeth Kübler-Ross, *On Death and Dying* (New York: Macmillan, 1969).

4. Ibid., 114.

5. Mary Lou Wiseman, *Intensive Care: A Family Love Story* (New York: Random House, 1982), 305.

6. See Kenneth L. Vaux and Sara A. Vaux, *Dying Well* (Nashville: Abingdon Press, 1996), esp. 9–10.

7. Rabbi Byron Sherwin, quoted in ibid., 125.

8. Carlos M. N. Eire, "*Ars Moriendi*," in Gordon S. Wakefield, ed., *The Westminster Dictionary of Christian Spirituality* (Philadelphia: Westminster Press, 1983), 21–22.

9. An adaptation of Desiderius Erasmus, "Preparing for Death," in John W. O'Malley, ed., *Spiritualia and Pastoralia,* vol. 70 of *Collected Works of Erasmus* (Toronto: University of Toronto Press, 1998), 400.

10. Martin Luther, *Confitemini, Psalm 118:1,* as quoted in Eberhard Jüngel, *Death: The Riddle and the Mystery* (Philadelphia: Westminster Press, 1974), 132.

11. Robin Marantz Henig, "Will We Ever Arrive at the Good Death?"

12. Jon M. Walton, "Thanks at All Times," a sermon preached at First Presbyterian Church, New York, NY, November 23, 2008.

13. Douglas John Hall, *Why Christian? For Those on the Edge of Faith* (Minneapolis: Augsburg Fortress, 1998), 173–74.

14. William F, May, "The Sacral Power of Death in Contemporary Experience," in Stephen E. Lammers and Allen Verhey, *On Moral Medicine: Theological Perspectives in Medical Ethics* (Grand Rapids: Eerdmans, 1987), 181.

15. Lewis Thomas, *The Youngest Science: Notes of a Medicine Watcher* (New York: Penguin Books, 1995), 56.

16. John Carmody, *Cancer and Faith: Reflections on Living with a Terminal Illness* (Mystic, CT: Twenty-third Publications, 1994), 54.

17. John Fanestil, "Graveside Hope: A Passion for Funeral Ministry," *Christian Century,* March 6, 2007, 25.

18. *The Book of Common Prayer* (New York: Church Hymnal Corp., 1979), 462.

19. Ibid., 465.

20. *Order of Christian Funerals* (New York: Catholic Book Publishing Co., 1989), 28.

21. Fanestil, "Graveside Hope," 25.

Chapter 7. The Marks of a Good Funeral

1. Stella Adler, *The Art of Acting,* ed. and compiled Howard Kissel (New York: Applause Books, 2000), 30.

2. Ibid., 24.

3. Ibid., 65.

4. Ibid., 104.

5. David Van Biema, "Mother Teresa's Crisis of Faith," *Time,* August 23, 2007, available at http://www.time.com/time/world/article/0,8599,1655415-1,00.html.

6. N. Richard Nash, *The Rainmaker: A Romantic Comedy in Three Acts* (New York: Samuel French, 1954), 89.

7. Jonathan Z. Smith, "Earth and Gods," *Journal of Religion* 49/2 (April 1969): 113.

8. Walter Brueggemann, *The Land: Place as Gift, Promise, and Challenge in Biblical Faith,* rev. ed. (Minneapolis: Fortress Press, 2002), 2.

9. "Funeral," *Evangelical Lutheran Worship,* Leaders Desk Edition (Minneapolis: Fortress Press, 2006), 668, 670.

10. Brueggemann, *The Land,* 2.

11. Ibid., 4.

12. Ibid.

13. Ibid., 3.

14. Kathleen Norris, *The Cloister Walk* (New York: Riverhead Books, 1996), 373.

15. Ibid., 376.

16. David Wendell Moller, *Confronting Death: Values, Institutions, and Human Mortality* (New York: Oxford University Press, 1996), 240.

17. Elizabeth A. Johnson, *Friends of God and Prophets: A Feminist Theological Reading of the Communion of the Saints* (New York: Continuum, 2003), 70.

18. The list of purposes of a good funeral is expanded and adapted from a list found in Paul Waitman Hoon, "Theology, Death, and the Funeral Liturgy," *Union Seminary Quarterly Review* 31/3 (Spring 1976).

19. Hoon, "Theology, Death, and the Funeral Liturgy," 175.

20. Ibid., 177.

Chapter 8. Planning the Funeral

1. Tom F. Driver, *The Magic of Ritual: Our Need for Liberating Rites That Transform Our Lives and Our Communities* (San Francisco: HarperSanFrancisco, 1991), 30.

2. Robert W. Hovda, *Strong, Loving, and Wise: Presiding in Liturgy* (Collegeville, MN: Liturgical Press, 1981).

3. Adapted from the English translation of the Hebrew done by "The Yahrzeit Organization" and found at http://www.yahrzeit.org/kaddish_eng.html.

4. Robinson Jeffers, *The Collected Poetry of Robinson Jeffers,* vol.1, ed. Tim Hunt (Stanford, CA: Stanford University Press, 1991), 178.

5. Leon Wieseltier, *Kaddish* (New York: Alfred A. Knopf, 1998), 26.

6. Ibid., 39.

7. Ibid., 585.

8. *The Order of Christian Funerals* (New York: Catholic Book Publishing, 1989).

9. *Evangelical Lutheran Worship,* Leaders Desk Edition (Minneapolis: Fortress Press, 2006).

10. *The Book of Common Prayer* (New York: Church Hymnal Corp., 1979).

11. *The Book of Common Worship* (Louisville, KY: Westminster John Knox Press, 1993).

12. *The Great Book of Needs: Occasional Services* (South Canaan, PA : St. Tikhon's Seminary Press, 1999).

13. Stan Friedman, "Sacrifices at Funerals: The Culture Is Changing," on the Web site of the Evangelical Covenant Church, http://www.covchurch.org/sacrifices-at-funerals-culture-is-changing.

14. *Evangelical Lutheran Worship,* Pew Edition, 279.

15. Ibid., 280.

16. *The Book of Common Prayer,* 499.

17. Ibid., 491.

18. Ibid., 492

19. *Evangelical Lutheran Worship,* Pew Edition, 281.

20. *The Order of Christian Funerals,* 83.

21. *The Book of Common Worship,* 916.

22. *Celebrate God's Presence: A Book of Services for The United Church of Canada* (Etobicoke, ON: United Church Publishing House, 2000), 451.

23. *The United Methodist Book of Worship* (Nashville: United Methodist Publishing House, 1992), 143.

24. The terms "naming" and "witness" for the actions of this section of the funeral are taken from *A Service of Death and Resurrection* (Nashville: Abingdon Press, 1979), x, 58–61.

25. *The Book of Common Prayer,* 496.

26. The pioneering anthropological work on human rites of passage is Arnold Van Gennep, *The Rites of Passage* (Chicago: University of Chicago Press, 1960).

27. "The Funeral Service," Orthodox Church in America, http://yya.oca.org/TheHub/StudyGuides/ContemporaryIssues/LifeandDeath/LifeDeath%20Sessions/Session2.htm.

28. *The Book of Common Worship,* 922–23.

29. Dennis L. Bushkofsky and Craig A. Satterlee, *The Christian Life: Baptism and Life Passages, Using Evangelical Christian Worship,* vol. 2 (Minneapolis: Augsburg Fortress, 2008), 174.

30. The name "Sending" for this section comes from *Evangelical Lutheran Worship,* Pew Edition, 283.

31. Bushkofsky and Satterleee, *The Christian Life,* 175.

32. *Evangelical Lutheran Worship,* Pew Edition, 283.

33. *The Book of Common Prayer,* 499.

34. Ibid., 501.

35. Ibid., 502.

36. Ibid., 833, altered.

37. Frederick Buechner, *Beyond Words: Daily Readings in the ABCs of Faith* (New York: HarperOne, 2004), 409.

38. *Order of Christian Funerals, Appendix 2: Cremation* (New York: Catholic Book Publishing, 1997), 6.

39. Richard Peterson, "Cremation Memorialization for the Next 1,000 Years," an address given to the Cremation Association of North America, August 21, 1998, and reported in H. Richard Rutherford, *Honoring the Dead: Catholics and Cremation Today* (Collegeville, MN: Liturgical Press, 2001), 22.

Chapter 9. Telling the Truth about Life and Death

1. The account of Bossuet's funeral oration for Anne of Gonzaga is largely taken from Edwin C. Dargan, *A History of Preaching*, vol. 2 (Grand Rapids: Baker Book House, 1970 [original ed, 1906]), 91–98.

2. M. De Voltaire, *A Philosophical Dictionary*, vol. 1 (London: W. Dugdale, 1843), 117.

3. *The Order of Christian Funerals* (New York: Catholic Book Publishing, 1989), 8, emphasis added.

4. Philip H. Pfatteicher and Carlos R. Messerlu, *Manual on the Liturgy: Lutheran Book of Worship* (Minneapolis: Augsburg Publishing Co., 1979), 360.

5. Charles Hoffacker, *A Matter of Life and Death: Preaching at Funerals* (Cambridge, MA: Cowley Publications, 2002), 13.

6. John Allyn Melloh, "Homily or Eulogy? The Dilemma of Funeral Preaching," *Worship*, 67/ 6 (Nov. 1993): 505–6.

7. John Leland, "It's My Funeral and I'll Serve Ice Cream If I Want To," *New York Times*, July 20, 2006, available online at http://www.nytimes.com/2006/07/20/fashion/20funeral.html.

8. Hoffacker, *A Matter of Life and Death*, 14.

9. http://tlsohio.org/Worship-Music/Sermons/MassoftheResurrection.pdf.

10. Carolyn Burns, in Patricia Anderson, *All of Us: The Meaning of Death* (New York: Dell, 1998), 233–34.

11. Lynn Caine, *A Compassionate, Practical Guide to Being a Widow* (New York: Penguin, 1988), 17–18.

12. Lynn Caine, *Widow* (New York: Morrow, 1974), 148.

13. Elizabeth A. Johnson, *Friends of God and Prophets: A Feminist Theological Reading of the Communion of the Saints* (New York: Continuum, 1998), 190.

14. Patrick D. Miller, "Heaven: A Homily," *Presbyterian Outlook*, Oct. 10, 2005, www.pres-outlook.com/opinion/editorials/491.html.

15. See William F. May, "The Sacral Power of Death in Contemporary Experience," in Stephen E. Lammers and Allen Verhey, *On Moral Medicine: Theological Perspectives in Medical Ethics* (Grand Rapids: Eerdmans, 1987), 181.

16. William Sloane Coffin, "Alex's Death," in *The Collected Sermons of William Sloane Coffin: The Riverside Years*, vol. 2 (Louisville, KY: Westminster John Knox Press, 2008), 4.

17. John Killinger, *Experimental Preaching* (Nashville: Abingdon Press, 1973).

18. John P. Meier, "Catholic Funerals in Light of Scripture," *Worship* 48 (April 1974): 212.

19. John Fanestil, "Graveside Hope: A Passion for Funeral Ministry," *Christian Century*, March 6, 2007, 27.

20. Walter R. Bouman, "Homily," preached at Trinity Lutheran Seminary and Bexley Hall, Columbus, OH, May 18, 2005, available online at http://www.crossings.org/thursday/2005/thur060205.shtml.

Appendix

1. *The Book of Common Prayer* (New York: Church Hymnal Corp., 1979), 499, language altered.

2. Ibid., 493.

3. *The Book of Common Worship* (Louisville, KY: Westminster John Knox Press, 1993), 911.

4. Center for Disease Control and Prevention, *Understanding Suicide Fact Sheet, 2008*, http://www.cdc.gov/ncipc/pub-res/suicide_factsheet2008.pdf.

5. See Roslyn A. Karaban, *Complicated Losses, Difficult Deaths: A Practical Guide for Ministering to Grievers* (San Jose, CA: Resource Publications, 2000), 41.

6. Ibid., 33–54.

7. *The Book of Common Prayer*, 494.

8. S. J. Ventura et al., *Trends in Pregnancies and Pregnancy Rates by Outcome: Estimates for the United States, 1976–96*, Document 21/56 (Washington, DC: National Center for Health Statistics, 2000), 2. The actual figures (for 1996) are an average of 3.2 pregnancies per woman, with 2.0 live births, 0.7 abortions, and .5 miscarriages or stillbirths.

9. Often the benchmark of twenty weeks of pregnancy is used to distinguish between a miscarriage (or spontaneous abortion) and stillbirth, but there is nothing set in stone about such a number.

Index